PEOPLE BEFORE PROFIT:
THE INSPIRING STORY OF THE
FOUNDER OF BOB'S RED MILL

Ken,

Let's Do Good ~~AND~~ Make Money.

Just like Bob!

Ken

1-15-13

People
Before
Profit

THE INSPIRING STORY OF THE
FOUNDER OF BOB'S RED MILL

KEN KOOPMAN

INKWATER
PRESS

PORTLAND • OREGON
INKWATERPRESS.COM

Edited by Linda Franklin
Bob's cover photo: Nancy Garner; Bob's Red Mill cover photos: Masha Shubin; Back cover photo: Eric Griswold, Eric Griswold Photography
Unless otherwise noted, all photos are from the Bob Moore family or Bob's Red Mill Natural Foods, Inc. archives.
Cover and interior design by Masha Shubin

Scripture quotations are taken from the Holy Bible, New Living Translation, copyright ©1996, 2004, 2007 by Tyndale House Foundation. Used by permission of Tyndale House Publishers, Inc., Carol Stream, Illinois 60188. All rights reserved.

Publisher: Inkwater Press | www.inkwaterpress.com

Paperback
ISBN-13 978-1-59299-726-8 | ISBN-10 1-59299-726-0

Kindle
ISBN-13 978-1-59299-727-5 | ISBN-10 1-59299-727-9

ePub
ISBN-13 978-1-59299-728-2 | ISBN-10 1-59299-728-7

Printed in the U.S.A.
All paper is acid free and meets all ANSI standards for archival quality paper.

1 3 5 7 9 10 8 6 4 2

Dedicated to
Charlee, the First Lady of Whole Grains

TABLE OF CONTENTS

PROLOGUE

O N HIS EIGHTY-FIRST BIRTHDAY, BOB MOORE GAVE HIS COMPANY TO his employees. To some observers, this gesture could have been interpreted as an old man's desire to walk away from his business, or to dump a struggling enterprise on unsuspecting workers. Not so in the case of Bob's Red Mill Natural Foods. The company was cash rich and in the midst of another record-shattering fiscal year. In fact, since 2002, Bob's Red Mill has averaged an impressive 24.7% annual increase in sales. Its whole grain products were available in nearly every grocery store in North America, and the manufacturer of more than three hundred natural, organic, and gluten-free products was expanding internationally.

Quartz millstones slowly turning twenty-four hours a day produced distinctive, stone ground whole grain flours, cereals, meals, and mixes that were packaged in transparent bags, stacked on pallets, and loaded into trucks bound for every part of the United States and Canada. Consumers bought into the company's mantra, *Whole Grain Foods for Every Meal of the Day,* by filling their baskets with hot breakfast cereals; whole wheat flours for baking; mixes for cornbread, biscuits, cakes, and cookies; and ancient grains such as quinoa, kamut, and amaranth for side dishes, salads, and entrees.

Sales got a boost – and continue to grow – as a result of the USDA's unveiling of the new Dietary Guidelines for Americans on January 12, 2005. For the first time, people were given specific recommendations for whole grain consumption, separate from those for refined grains. The federal nutrition policy suggested they eat at least three one-ounce-equivalent servings of whole grains each day. Good news for the miller of whole grain natural foods, who since the mid-1970s had been promoting the benefits of eating whole grains as part of a healthy diet.

No one who knew him doubted Bob Moore, at eighty-one years young, would continue at the helm of Bob's Red Mill. It wasn't just that his name was synonymous with the company, or that his face was plastered on every bag. Or the fact he was a true believer in eating whole grains for every meal of the day, and was in excellent health. If this great-grandfather were to appear on the TV show *Survivor*, the consensus vote from his 209 employees would be that Bob would win. Known for his high energy and tremendous work ethic, they knew he would certainly "outwork" any contestant he went up against.

"I started working for Bob twenty years ago when I was thirty-two and he was sixty-one," remarked Bo Thomas, Superintendent of Engineering and Maintenance. "And he was running circles around me then! Now at fifty-two, I'm beat at the end of the day, and here comes Bob in his eighties, and as strong as ever. I absolutely cannot figure out where he gets so much energy. I guess he has a strong constitution."

Those who know Bob's story know his mettle has been honed by fire – literally. How many business owners at nearly sixty years of age would mount a comeback after they lost everything in a fire? Maybe some, if the insurance payoff was sufficient. But if the payout only covered the amount owed on the building, as was the case in the 1988 arson fire that destroyed Bob's business, most men would walk away, take early retirement, or go get a job working for somebody else.

Bob couldn't do that. It wasn't in his DNA to give up. And on February 15, 2010, it certainly wasn't part of his make-up to cash in, walk away from the business he loved, and retire. Given that the average retirement age in America is sixty-two, and the average length of retirement is eighteen years, most "Bobs" would be living on borrowed time. Most men on the road to retirement typically quit going to work every day in order to pursue pastimes such as golf, gardening, travel, and other hobbies. It wasn't for lack of outside interests that Bob never considered retirement. He loves to restore old cars, and in nice weather enjoys driving one of his two 1931 Ford Model A's to work. He is an accomplished musician, known to serenade the team on his violin, or trade off with several of the musically inclined at work who have the liberty to sit at the piano outside the break room and play a few tunes. One of the true joys in his life is playing the boogie-woogie blues on his Steinway & Sons nine-foot concert grand piano at home. He is a voracious reader, consuming books about ancient civilizations, archaeology, and his favorite study subject, the Scriptures. He loves to travel, to drive on roads he's never been on before, and, of course, his passion – visiting old flour mills.

By turning the tables and giving the gift of his company to his employees at his birthday party, Bob forever affected the livelihood of his two hundred employees. "It's been my dream all along to turn this company over to you – the people who made this all possible – and to make that dream a reality on my birthday is just the icing on the cake," he told them at an all-company meeting held at the headquarters office in Milwaukie, Oregon.

Management had earlier announced at each of three employee shift pizza parties that through the implementation of a new Employee Stock Ownership Plan (ESOP), Bob's Red Mill Natural Foods would become an employee-owned company. The generosity of founders Bob and Charlee Moore and their minority partners, Chief Financial Officer John Wagner, Executive Vice President of Sales and Marketing Dennis Gilliam, and Vice President of Sales Robert Agnew was not lost on the assembled crowd.

Production line workers, warehousemen, mill operators, maintenance crews, customer service reps, office staff – they all milled about in various stages of bewilderment. The collective response ran the gamut of emotions: shock, tears, questions, blank stares, and smiles. They were thrilled to learn about the future contributions to their retirement. "I thought some of them were going to kiss me," Bob recalls. "It went over very, very well."

Even though some of the details were fuzzy regarding what an employee-owned company meant to them personally, there was no misunderstanding about their main concern – Bob Moore was not leaving the company. He and the current management would not change. There was no intention of ever selling out to some bigger corporation.

Not that there weren't offers. In fact, Bob's executive assistant, Nancy Garner, figured in the five years she had been with the company she had fielded at least one call a week from someone wanting to talk to Bob about buying the company. That's more than 250 inquiries. And Nancy thinks that estimate is low. And why wouldn't a savvy buyer be interested? The company had been growing at an average twenty percent clip since 1990. They had no debt. The management team was strong (most had been in place at least ten years). Their retail partnerships and distribution channels were solid. Their niche, the healthy foods category, was trending up. Their 325,000-square-foot manufacturing facility, which they had moved into in 2008, was three times larger than their previous space and provided ample room for expansion. Supplier sources were secure. And the best part – the international market for whole grain products was busting wide open.

Bob's Red Mill employees knew they had a good thing going, but they really didn't understand how good it was about to get. In addition to their regular salary (which for hourly workers was more per hour than the prevailing wage), Bob's Red Mill offers a traditional retirement plan called a 401k, and matches dollar for dollar up to four percent of employees' contributions to the plan. This is all on top of a monthly bonus structure where everyone shares in a type of profit-sharing pot of money tied to monthly goals. This unique profit-sharing program has been in existence since the 1980s, and as far back as anyone can remember, there have only been a few months when an extra bonus check has not been handed out (the extra amount employees received in the 2011 profit-sharing program was a whopping $2,788,093).

And now there was the Bob's Red Mill Employee Stock Ownership Plan. The details of the plan would be communicated at a later date, but that Monday it was important for them to hear this more than once – it *was solely funded by the employer* and not the employee. The employees did not have to pony up any cash to buy stock. Bob and his partners had decided to totally fund the ESOP through the business. They did not go to the bank and leverage it with a loan. No one in this new employee-owned company would have to pay a dime to become owners. It was given to them.

According to Joe Burt, owner of Pension Plan Specialists, who consulted with the partners in the ESOP development, it is uncommon to find another business owner who provides this level of bonusing to employees.

"As far as I'm concerned, you aren't going to find another human being who is as generous with his money and his employees as Bob," he says. "I mean, this is unheard of. Monthly bonus structures, profit sharing, 401k match, and an ESOP. You name it, he has provided it."

Burt continues, "And if you have ever been with Bob, if you walk through the restaurant or you walk through the mill, he is adored. He is literally adored. Not just respected, but adored by his employees. Another thing very important to Bob was that his employees understood the ESOP was not a replacement for any of those other benefits the company was already providing. This was in *addition to* the other benefits. It is just amazing he has taken that stance."

"To me, this is the ultimate way to reward employees for their contributions to our ongoing success and growth," Bob says. "Truly, and you need to hear me on this, it was the *only* business decision I could personally make."

That sentiment, which was picked up by scores of business writers and journalists around the country, struck a chord with the American public. They were used to the media reporting on corporate greed, bosses behaving badly, and employee frustration in the workplace. It seemed like you couldn't turn on the nightly news without hearing a story about a Bernard Madoff–type swindler cheating his constituents out of millions of dollars, or some corporate muckety-muck emptying the company coffers and leaving his beleaguered employees to pick up the pieces or hit the streets.

Unemployment was in the double digits with fourteen million Americans unemployed. Banks were closing. Economic forecasts were dismal. Americans' confidence in the corporate world was shaken. The only business news was bad news.

Then this, from *Forbes.com*:

> I'm feeling optimistic. I have recently seen a story that gives me hope that we could see a shift in the way leaders of corporations view their responsibilities.

The writer, referencing the *ABC World News* story on February 18 about Bob Moore turning over ownership of his multi-million-dollar company to its employees, went on to say:

> ...surely Moore could have pocketed more than a bundle by selling to a large food producer looking to expand in the organic, health food, and gluten-free segments – the markets that Bob's Red Mill serves. But instead, the leader felt an obligation to the people who helped him build his company over the past thirty years. This wasn't an obligation served by typical corporate responsibility. Instead, Moore believed this was "the only business decision he could make." Altruistic? Perhaps, but nonetheless, remarkable. Is it possible that coming off a decade where we have too many examples of corporations behaving badly, that we will see a return of ethics in the workplace? Is it too much to hope for that instead of sending jobs offshore, over-working employees, cutting benefits, and answering only to Wall Street, that we will see businesses once again focusing on their corporate responsibilities to their employees?

If one were to ask his employees or the legions of Bob's Red Mill fans, "Is this a return to ethics and corporate responsibility at Bob's Red Mill?" they would answer, "No, they never left."

Following the press release that went out announcing the ESOP and the ensuing national and international media coverage, the company's online message boards were flooded:

> Saw the news story and just had to say THANKS. With greed running rampant these days, and people struggling to get by, such an action offers a little light. It also makes me want to do business with a company like yours. Now if only we could get people like Bob to run the banks, utilities, maybe even the government...well, I know it sounds delusional, but thanks for the moment of joy! *Jill from Illinois*

> You sir are an amazing man. Your story on ABC brought tears to my eyes. The world needs more unselfish people like you. It's very comforting to know you 'get it!' You are a gift to your employees; just like they are a gift to you. *Brad from Michigan*

> You are an inspiration! What a great thing you did for your employees. It's so refreshing to read something positive from a captain of industry. Thanks for being one of the good guys! *Maggie from Ohio*

> Your story shows the love for your company and employees and is a perfect example of how we should all behave in this "me-first" world. *Diane from Illinois*

> What you, Bob, have done is something every businessman should learn. *John from Florida*

Of course, Bob's Red Mill wasn't the only company in the United States to implement an ESOP in 2010, but according to industry observers, no other company has garnered so much attention for it.

"I would venture to say that no other ESOP in the history of ESOPs has gotten this kind of media coverage, this kind of national acclaim," relates Burt. "I would attribute that partly to the recession, because this was such a positive business story that surfaced from a sea of doom and gloom. On the other hand, Bob has become such a media darling, and every national news interview he did seemed to spark another one."

There were at least 11,400 ESOPs in place at the beginning of 2009, according to the National Center for Employee Ownership, a nonprofit organization that monitors trends in stock bonus plans and profit-sharing programs in America. As of 2007, there were about fourteen million participants with nearly one trillion dollars in assets.

So why did a little ESOP for 200 employees at a relatively small natural foods company in the Pacific Northwest garner so much attention? *People* magazine dedicated a two-page spread to it. MSNBC TV called Bob "awesome," "a hero." *The Huffington Post, BusinessWeek, MSN,* and *USA Today* blogged about it. National nightly news programs like *FOX and Friends* and *ABC World News* fawned over him. TV stations in Washington, D.C., Massachusetts, Maryland, California, Kansas, Missouri, Arizona, Michigan, Idaho, Montana, and Washington ran stories on their news broadcasts. Business outlets like *Inc. magazine, CNNMoney.com,* and *Forbes* followed the story. *NPR,* a radio station in South America, and a half dozen Northwest stations interviewed Bob. It was front page news in Oregon's daily newspaper, *The Oregonian,* and the state's regional papers picked it up, too. Portland's TV personalities talked it up on their morning news programs, and the business story was covered on the evening news as well, from Seattle down the I-5 corridor to Eugene and Roseburg.

"It became the feel-good story of the recession," explains Craig Ostbo, principal at Koopman Ostbo Marketing Communications, the long-time agency for Bob's Red Mill. "That's the only explanation we have. We sent out a press release. And the media started calling. And calling and calling and calling. It started with Diane Sawyer's people from *ABC World News* the day after we broke the news, and the media attention didn't stop for weeks."

The headlines on newspapers, magazines, blogs, trade magazines, and news stories across the country told the story: "A Gift in Hard Times." "Act of Kindness." "Bob's Red Mill Employees Get Set for Life." "Best Boss Ever." "Good News for a Change." "Work Here and Own it." "Bob Leads the Way Again." And Bob's favorite: "Bob's Red Mill Now an Employee-Owned Company."

"I have people right now who have been with me 30 years," Bob says. "They were just committed to staying with me. So, the logical thing for me to do was give them the company. It's the only business decision I could make. I could not sell the company. I just couldn't sell it. I don't think there's anyone worthy to run this company but the people who built it."

To call Bob Moore a "hands-on boss" would be a gross understatement. He seems to be everywhere all the time. His boundless energy takes him on at least two complete facility tours a day. And that's not counting the one-mile trip to the Bob's Red Mill Whole Grain Store & Visitors Center where he usually stops in for breakfast or lunch. The 15,000-square-foot building is painted bright red with white trim, and features an eighteen-foot working waterwheel. It was one of Bob's many goals in life to come to work at his own American classic flour mill facility. So, fifteen years after his original red mill burned to the ground, he built this one.

The parking lot is almost always full (except on Sunday when the place is closed). Long hair, gray hair, purple hair, the "mill store," as it is known to the locals, attracts an eclectic mix of Birkenstock-wearing, bulk-buying, diet-minded, healthy, and healthy "wanna-be" customers. At breakfast, there are usually a couple of Bible study groups not talking in hushed tones in corners of the upstairs seating area. Downstairs, among the aisles of packaged whole grain products, cooking supplies, books, and kitchen gadgets, shoppers interact with the well-informed retail staff. A line in the back by the kitchen extends beyond the row of twenty-five-pound sacks of flour, and usually ends up in front of the museum-type display of actual working millstones that are powered by the waterwheel outside. The smell of fresh baked bread permeates the air. One can't help but feel healthier just reading the menu, featuring "whole grain this" and "heart healthy that." Of course, there's the rack of Kettle Chips next to the cash register, but hey, they're fried in the good fat.

The industrial neighborhood where blue-jeaned workers make saw chains and parts for jet engines and gas turbines creates a brisk lunch business at the deli counter. The perfume of oil and grease temporarily displaces the more delicate scents from the morning's predominantly female shoppers. Man-size portions of pastrami and roast beef are piled up on sandwich bread made hours earlier from whole wheat flour milled just down the road. The mostly male crowd spills outside where patio seating, a waterfall, leafy trees, and Bob's favorite classical music playing in the background provide the contrast to their ear-plug-wearing manufacturing duties.

Striding into the mill store, Bob is treated like royalty. Kids point and tell their mommies, "Look, it's the man on the package." He wears the same distinctive poplin driving cap in person as he does in every picture in print ads and on every package. He buys them from third-generation haberdasher John Helmer in downtown Portland and wears them religiously because his doctor told him decades earlier he was a candidate for melanoma cancer if he didn't cover his balding head. Rarely seen in his "civvies," as he calls any attire not branded with a Bob's Red Mill logo, he's a fixture in tan pants, and any one of a half dozen pastel colored long-sleeve shirts. With his bright red vest jacket with "Bob" embroidered on it, it's kind of hard to miss him. Regular customers get a boisterous "Hi, how are ya? Good to see you," from the white-haired and -bearded celebrity. He doesn't have a "Ho Ho Ho" kind of laugh – it's more of a "HA!" – but with his white beard and red vest...well, let's just say Macy's could use him to spell you-know-who come December.

Bob loves people. Can't get enough of them. Wants to be surrounded by them all day. Would love nothing more than to stop and visit, chat, engage, learn, encourage...and then move on to the next person. Young, old, man, woman, it doesn't matter. He's an interesting and interested talker.

He's a conversational pinball, bouncing around from table to table. He wants to know if their meal is to their liking. Have they tried his baked-from-scratch biscuits? Would they like some more coffee? What do they think about the weather, today's headlines? He's full of recipe ideas, trivia, advice, banter, and questions. All delivered with a twinkle in his eye, a wink here and there, and a hearty laugh.

Watch the people in his wake – they're smiling. Well, mostly. There was the lady who waited patiently while Bob had his picture taken with one adoring fan and then his hand shaken by an elderly gentleman who advised, "You need more drinking fountains on the tour of your plant." As Bob was taking note, the patient lady, in full frown now, marched up to him and spat out, "I don't like your chili; not enough meat! I like Dinty Moore and I like Nalley's, *but I don't like your chili!*" She huffed and walked away, before Bob could tell her he only serves vegetarian chili.

To most people, though, Bob's aura seems to linger, momentarily brightening their day and somehow depositing a positive feeling that sticks with them, much like the bowl of his steel cut oats they had for breakfast. Is it marketing? Yes. Bob is the consummate promoter. But is it real? You bet. There's no fooling around when Bob Moore gets on his soapbox and starts talking about what he believes is the right way to eat. He can quote chapter and verse (he'll refer you to Genesis Chapter One in the Old Testament) that extols the virtues of and need for consuming whole grains, with their reproductive germ left intact. His sincerity is undeniable. His commitment evident.

Bob is an on-fire evangelist for whole grains and healthy eating. He's passionate in his beliefs that large corporate food companies are contributing to the obesity epidemic affecting the youth of today with their sugary cereals, high-fructose corn syrup beverages, and super-sized portions. He rues the advertising messages targeting kids, the ones idealizing consumption habits that are counterproductive to optimal health.

But overall, he remains optimistic. It's in his nature to remain positive.

Back at the manufacturing plant in his second-floor corner office, Bob gazes out the expansive windows and marvels at the sight of blue sky, green trees, and the bustling traffic heading east and west on Highway 224. He is very grounded in his love of the Earth, nature, the elements, and the creatures that inhabit his surroundings. A tirelessly curious human being, Bob can be found at his desk at 6 a.m. reading a book on archaeology or some ancient civilization. He usually has a half dozen books he's reading at one time, three or four at his nearby home in Milwaukie, and the rest lying open on his desk at work where he left off the day before.

By 7 a.m. when the day shift starts to arrive, Bob can't help but turn his focus to the cars driving into the parking lot directly below his point of view. It's not attention deficit disorder, but the man is compelled to want to know what is going on in his vicinity. He pops out of his chair to get a better look at the new company pickup his maintenance supervisor just drove onto the lot. Later, he's back at the window pointing out an all-electric car one of the production line engineers is driving, citing the number of miles he drives it to work each day (four), miles per charge (twenty), and other tidbits he's gleaned from the guy. Another time, it's his grandson Keith Moore, a state-certified journeyman electrician and benefactor of a new alternator Bob just paid for to go in the used car he bought him. Then an email pops up on his smart phone. It's an announcement about a single order, $81,500, one of the company's biggest to date. He must write back immediately:

SUBJECT: The Big Amazon Order

Hi Den,

I would enjoy looking at a copy of this order, the number of SKU's, the quantity of each, etc. Surely we can learn something from perusing such a large order. It certainly tells us what our customers want by way of product since Amazon carries such a broad range of our line. So, if you set all of our products out on a table and then you turn the public loose, and at the end of the day you see what they have picked and what they have left, it is kind of like that. Let's get a copy and share it with Robert, Trey, Matt, and others. Thanks for the information. Bob.

As employees start to arrive, Bob has a wave or a word for each of them. He wants to know how their weekend was, what they are working on today, how their family is doing. Anyone and everyone is invited to pop in. There is never a closed door to his corner office. He can't sit still for long. If the hallway is quiet on his end of the building, he'll take a walk through sales and marketing, accounting, customer service, and the research lab. His favorite place, though, is the machine shop downstairs. It's there where he can get his hands dirty with "his guys," mechanics, electricians, welders, and maintenance workers. It's with this crew that he can relate to the best. It's where he got his start – building motors, fixing machines, tuning engines, figuring out how to make things run better.

And his favorite thing? That's easy.

"If I had to pick the one thing I love the most about my life today, it's my people," Bob says at age eighty-one. "I just love them. I have a great relationship with the most wonderful people."

Other businessmen well past the generally accepted retirement age of sixty-five might have a different idea about their favorite thing. Golf, travel, financial freedom, a second home somewhere warm, for example. But Bob has his own way of looking at things – some might call it an unconventional approach to life. On her prime-time national news broadcast, ABC's Diane Sawyer described it as, "a story we really love; hope you do, too."

PEOPLE BEFORE PROFIT

THE OLD MILL

T HE CALL CAME IN AT 12:30 A.M. FIRE ON ROETHE ROAD.
Volunteer firefighter Dean Hauck had stayed up late to watch Game
4 of the NBA Playoffs between the Detroit Pistons and LA Lakers. His
hometown Portland Trail Blazers finished second to the Lakers in the
Pacific Division, but lost in the first round of the playoffs for the third year
in a row. So he was rooting for anyone who played LA. Besides, Dennis
Rodman was his favorite player. Watching the game at home that evening in the duplex he shared with his twin sister, the twenty-five-year-old
basketball fan whooped and hollered every time Rodman got a rebound
or scored a point. He finished the game with seven of each. The Pistons
won 111–86 to even the series at 2–2, and in typical Rodman fashion he
finished the game with five fouls in nineteen minutes of action.

So with only about ninety minutes of sleep, Dean was a bit groggy
as he fumbled to turn off the Plectron beeper the City of Gladstone
provided for the members of its all-volunteer fire department. The siren
atop the nearby fire station was still wailing its alert as Dean jumped into
his pickup and started his two-block drive. The residents of the Portland

bedroom community were turning over to go back to sleep as the siren ran down and Dean hustled into the station.

He was the first engineer to arrive, so after gearing up, he jumped into the driver's seat, received the details of his destination – and then froze. Big barn. The 4000 block of Roethe Road, just west of McLoughlin Boulevard.

For the past year, Dean had been working as a warehouseman for Moores' Flour Mill in Milwaukie, Oregon. His job was to store and distribute finished products – such as specialty flours, hot breakfast cereals, cornmeal, and baking mixes – in a building across the street from where they were manufactured. At the mill, owner Bob Moore used two-thousand-pound quartz millstones to grind wheat, oats, corn, barley, and other grains, and then package them in small bags for sale in their onsite retail store, as well as to local grocery stores. Since it opened in 1979, people from all over the Portland area would visit Moores' Flour Mill to buy their whole grain flour, steel cut oats, polenta, pancake mixes, and dozens of other "stone ground" products Bob and his wife Charlee took such great pride in manufacturing. And Bob liked nothing more than to take his customers on tours of his beautifully restored forty-year-old wooden flour mill.

All that changed in dramatic fashion in the early morning of Wednesday, June 15, 1988. June in Oregon is festival month, partly due to the hoped-for end of soggy conditions citizens tolerate from October to May, but primarily because it's Portland Rose Festival time. The region's annual blowout party was about to kick off its eighty-first season, a three-week stretch of parades, carnivals, races, a queen coronation, and the much-anticipated visit of U.S. Navy ships that unloaded hundreds of sailors to experience the best and worst Portland has to offer.

The night of the fire also pre-empted the fireworks and hoopla of that weekend's Milwaukie Daze Festival, a quirky down-home celebration featuring beer gardens, carnival rides, concerts, and art shows. Many of the seventeen full- and part-time employees of Moores' Flour Mill were planning to indulge in one or both of the mid-June offerings. But the burning of the big red wood building at 4001 Roethe Road that Tuesday night changed the plans – and lives – of everyone associated with the nine-year-old company.

When Dean turned the fire truck right onto McLoughlin Boulevard, the main drag from Gladstone through Milwaukie and into Portland, he flipped on the siren so he could race through the red stoplights. In the distance he saw smoke and the glow of a very angry fire. It was at that moment a switch went off in his head, and he said to himself, "Oh crap, what am I gonna do for a job now?" Hoping it wasn't, but now knowing it was, his place of employment that was burning, Dean began playing the tape in his head that repeated the same questions over and over. "How am I going to pay the rent?" "I've got a car payment, what do I tell the bank?" "Where am I going to find a job?"

Tuesday, June 14, 1988, was a typical day in the life of Bob and Charlee Moore. Bob rose early as he usually did, dressed, and headed down to the Bomber Restaurant for breakfast. Charlee enjoyed her quiet mornings at home as she readied herself for work. Most mornings Bob arrived at the aviation-themed restaurant just after it opened at 6 a.m. Owner Art Lacey already had the coffee on and was seated at his usual table with Wes Tarr, a local contractor known as "The Construction Doctor." Five days a week for more than four years, Wes would meet Art at 4:30 a.m. at the back door, ready for coffee and conversation. Bob Johnson, for whom nearby Johnson City was named, was one of Bob's friends from Kiwanis, and he usually showed up as well.

Bob, Wes, Bob, and Art talked about the usual stuff that bright sunny mid-June morning – their business, the weather, politics, movies, and the news. *Bull Durham* with Kevin Costner and Susan Sarandon was opening the next day in Hollywood. Of course, they commiserated, they would have to wait a couple of weeks to see a first-run movie here in the Pacific Northwest. And they debated what it might mean to their respective businesses if Michael Dukakis, who had just clinched the Democratic nomination for president the week before, were to win over Vice President George H. W. Bush, the Republican nominee.

Over a bowl of oatmeal (of course), Bob gave the guys an update on his business. The company had just celebrated its ninth anniversary in May and he was projecting a thirty-four percent increase over 1987's sales total of $1,604,558. Bob kept meticulous records. Every day on a desktop calendar he would write down the day's retail and wholesale sales numbers. Then at the end of the month, he would document sales figures for total retail and wholesale, as well as daily averages for each. For example, May's total sales were $204,387. Wholesale business accounted for $182,068 and retail $22,319. The daily average of $8,175 in combined sales was a very good number. Revenue from his little retail store remained steady, but thanks to Fred Meyer, Safeway and other grocery chains that carried his Bob's Red Mill branded products, Bob's wholesale business was growing month over month.

Business was so good, he told the guys, he felt compelled to share the profits with the people who made it possible – his employees. He explained that as of June 1, he had instituted a new year-end bonus program.

That memo, along with the bulletin board and the wall it was posted on – everything, in fact – burned to the ground later that night when a suspected arsonist lit a fire in the dumpster and pushed it up against the old wooden mill.

After locking up that evening, Bob made the one-mile drive home and settled in for a relaxing evening. He couldn't know that as he was getting into bed about eleven that night, there was a young woman from Southeast Portland who may have been preparing for her nightly ritual of crossing into Clackamas County from neighboring Multnomah County to cause damage to businesses and storefronts along McLoughlin Boulevard, the main thoroughfare through Milwaukie. The Clackamas County Sheriff's Office, on the other hand, was well aware of Kathleen Susan Anders and her night-time antics. They dubbed her the "CRX Lady," because between January and May of 1988, either she or her car had been spotted more than fifty times at locations in the county where fire or burglar alarms had been activated. She usually used a rock or a crowbar to break windows and set off alarms, but had escalated her repertoire to setting fires in dumpsters. It became a nightly routine for graveyard shift sheriff David Byrne to either pull her over or chase her back into Multnomah County. Police had ticketed her seventeen times for a variety of infractions in five months.

Charlee was the one who heard the phone ring sometime around midnight. She went downstairs to listen to the recorded message. The frantic voice was from one of their employees, Nancy Winston, who lived near the mill, Charlee will never forget the words, "If you get this message, call me right away."

"I could hear the sirens," she said. "In my heart, I knew our mill was on fire."

Bob was up and out the door first, racing down the road to get to his beloved mill. Charlee followed minutes later. Their worst fears were realized when they drove up to Moores' Flour Mill and saw the building engulfed in flames. As they huddled together in front of the burning mill, still trying to grasp what was happening, the realization that the building would not be standing in the morning started to wash over them. Bob recalls experiencing a state of numbness that temporarily blocked his emotions. A wall of flame that once constituted the east side of the mill store came crashing down, jarring his senses and bringing him back to the reality that all his equipment, supplies, machines, finished product, and treasured millstones were in the process of being destroyed. The thought of somehow trying to save those hundred-year-old stone grinding wheels propelled him into action.

After making sure Charlee was all right, Bob began searching for the fire marshal. He spied him over by one of the trucks. James Hart, fire marshal and assistant chief of the Oak Lodge Fire Department, knew Bob from the routine inspections of the mill he had made over the years. An old wooden flour mill bordering a residential area was definitely on his radar. After offering his condolences, Hart asked Bob if there was anything he could do. He said he had lots of available personnel and the trucks had plenty of water.

"I said, 'Yes, could you please try to save my millstones.'" Bob pointed out the mill room, and also the office where all his records were stored. Hart immediately dispatched a couple of firemen to each location. Bob watched as the men cut holes in the sides of the building. As soon as the openings were big enough, crews with fire hoses were directed to shoot water into those areas.

Would this be the end of the line for these century-old grinding wheels? They were the foundation of every miller's business. Bob's three pairs of French buhr stones were the heart of his grain milling operation. Without them, there would be no stone ground flour, wheat, barley, or rye. The premise of Moores' Flour Mill, the philosophy of its owner – that you stone grind a pound of grain and you get a pound of stone ground goodness, nothing added and nothing taken out – was in jeopardy. He abhorred the mass production of "roller-milled" white flour because the process removed the bran and germ of the wheat kernel, stripping it of its natural vitamins, minerals, and disease-fighting properties.

If he couldn't mill the old-fashioned way with millstones, he would simply walk away from the business. Because stone ground whole grains was more than a business to him. Ever since Charlee had convinced him to eat a healthy whole grain diet, his soul was invested in the lifestyle. He had become a whole grains evangelist, and nothing could deter him from his commitment.

Except maybe a fire that was in the process of destroying everything he had. As the rest of the building burned, Bob approached the fire marshal again. Hart could tell from the quizzical look on his face what he wanted to know. "It was arson, Bob. Looks like somebody pushed your dumpster up against the side of that open shed and lit it on fire."

Bob looked hard at the area the fire marshal was pointing out. That shed was where he stored old flour sacks and large paper bags that had held hundreds of pounds of grain. Given the hot, dry weather they'd been having, and the flour dust and residue in the storage shed, any spark or flame would instantly ignite those materials. And probably create a small explosion as well.

As Bob struggled to comprehend who could have deliberately come onto his property with the intent to destroy his business, a singular thought began coursing through his brain. As emotionally spent as he was from the night's tragic unfolding, he felt an inner peace. While others in his place might have cursed God, Bob held fast to his belief that everything happens for a purpose, that God is always in control, no matter what.

And then, in the midst of the still frantic activity around him, and with the flames finally starting to subside, his mind turned to his employees. Seventeen souls that counted on him. A dozen families that put food on the table because they had a job at the mill. His emotions raw, he felt a sadness come over him, as the sensation of letting down the good people who worked for him started to sink in. A heaviness settled on him as he started thinking about the reality of tomorrow. Yesterday he had a thriving business. He was on track to gross two million dollars that year. Everyone was excited about the new profit-sharing program he had just announced. Fred Meyer and Safeway had been increasing their orders month after month. Now he didn't have a mill to produce a product. He didn't have a place for his employees to work. For nearly ten years, this is where he had spent most of his waking life. This is what he loved to do. Now, at fifty-nine years old, it had all been taken away from him.

The next couple of days were a blur. Police officers and fire investigators needed to interview him. Employees posed questions he couldn't answer. Retailers he had been supplying were itching to know if their orders would be filled. Bills were coming due and there were bank loans to consider. Condolences flooded in from friends and loyal customers. And the media kept calling, wanting to know what he was going to do next.

Bob had been interviewed by several journalists in the days after the fire, but none with quite the panache of TV newsman Paul Linnman. The KATU anchor for the local ABC affiliate was the closest thing to a "news celebrity" in Portland, having gained fame for his coverage of the infamous "Exploding Whale" story (it was so popular that Linnman eventually wrote a book about it). On November 12, 1970, the twenty-three-year-old rookie reporter and cameraman Doug Brazil were on the Oregon coast to witness the planned disposal of a whale carcass. The forty-five-foot-long sperm whale had died as a result of beaching itself near the town of Florence. Consultation with officials from the U.S. Navy culminated in the decision to try to disintegrate the estimated 16,000-pound behemoth by blowing it up with dynamite. A half ton of explosives was used, and the ensuing magnificent explosion was caught on film as Linnman narrated. As large body parts rained down on nearby buildings and parked cars, his voiceover was peppered with humor. He joked that "this land-lubber newsman had become a land-*blubber* newsman" as squishy whale parts landed on the assembled crowd. His alliterative "the blast blasted blubber beyond all believable bounds" caught the attention of Pulitzer Prize–winning humor columnist Dave Barry, who described the "Exploding Whale" story as the funniest single news event he had ever seen.

There was nothing humorous about Linnman's interview with a stoic Bob Moore days after the fire. As the two walked the inhospitable property, the only evidence the place used to be a thriving milling operation was an antique printing press employees used to print labels on paper sacks. The rest was pretty much a charred mess.

In the somber opening to his news story that night, Linnman stated, "Businesses that experience a fire usually bounce back better than ever, finding new life and big insurance payouts. But that's not the case with Moores' Flour Mill. Channel 2 News learned today that despite rapidly growing business and a devoted clientele, it may be over for Moore."

He described Moores' Flour Mill as "something of an institution in the community…as a popular retail outlet and attraction." From a much earlier interview, a beaming Bob Moore was quoted as saying "people come out here to see this marvelous old building with all its marvelous old milling equipment, and they say 'Good grief, you're for real!'"

"But whatever magic Moores' Flour Mill had went up in smoke early on June 15; the fire was arson-caused," Linnman reported. "Insurance didn't cover Bob Moore's losses, and he says the cost of rebuilding is astronomical. And while Moore at first said the mill would make a comeback, that's now in doubt."

As a beleaguered Bob Moore looked into the camera during the interview, one could see the angst on his face. The agony of the previous few days had taken its toll. He looked crestfallen. His shoulders stooped. When asked what he was going to do now, he haltingly responded with, "Well, we thought we'd pretty well made a decision today. I don't know. Then you came out, and...I don't know. We really have criss-crossed between chucking the whole thing, and, uh, I don't know." He looked back at the reporter, shook his head a couple of times, and finally said it "I really don't know what I'm going to do, Paul. I just don't know."

CHAPTER 2

A FAMILY BUSINESS

A S FAR BACK AS HE CAN REMEMBER, BOB MOORE KNEW WHAT HE wanted to do in life. He would go into business with his dad. Just like his dad had done with his father. They talked about it constantly. Late into the night in their Los Angeles home, father and son would dream about the company they would someday own together. He can remember that even as an eight-year-old, their discussions always centered on building things and selling them – machinery, motors, and electrical equipment. That's because Bob's dad, Ken, worked at the time as a salesman for the Independent Addressing Machine Company. He sold the electric motor–driven machines that stamped out mailing addresses and labels for magazines and other printed material. Bob's grandfather, Frank, had started the company in 1930 during the Great Depression. In fact, he opened his doors only months after the U.S. stock market crashed on Black Tuesday (October 29, 1929). Given his entrepreneurial spirit, he might have been buoyed by the optimistic words of American business icon John D. Rockefeller, who said, "These are days when many are discouraged. In the ninety-three years of my life, depressions have come and gone. Prosperity has always returned and will again." While the stock market did initially reverse its devastating decline in the first part of 1930, returning to pre–October 1929 levels by April, the nation's income continued to drop and the domestic economy plummeted.

Frank struggled to make ends meet in the mid-'30s, and felt if he could just convince his son to come work for him, he might be able to turn things around. Deep down, Ken wanted to go into business with his dad. But he and his young bride, Doris, had just welcomed their first-born son into the world less than a year before his dad had started the addressing machine company. It was too risky for a twenty-five-year-old family man to go all-in on a Depression-era startup.

So, to support the three of them, Ken found jobs in sales – at a newspaper and on a bread truck route. But when he turned thirty-three, the lure of working side-by-side with his dad in the family business was too great to resist anymore. He moved the family from San Bernardino back to Los Angeles and took a sales job at the Independent Addressing Machine Company.

Bob remembers those three years as some of the best of his life. Grandfather and father working together. And when they weren't at the office, they were talking shop. Bob was only nine, but he vividly recalls the conversations, especially on the weekends, when he would sit with his dad and grandpa and listen to their stories about the addressograph business. Mostly he was interested in hearing about the equipment they used. He was fascinated by the workings of the machines that stamped out the plates and printed addresses onto the envelopes. When his dad had taken him to the plant, he stood close to the large steel frame of the addressograph machine, mesmerized by the sights and sounds of the stamping process. Wide-eyed, he watched as the operator used a foot pedal to stamp out the addresses, swapping out the assembly plates in sequence, sort of like slides in a slide projector. The assembly plates came from steel cassettes that looked like library card catalog drawers. In a blur, a rapidly moving inked ribbon popped into the space between the raised type and the mail piece to create the stamped impression.

Bob was also very curious about the business aspects of the operation.

Since he believed he would someday be working at the Independent Addressing Machine Company, and probably owning it himself one day, he felt obliged to learn all he could about running the place. He wanted to know about the distribution process, the sales cycle, the costs to buy materials and fulfill orders. He figured if he were going to be president of the company, he should also know about the finances, salaries, banking relationships, etc.

But when it came to discussing the numbers, granddad and dad grew distant. Then the arguments would start. The sixth-grader didn't pick up on it then, but every time the issue of money came up, voices would be raised and the conversation became more heated – until one or the other would change the subject. That conversation changer went over Bob's head, and it certainly didn't dissuade him from jabbering on about how the three generations of Moores would one day be in business together.

"It was always 'when' we would go into business together," Bob recalls. "It was never 'if.'" Looking back, he describes the concept of father and son going into business together as "permeating every aspect of our lives."

"We didn't even have to talk about it sometimes. We knew. It was just an important ingredient in our relationship."

Bob's first indication that something had gone terribly wrong at the Independent Addressing Machine Company was when the sheriff came to the door and told his mom he had a court order. As the scared little boy watched, the stern man with the clipboard began checking items off on a list he had. He told his mom he was looking for property that belonged to the Independent Addressing Machine Company. When she asked why, he told her it was for the bankruptcy proceedings.

Devastated, mom and son stood by while the sheriff gathered up a couple of things, including a typewriter that dad had brought home from the office. Even today, Bob doesn't know if his dad brought the typewriter home to salvage it because he knew the company was going broke. But apparently somewhere, it was on a list. What he did find out was the company didn't have enough operating capital to buy raw materials.

"When dad would bring in the business, it was the worst thing in the world because they couldn't fulfill the orders."

It was 1940, and the ten-year run for the Independent Addressing Machine Company was over. Bob doesn't know who was more disappointed – his grandfather for convincing his dad to quit his good-paying job and join the family business or his dad for accepting the job. Either way, Frank and Ken Moore's dreams of having a business together were over.

But not Bob's. Sure, he was only eleven years old, but he was convinced nothing could get in the way of working together with his dad. Even as Ken and Doris Moore struggled to pay the bills in the aftermath of the bankruptcy, they encouraged their only child to dream big dreams. Neither father nor son was deterred from planning for the eventuality of starting a business. Maybe their late-night conversations helped assuage his dad's feelings of failure. They certainly encouraged the soon-to-be teenager. He didn't care much for his schoolwork, and he had no problem staying up late on weeknights researching money-making ventures and writing up business plans. With books, papers, and charts spread out on the dinner table, the two would share pot after pot of coffee. And his dad would smoke. In fact, both Mom and Dad smoked. His dad wouldn't put out his last cigarette of the night until his mom called out from the bedroom what she had to say almost every school night: "Will you two quit talking and go to bed!"

Bob's entrepreneurial bent wasn't shaped solely by his dad's side of the family. His great-grandfather on his mother's side started several businesses, invented stuff, and even wrote a book. Jacob Yost and his wife Sarah raised seven children, and all worked in some capacity for Yost Yeast, the family business. During that time, 1895–1905, everybody baked their own bread. Since ancient times people have used yeast for baking and fermentation. For bread baking, it was an essential leavening agent that would cause the dough to rise and give the baked product a soft and spongy texture. So, having quality yeast in the kitchen was a must.

Fleischmann's Yeast was the dominant commercial brand, but small mom and pop operations provided locally sourced options as well. What

**Bob's Great-Grandfather Yost at the Arkansas
City Independence Day parade (1901)**

started out as a small home-based business in their modest Arkansas City, Kansas, neighborhood grew to become a thriving concern with multi-state distribution.

Daughter Daisy Yost Barnes would later write, "It was a dry-crumb yeast that mother started making in her kitchen in a small way. My brothers started selling it in the neighborhood and around town until there was enough demand for it that grocers were asking for it."

A grocery store owner told them they needed a trade name for the product, so they came up with "Sunflower Brand" of Yost's Homemade Yeast. They applied lithograph labels to the small packages of yeast with a picture of a sunflower and a bread recipe. When production outgrew the parlor, which had been converted into a drying and packaging room, the Yosts built a factory at the corner of D Street and Gravel Street. Jacob planted peach trees on the ten-acre lot, as he learned the dry crumbled peach leaves had the same effect in making the yeast as did hops, which he had been buying.

The "Sunflower Brand" was doing so well it caught the attention of a competitor who offered to buy the Yosts out. The Yeast Foam Company "made a good offer to buy out the business, but my father and brothers thought it was doing too well for what they offered," Daisy wrote. The bigger competitor then tried a different strategy. They started mailing out free sample packets from the Yeast Foam Company to households in the Yost's territory. As business declined, Daisy lamented, "It then became the old story of Big Business overcoming a small one." Jacob wouldn't sell out, but after ten years he was ready to move on. He had actually been spending less time at the yeast factory and more time on a new business venture.

His new revenue-generating scheme was all about "greenbacks, gold, and silver." In his book, he described it as *"The Hen as a Money-maker"*:

> The hen converts grass into greenbacks, grain into gold, and for the sand and gravel she returns us silver. The hen yields the farmer more for the investment than any other animal, and gives him the least trouble. She asks nothing of him unless he chooses to give it to her, but if he so chooses to supply her needs, she returns the compliment many fold and places at his disposal an article which is demanded in his domestic economy.

According to family history, Jacob had a love affair with hens, and had been raising chickens for as long as anyone could remember. He eventually turned it into a business at a scale large enough to supply fryers and fresh eggs to the Fred Harvey Eating House and other local hotels and restaurants in the Arkansas City area. The industrious inventor also built the machinery and equipment needed for a large-scale chicken-raising operation, primarily incubators and brooders. His *Kansas Incubator No. 1* had a capacity of 300 eggs and featured a device that turned all the eggs in each tray at the same time without touching the eggs. As incubators are a substitute in the poultry industry for sitting hens, Jacob would show off his invention to his war veteran buddies at the Old Soldiers

Reunion, timing the incubator to hatch baby chicks during the annual Fall meeting.

In the introduction to his book *The Care, Cure, and Protection of Poultry*, which was registered in 1895 with the Library of Congress in Washington, D.C., he was proud to share his knowledge with budding chicken ranchers:

> In putting out this book, I have kept in mind to whom it will be of most benefit. I have ten years experience in the raising of poultry and if that experience is worth anything to those interested in the business, I will feel that I have done well in departing desirable information, as well as gaining a profit for myself. The description of the machines and buildings are carried out minutely so that the boys and girls can read them intelligently and by the assistance of the materials and a few tools they will find all the information necessary to carry out everything essential to a successful end.

But at age fifty-nine, the strain of running a chicken and egg operation, as well as trying to fend off a bigger competitor in the yeast business, became untenable. So, Jacob and Sarah put their house up for sale, sold their other properties, and moved the family to Southern California.

The family settled in Orange County, and while their parents enjoyed a nice retirement, the siblings who moved west with them found new careers not related to the old family business. One son, Charles, however, parlayed his sales experience in the yeast category into a position with the Continental Baking Company. He started as a salesman and worked his way up the corporate ladder, ultimately making it to senior management. The company was in the business of baking and selling bread, cake, and other related bakery products. They were widely known for their two leading brands – "Wonder" for its bread products and "Hostess" for its cake products. One might conclude it was inevitable Bob would end up in the baking business. After all, his great-grandfather was in the yeast business; his great uncle was a bigwig at a bread and cake company, and even his dad spent several years surrounded by bread – literally. Shortly after Bob was born, his dad's Uncle Charles used his influence at the Continental Baking Company to land Ken Moore a bread delivery job. They gave him a boxy 1931 Dodge truck, filled it to the top with Wonder bread and Hostess cakes, and provided a map with grocery store destinations. Only problem was the route was in San Bernardino County. While the orange groves of Orange County marked the outskirts of Los Angeles in the 1930s, the desert and mountains of San Bernardino represented the outer limits of civilization at the time. It was a brand new route, and covered hundreds of miles of sand-swept back roads. Ken, sometimes with little Bobby aboard, would make the rounds – Yucaipa, Beaumont, Banning, taking them tantalizingly close to Palm Springs; but the territory veered east toward the San Bernardino Mountains. At least they got to tour the national forest and the resort towns near Big Bear Lake and Lake Arrowhead. Bored or not with the monotony of the long drive, Bob remembers his dad whistling. All day long. It was hard to hear the tunes some days, what with there being no door on the driver's side, but the son in the bouncy passenger seat has never forgotten the beautiful sound.

Bob treasured the good memories of father and son together in the Wonder˙ bread truck. They spent seven years in San Bernardino, long enough that dad expanded the business so another driver took over the bread route and Ken managed the cakes and other baked goods. And it was during those early formative years that the youngster began dreaming about working with his father. He idolized him. Loved being around him. Couldn't wait until he was old enough to join his dad in a company that they would start together. It was in his blood. His great-grandfather worked with his boys. His grandfather brought his dad into the family business. And someday Bob would work for his dad.

Except it didn't work out that way. Before son and father could realize their dream of going into business together, Ken Moore, a heavy smoker, died of a massive heart attack at just forty-nine years old. All the planning. All the late-night conversations. All the dreams. Gone in a heartbeat.

Even today, an eighty-one-year-old Bob Moore admits he still misses his dad terribly. Still thinks about him every day. Still wonders "what if."

CHAPTER 3

WHISTLING AND DIXIE

Maternity

There once was a Square, such a square little Square,
And he loved a trim Triangle;
But she was a flirt and around her skirt
Vainly she made him dangle.
Oh he wanted to wed and he had no dread
Of domestic woes and wrangles;
For he thought that his fate was to procreate
Cute little Squares and Triangles.

by Robert W. Service

Robert W. Service was Doris Learnard's favorite poet. He was a bit wild for her strict Methodist upbringing, but the eighteen-year-old Long Beach woman was becoming quite the independent thinker. The denomination's *Book of Discipline* prohibited drinking and promoted a strict and legalistic religious lifestyle. Some of the straitlaced practices for women in the church were to wear no make-up and never cut their hair. Accordingly, Doris's mom, Gertrude, and her two aunts, Daisy and Rosie, wore their long locks in tightly rolled buns.

So, it was a bit of a break from the ol' Methodist mold to hear "Aunt Doris" on radio station KGER reciting poetry from the author of such bawdy bar-room ballads as "Infidelity," "Virginity," and "Laughter." Doris had gotten the job at the Southern California radio station through family connections at the Methodist Church they attended in Long Beach. Station owner C. Merwin Dobyns, an independent oil operator and retail shoe merchant, established KGER on December 12, 1926, primarily as a religious radio station with a variety of Christian programming. KGER initially had a whopping transmitter power of one hundred watts, certainly a strong enough signal to hear the broadcast several blocks from the Dobyns Footwear Building at 435 Pine Avenue in Long Beach. Dobyns hired Doris to be the radio station's receptionist, but within a few months he gave her her own program. Opening with the distinctive "clop clop" sound of horse hooves (okay, they were probably coconut shells banged together, but, hey, the entrepreneurial Dobyns was selling "shoes" downstairs, after all), the "Aunt Doris" program would feature her poetry reading, some Bible lessons, and local music provided by the likes of the Long Beach Municipal Band.

In the early '30s, most people got their news from newspapers, but a few pioneering radio stations were beginning to add news to their broadcasts. In order to keep up with the competition, Dobyns decided to add a news program to the show,[1] so he contacted the local newspaper, the Long Beach *Press-Telegram*. He asked if they could send someone over every morning with the news highlights of the day. The *Press-Telegram* wanted the free advertising, so they assigned twenty-two-year-old Kenneth Earle Moore to be the runner. When he climbed the stairs to the second-floor offices of KGER and saw the pretty young woman sitting

---

1 Well-known Los Angeles newsman Clete Roberts was part of the KGER local news team early in his storied career. With his trademark mustache and signature sign-off, "I bid you a pleasant evening," Roberts was a TV news fixture in Southern California for more than thirty years.

at the receptionist desk, Ken determined he would be more than happy to come back every day to deliver the newspaper. The nice young man would tarry at the front desk, ostensibly to circle with his red pen the top news stories to be read on the radio that day. But his true intentions became clear when he asked Doris out on a date.

Doris's dad had died when she was a young girl, so she couldn't seek his approval of her new beau. But she certainly had it from her mom and her two aunts. They adored Ken. Even though he smoked and probably had a drink now and then, they looked past those bad habits and believed he had a good heart. It was obvious the two twenty-somethings were in love. A whirlwind romance culminated in a wedding on May 15, 1928, and Ken and Doris Moore started their new life together. The newlyweds decided a change of scenery was needed, so they packed up and moved north to live with Ken's aunt and uncle in Portland, Oregon.

Otto and Nellie Brandes owned a creamery on Front Street, but the rural setting of the Pacific Northwest was quite a departure from the city life and pleasant weather Ken and Doris had become accustomed to in Southern California. Jobs were hard to come by in an economy heading into the Great Depression, and Ken soon figured out he wasn't interested in a blue-collar career at the creamery. And he hated the cold and the rain. February, 1929, was especially intolerable, as several cities in Oregon established all-time low temperatures, including Pendleton at minus twenty-eight degrees. The only good thing about that unbearably cold month was the birth of their first child. A boy. Robert Gene Moore was born in Portland on February 15, 1929. They called him "Bobby," and his dad couldn't be prouder he had a son.

Doris missed her family terribly, and the new father couldn't wait to show off his pride and joy to the relatives back in California. So when little Bobby was about six months old, they stuffed their meager belongings into a couple of old suitcases and boarded a Greyhound bus bound for Los Angeles. The trip was memorable, at least for the parents, who years later would laugh together as they told the story of their baby's diapers being full the entire trip.

Doris and Ken Moore with four-year-old Bobby (1933)

Back in Southern California after his relocation experiment in Oregon, Ken Moore had to rely on relatives once again to find a job. He'd tried the newspaper business in Long Beach, slogged through a miserable year at his uncle's creamery in rainy Portland, and now found himself in San Bernardino driving a bread route thanks to his great-uncle's influence with the Continental Baking Company.

Family was important to Doris and Ken. They regularly made the 140-mile round-trip drive to Long Beach for holiday gatherings and weekend visits. With their little toddler in tow, mom and dad were favored guests at the combined family picnics. Great-grandpa Yost was going deaf, and the gruff old man kind of scared him, but Bob treasures the pleasant memories of a large extended family. There were lots of cousins and kids his age to play with. And his mom's mom and her two sisters always fawned over little Bobby. It seemed to him that Grandma Gertrude and great-aunts Daisy and Rosie were always around, and it provided a very stabilizing effect to the youngster who was an only child for fourteen years. Or maybe it was because the three sisters lived so long that Bob felt their ongoing presence so distinctly. They each lived more than one hundred years. And all three of them died the same year, 1998.

Growing up in San Bernardino was a happy time for young Bobby. He felt free. Sure, it was the 1930s and there was the Depression, but his dad had a steady job and the family didn't want for anything. Maybe it had to do with the fact that Ken Moore whistled. Beautifully. All day. The sound was comforting and reassuring. When his dad whistled, Bobby felt everything was going to be okay. While he idolized his dad, Bobby was very close to his mother as well. As a homemaker, she had the time to spend with her only child. She would wake him up in the morning, feed him breakfast, and then walk him to school. And she was there when he got home. There were few, if any, restrictions placed on him. San Bernardino was a small town in the 1930s, and moms and dads didn't have to worry about letting their kids run loose. Especially in the summertime, when it was scorching hot in the valley. Bob remembers getting up early on Saturday mornings, throwing on a pair of shorts, and running barefoot out of the house to play with friends. One 110-degree day he remembered his feet burning after he ran across the street in front of his house. Looking back, he could see the imprint his bare feet had made in the melted asphalt. Some Saturdays he wouldn't get back until dark. Total freedom. But there was a catch. And Bob vividly remembers a conversation with his dad when he was seven years old.

"He talked to me about freedom. He was such a great talker. 'This is a free country,' he would say. 'As long as you don't disobey the law, you have freedom. And it's only free to people who obey the laws of the land. Just remember that.' That was a very important life lesson for me. My dad was a great philosopher about things. Here he was preaching to me about freedom when I was only seven years old. I think he liked me. My mom liked me, too. And I liked them."

There was somebody else Bobby liked at the time, too. Her name was Dixie and she was in his third-grade class. And whether it was because of the popular 1936 rendition of the song "Is It True What They Say About Dixie?" by Ozzie Nelson and his Orchestra, or his budding fascination with the opposite sex, Bobby felt a strong attraction for the pretty girl.

"My dad had huge respect for womankind," Bob recalls. "He was always telling me how you open the door for them, how you should treat them. I was aware of the difference, the fascination, an attraction, a genuine curiosity, I think, for the opposite sex. And even when I was in the third grade, he made me aware of a responsibility toward them."

Dixie lived in the same neighborhood, and every now and then Bobby would find himself walking her to school (although from her perspective he admits she probably felt they were "walking to school" vs. "Bobby was walking me to school"). Either way, Bobby surmised she must have been attracted to him because of one particular incident on their walk to school.

Their route took them through a new housing development where several homes were under construction. On previous trips, Bobby had rummaged through the piles of discarded lumber, collecting nails and boards he would bring home and build things with (this trait of sourcing scraps and discarded building materials to save money and cobble things together became a lifelong endeavor and a source of satisfaction for the future miller). Their detour through the side yards of the half-built wooden structures led the two third-graders to a pile of stacked lumber, which they scrambled up and then perched themselves on the top with feet dangling over the edge.

Bob doesn't recall how long they sat there, but he does remember getting close to the opposite sex was extraordinarily fascinating. "I guess I was able to say enough things that kept her interested in sitting up there with me for a few minutes…and it wasn't planned or anything like that, but then I just leaned over and kissed her on the cheek. I can still remember that moment to this day – how I felt; and how she reacted."

Dixie jumped off the stack of boards. And took off. She ran all the way to school. And by the time little Bobby had recovered from his mountain top experience and made his way to the schoolyard, all the kids knew about the stolen kiss. Dixie had blabbed to everybody. And the jeers and ribbing started immediately. It was the most embarrassing thing that had ever happened to the red-faced eight-year-old.

"It was a little slice of my life that stands out in modest detail. It was simply an impulse and can't be interpreted in any other way than just my full fascination with this creature that was different than me, smelled different, looked different, felt different. I never touched her, and I certainly never kissed her again. Obviously, I rather avoided Dixie after that."

His parents were affectionate toward each other in the presence of their only child, and that probably contributed to what Bob feels was a healthy and normal upbringing. Whether they ever knew about the kissing incident, he doesn't know; but he wasn't able to hide his subsequent expulsion from the third grade. Getting kicked out of elementary school today certainly wouldn't happen without parents' knowledge, but apparently in 1938 the communication between school and home was spotty. Anyway, Miss West didn't always appreciate the antics of her rambunctious third-grade student. He just wouldn't stop talking in class, even when she told him to be quiet.

CHAPTER 4

FREEDOM

B OB ADMITS AS A YOUNGSTER HE WAS INTERESTED IN EVERYTHING BUT
school, and his mind would wander. In today's world, teachers
would probably label him ADHD and send him to a special class for
disruptive kids. But back then, after an especially intolerable outburst,
Miss West lost her patience and took immediate action. She escorted
him to the cloakroom, took out the paddle (the kind that had the split
down the middle so when they hit you with it, it sounded like it broke a
bone, Bob recalls) and walloped him a few times. Even that didn't stop
him from talking back, so she kicked him out of school. Told him not to
come back until he had learned his lesson and wouldn't be so talkative in
her classroom.

Well, to an eight-year-old who didn't like school anyway, that was a
sentence he quite enjoyed. And since Miss West didn't inform his parents he had been expelled, it became the perfect opportunity for a secret
holiday break. Bobby told no one. The little rascal went home that afternoon at the normal time, ate dinner with his folks and went outside to
play with his friends as he usually did. The next morning he played along
with the regular routine, but when his mom walked him to school that

day, he tarried a bit and as soon as she was out of sight he took off. All day long he roamed the streets of San Bernardino, enjoying his freedom and reprieve from school.

He hopped a fence bordering Blazedell's Auto Park where they lived and spent hours exploring what he remembers was the largest farm in an incorporated city in the United States at the time (for years Bob saved the *Ripley's Believe It or Not* story about their unique neighbor). He jumped on the back of one of Mr. Field's horses and just sat there while the bored animal munched on grass. When the train came chugging up the pass on the railroad tracks that ran behind the property, he ran over and leaned in as close to the diesel locomotive as he dared, just to feel the whoosh of the fast-moving air and smell the metallic tailings of the huge machine. When he got tired, he would wander over to the large barn, climb up into the rafters, and spend hours observing the operations of the working farm. Always fascinated with machinery, his attention would be fixed on the tractors that plied the fields. It was harvest time, and the future grain miller remembers being mesmerized by the process of the cutting, bailing and transport of what was reaped that day. And the smells stuck with him forever.

The little truant's Huck Finn experience came to an inglorious end when word finally reached his parents. The three days of being AWOL from school only served to solidify the third grader's disdain for the confines of the education system. He was much more interested in cars and anything mechanical. He wasn't a bad kid, but neither was he a good student. He made choices as a youngster that he regrets today. Given the opportunity to learn certain scholastic building blocks, Bobby opted out. Some people never learned to swim, Bob never learned how to cursive write. For the rest of his life, he would print every letter of every word he wrote. He was proficient at it, and fast, but it has remained one of those missed opportunities that still sticks in his craw. As much as he loves the written word today, especially hand-written notes and letters, he still wishes he could produce the more elegant and seemingly lost art of cursive writing.

The third grade was so memorable to Bob because right in the middle of the school year his dad succumbed to *his* dad's petition to come work for him at the Independent Addressing Machine Company. So, Ken Moore quit the San Bernardino bread route his uncle had gotten him and moved to Los Angeles to join his father in the family business. It was 1938, a transitionary time for the country – post-Depression and pre–World War II. Ken, Doris, and their son were moving from "the Wild West" to downtown L.A., and while that meant being closer to aunts, uncles and cousins for nine-year-old Bobby, he would have to adjust to a new school, new teacher, and hopefully, new friends.

Thank goodness for the seating arrangement in Mrs. Mockman's third grade class. She assigned the new kid to a desk right behind the prettiest girl in the school. Her name was Diana Rogers. She was taller than he was, kind of willowy, but it was her long hair that dazzled him. He had a hard enough time focusing on his lessons, but this beautiful creation sitting two feet in front of him precluded him from paying much attention to the teachings of Mrs. Mockman.

"I was an only child until I was fourteen years old with no other female influence in my life except my mother's, so I was keenly aware of the difference between the sexes. I didn't know anything about them at all; they were mysterious to me. But at the time, I thought it was very pleasant."

The suave admirer didn't try to pull a "Dixie" on the cute Diana, but later, she became the first girl he ever dated. Bobby asked his mom and dad if they would go on a double date with the two twelve-year-olds, and they said "yes." Bob doesn't remember the movie the four of them saw, but he was sure they had a great time. The two remained friends for many years. Bobby and Diana's older brother Fred got involved in Scouts together, but it was probably just a veiled ploy for Bobby to hang around Fred's sister after school. Diana was on his radar even after the two graduated from high school. Bob remained an admirer, although from a distance, as the young lady blossomed with a career as a Hollywood entertainer. She became one of the "Earl Carroll Girls," a collection of beautiful women who in the 1930s and '40s sang and danced at clubs

Mr. Carroll owned in New York and Los Angeles. According to author Ken Murray who wrote *The Body Merchant*, Earl Carroll was "the most notorious connoisseur of female flesh in the history of show business."

Guests at the Earl Carroll Theatre Restaurant in Hollywood received postcards with glam shots of his girls on one side and this printed on the other:

> This favorite gathering place of celebrities from radio and screen is located in the heart of romantic Hollywood. The most distinctive theater in the world. Luxuriously appointed. Beautifully decorated. With its all-star cast, outstanding shows and sixty of the most beautiful girls in the world adoring the lavish review is a MUST on your list of the best in entertainment. Dance to a famous orchestra. Watch a coast-to-coast CBS broadcast and enjoy the superb dinner, created by world renowned chefs. The cost is remarkably little: $3.30 includes a deluxe dinner or $1.65 without dinner, plus tax. You are welcome early, stay late and never buy a drink unless you want to. Evening clothes are not required and ladies may come in unescorted. A visit to Earl Carroll's is a breath-taking, memorable experience.

After they had addressed the cards, guests would give them back to the waiters, who would forward them to Mr. Carroll to be mailed. A clever marketing tool, the "Earl Carroll Girls" postcards canvassed the world, prompting many male recipients to schedule a visit when they traveled to Southern California.

While Bobby's interest in the fairer sex remained piqued (including an infatuation with Jewel in the fourth grade), he got involved in another lifelong pursuit – music. His parents enrolled him in the National Institute of Music and Arts and signed him up for violin lessons. Throughout his grammar school years, it was violin and orchestra practice on Wednesday nights. And then one day his parents surprised him by bringing home an old piano they had purchased for five dollars. It was so big they had to take off the front door and even remove the door trim to get it into the house. It landed in Bobby's bedroom, and forevermore either a piano or a violin would be a fixture in his life. He could have bought his parents' home many times over with the two expensive instruments sitting in his Milwaukie, Oregon, home today. The Steinway & Sons nine-foot concert grand piano and the 1812 Giovanni Trinelli violin from Scandiano, Italy, are valued well into six figures.

Cub Scouts became another Moore family activity while Bobby was nine and ten years old, with Mom as den mother and Dad the assistant Cub master. The group of eight neighborhood boys who were part of the pack attached to their grammar school on Western Avenue in Los Angeles met at the Moores' home. The future Earl Carroll girl's brother Fred Rogers was the Boy Scout "advisor" to Bobby's Cub Scout group. Doris reveled in herding the boys dressed in their Cub Scout uniforms on field trips to museums, science fairs, and sporting events. With her radio show background, she would slip into different characters and entertain the boys in her sing-songy voice, "Let's see here, what are we going to do today?" she would tease. Then she would shepherd them onto the streetcar and head downtown to Exposition Park, a 160-acre playground for kids and adults. One day it would be the Natural History Museum, where the boys would roam the halls for hours, gawking at the dinosaur exhibits, Indian artifacts, and historic displays. Another time they would spend half a day exploring the exotic flowers and beautiful landscapes at the Rose Garden. They made several trips to the California Museum of Science and Industry, and toured the National Armory as well. A real jaw dropper for the young sports fans was walking onto the field of the 100,000+ seat Los Angeles Memorial Coliseum. Here was where their heroes on the University of Southern California's Trojan football team played their home games, where the 1932 Summer Olympics was held, and where the National Football League's Los Angeles Rams began playing in 1946.

While his Cub Scouting days were fun and exciting, Bob looks back on the experience as an impactful and important formative phase of his young life. The organization's aim was "to help boys grow into good

**Ten-year-old Cub Scout/Musician in front of the
Moore family home in Los Angeles (1939)**

citizens who are strong in character and personally fit." Even at eighty-one years of age, no one would argue today that Bob Moore isn't the epitome of strong character and personal fitness. He possesses the same values and morals that were instilled in him as a child. That's not to say he couldn't be a little troublemaker sometimes.

One Halloween when he was twelve, Bobby and his mom carved a scary face on a pumpkin. He wanted to see how brightly the candle inside illuminated the jack-o'-lantern, so later that night he placed it on the window sill of the family bathroom and went outside to admire his monstrous creation. When he got outside and looked up at the ghoulish sight, it was bright all right. He had placed the pumpkin too close to the curtain, and the flickering candle had ignited the lacy window covering.

Screaming "FIRE," Bobby raced back into the house. By the time he got to the bathroom, his mom was already there beating down the flames. She got the fire out, and except for the burned curtains, there were just a few blackened spots on the window frame and ceiling where the paint was singed. The little pyromaniac was scared to death. Initially, because he thought he might have burned the house down. And secondly, because he expected a major whoopin'. But there was no spanking. No belt. The event passed unpunished. His mom and dad knew how bad their son felt, and they weren't the kind of parents who beat their child. This was a home filled with love. And mutual respect. It was when Bobby made the mistake of disrespecting his mother that he got the beating.

It only happened once. He was twelve or thirteen, but he never forgot the circumstances that led to his dad hitting him. Dad was sitting in his chair reading the newspaper. Mom was in the kitchen, and Bobby was standing in the doorway between the kitchen and the living room. Mom and son were having a discussion, which grew into an argument. And then Bobby did it – in a blatant demonstration of disrespect, he sassed his mom a good one. It wasn't like him to speak to his mother in irreverent tones, much less with a harsh word. But there it was, irretrievable; just hanging in the now silent air between the kitchen and living room. The next sound was the thud of the newspaper hitting the floor. Bob remembers his dad's eyes most of all. The hurt, the anger, the disappointment, all rolled up into one moment of fury.

"He hit me so hard I reeled backwards down the hall and into my bedroom, hit the wall, and ended up sitting down on the floor. He stormed into the room and slammed the door. 'Don't you ever speak to your mother that way again,' he said as he stood over me. He was mad. The maddest I had ever seen him. Here he was, the sweetest guy in the world. I know that day was harder on him than it was on me. I don't think he ever got over it. Later that night he came back into my room, and he was crying. He was so embarrassed because he got physical with me – and it was the only time he ever did – but he just loved my mom so much."

The violent episode devastated the Moore household for days. The uncharacteristic actions that unfolded that day rocked their world. A son learned that when it came to taking sides, the father sides with the mother. And he learned people are human. The experience opened his eyes to certain realities in life. That you can't take things back once they've been spoken in anger or acted out in a fit of rage. That there are ramifications to your actions. And, for good or bad, these are the life experiences that pile together to make you who you are.

Bobby wasn't afraid of his dad – ever. They knew each other too well to ever doubt where they stood in each other's eyes. Their bond was built on trust. And they shared a faith in each other that stayed strong because neither wanted to let the other one down. Bob remembers their talk, when he turned thirteen, about what freedom meant to the new teenager. To his dad, it meant being home by 9 p.m. But the independent young man who lobbied for a later curfew countered, "But, Dad, I would never do anything that you would be disappointed in. You've taught me right from wrong, so you don't have to worry."

The earned freedom Bob gained as a teenager extended into the kitchen as well. His mother gave him free rein to cook and bake as he pleased, and even though he would make an awful mess, she got a big kick out of her budding young baker. The Moores' kitchen was always open for Bob and his friends to experiment. On weekends he would bring his buddy Carl Holmes over and they would bake cookies, pies, and cakes. One day they tried to make a chocolate pie, and the future miller of flour and grains learned one of his first lessons about dough – less is more. Bob and Carl didn't know it at the time, but they soon discovered the more you work the dough, the tougher the crust. So, they were workin' it, workin' it, and workin' it. Then they formed it in the pie pan and let it bake while they made the chocolate pudding filling. When it was ready to eat, they got a sharp knife to slice it into pieces. Bob and Carl took turns trying to cut through the leaden crust. But it was so tough they couldn't make a dent in it. They finally gave up and ended up scooping out the chocolate pudding and eating it with spoons. But they weren't done with the hard doughy disk. Tearing it with their hands didn't work, so they took it outside and started tossing it around like a Frisbee. After several unsuccessful attempts to shatter it by flinging it against the fence, they got some clothespins and hung it on the clothesline. Target practice ensued. Utilizing rocks and other heavy objects, they finally succeeded in breaking their crusty creation apart. Mrs. Moore thought it was one of the funniest things she had ever seen. She got a kick out of her son's and his friend's antics.

Bob and Carl had better luck with the icebox cookies (after all, they were supposed to get hard when frozen). They would form the cookie dough into the shape of a small rolling pin, wrap it in wax paper, twist both ends to seal it, and put it in the icebox, which in those days was a non-mechanical refrigerator cooled by an actual block of ice. According to the recipe, they were supposed to wait a couple of hours until the dough was frozen, then cut the roll into little round disks, place them on a cookie sheet, and bake them for twenty minutes. The icebox cookies never made it into the oven. Invariably, the impatient teens would get bored waiting for the dough to harden. Before it was barely cool, they would open the freezer, grab the wax paper-wrapped dough, and start slicing off pieces. Down would go the raw cookie dough, and out the window went the recipe.

It wasn't that Bob couldn't or wouldn't adhere to the precise directions a pie or cookie recipe called for. What manifested itself in that "open kitchen" policy his parents granted him was a sense of total acceptance. "It seemed to me at the time to be a kind of passive love – not necessarily demonstrative love – but a way of letting me know, 'You're welcome here.' While I undoubtedly took it for granted at the time, having that freedom at home really affected who I was and who I became. My mom and dad did a nice job on me."

It's easy today to make the connection between the open, trusting relationship Bob's parents had with their son and the open-door policy

Bob enjoys with his employees at Bob's Red Mill. It's a rare occasion to see the company founder's second-floor corner office door closed. And it's common knowledge that anyone – from production line worker to executive vice president – can have an audience with the owner. All they pretty much have to do is walk by his door, and the ever-curious and alert CEO will wave them in. It's always a hearty "Come on in. How are you?" And then usually a handshake or a hug. No request or question goes unanswered. And usually a solution is reached on the spot. That's the way his parents treated him; that's the way Bob treats his employees.

CHAPTER 5

A BOOMING BUSINESS

LIFE WAS GOOD IN L.A. FOR THE MOORE FAMILY. THEY HAD MOVED TO a small house six blocks from Ken's parents, so Bob would often stop by his grandparents' house on his way home from school for one of Grandma's scratch biscuits. Although Ken's job as salesman at his dad's Independent Addressing Machine Company didn't last that long, Ken did well. He would come home at night, the sound of his trademark cheery whistle preceding him, with his ever-present cigarette in one hand. In the other, he would hold up a pamphlet, newsletter or magazine for which he had sold label-printing services. "Guess what I got today," he would announce, trumpeting his latest sales conquest.

Sometimes on weekends he would bring his wife and son to the plant to help stuff envelopes and package up bags of newly labeled mail bound for the post office. They didn't have zip codes in those days, so the family would group everything by city. Bob's favorite chore was sorting the monthly news publication produced by Metro-Goldwyn-Mayer Studios. MGM was the movie-making powerhouse located in nearby Culver City, and Bob was enthralled with the magazine's glamorous photos of the day's top movie stars. There were behind-the-scenes stories about the leading actors and actresses, as well as promotional photos of upcoming films. It was Hollywood's heyday, with two MGM blockbusters (*Gone With the Wind* and *The Wizard of Oz*) nominated for Best Picture at that year's Academy Awards. *Gone With the Wind* won the 1940 Academy Award, but, unfortunately, that year marked the demise of the Independent Addressing Machine Company.

While it set him back a bit, Ken wasn't about to let the bankruptcy of his dad's business slow him down. He had a saying that inspired him to keep moving forward, to find that next job: "Well, you can't sell out of an empty wagon." So, he moved on. And it didn't take him too long to find that next wagon to sell out of. It was for the National Supply Company in Torrance, a bit of a drive from their southwest L.A. home, but a father had to do what a father had to do. Especially when his wife was pregnant with their second child.

It was 1942 and the country was at war, which meant business was booming at the National Supply Company. Originally a foundry that manufactured and sold tools and parts for oil well drilling operations, the company began making tools for war. They fashioned gun barrels for battleships, heavy duty machinery for tanks, and landing gear for fighter planes. Because this type of large-scale metal working was new to the company, employees had to be trained, and some were enrolled in local colleges. National sent Ken to the California Institute of Technology in Pasadena to study metallurgy. The education paid off for the sales executive and the company, as government contracts wound down and new markets opened up in the private sector. One of the companies he called on was Kaiser Steel.[2] Located forty-five miles east of Los Angeles in Fontana (the plant was built inland from the Pacific Ocean so it would be out of range from enemy fire from the sea), it was one of the world's largest

---

2 A portion of the old Kaiser Steel Plant became the site of a racetrack called the California Speedway. And film makers have incorporated the ruins of the abandoned structure in movies such as *Black Rain* and *Terminator 2: Judgment Day*, with its unforgettable showdown between Arnold Schwarzenegger's character and the T-1000 cyborg.

steel plants. It supplied the steel for hundreds of wartime ships built on the West Coast during the early years of WWII.

Ken, as any good salesman would do, inquired as to what some of the Kaiser steelmakers' biggest cost-related challenges were. They referred him to an area of the plant where giant rolls of steel sheets were stored. Apparently, no one had spent the time to figure out what to do with remnants of the metal rolling process, particularly if a different thickness of steel was needed for another order. The workers would just readjust the rollers and produce a new roll. With his metallurgic training and knowledge of the hot-rolling and cold-rolling processes, Ken figured out a way to basically recycle the discarded rolls. He arranged for large flat bed trucks to haul the rolled steel away. Then he oversaw the "reprocessing" of the metal to Kaiser's specifications and had the finished product returned. He was a hero for saving the company money and ensuring the National Supply Company of a healthy contract. The coup earned Ken a promotion as the sales executive overseeing National's new industrial division. And his nightly updates at home about the experience entertained the Moore household for months. The conversation at the dinner table invariably featured some funny story about the "Kaiser rolls," especially when the bread basket was passed around.

Los Angeles's industrial role in the war was significant, with seventeen percent of the entire country's war production generated in the L.A. area. Its metropolitan area grew faster than any other major U.S. metropolitan area. By 1943, only thirteen states had a larger population than metropolitan L.A. It was home to one in every forty American citizens. It also held the largest concentration of Japanese wartime evacuees, with 80,000 of the 120,000 ethnic Japanese who were eventually evacuated to relocation camps.

One of those Japanese families lived two blocks from the Moores. The mom and dad with their young daughter owned the local neighborhood grocery store, Tom's Market, and they lived in the back. Bob's parents regularly dispatched him to run down to the market to pick up a few things for lunch or dinner. Mr. Tom would pull out a minced ham, slice off two or three pieces, do the same with a round of cheddar cheese, and wrap them in butcher paper. He would write down the charge (about thirty cents for the lunchmeat and cheese) on an index card; maybe thirty-five cents because Bob would usually sneak in a candy bar. Then he would file the bill in a metal box, alphabetized with all the other neighborhood families' grocery purchases. Everybody had a credit account, and when they got their monthly paycheck they would come in and square up with Mr. Tom. He would be sitting behind the counter, deftly adding up the last four weeks' charges, and Doris would always look over at her son with a knowing smile when she saw half a dozen Hershey's chocolate bars on the itemized list. "She was always good about stuff like that," Bob remembers.

And then one day the authorities showed up and escorted the Japanese family onto a bus. They were allowed to take some of their clothes, each of them with a suitcase, but that was the only possession they were permitted to take from their home, from their store. The market closed, and Mr. Tom, his wife, and their daughter were gone. Bob never saw them again, but he often wondered what happened to the young family. He heard they were among the 10,000 or so ethnic Japanese who were sent to the Manzanar War Relocation Center in Owens Valley. The internment camp was located 300 miles north of Los Angeles, about an hour's drive from Mammoth Mountain ski resort. Later in life when he was married and had three young boys, Bob made that round trip on I-5, Highway 14, and Highway 395 probably a hundred times when he moved from Los Angeles and opened a gas station in the town of Mammoth Lakes. Whenever he traveled that twelve-mile stretch between Lone Pine and Independence, he would gaze east of the 395 and wonder which of the 800 military-style wooden barracks that used to be there housed the Toms. Knowing that the family he liked as neighbors, who had once had their own private little rooms in the back of their store, were locked up there, surrounded by barbed wire fences, and forced to shower and go to the bathroom in communal latrines, was disturbing to him. The last time he drove that highway, he learned the National Park Service was re-creating the Manzanar Camp into a National Historic Site, putting on public display an inglorious American war story. Mr. Tom would have liked that.

The realities of war had unsettled their neighborhood, but what happened just nine days after Bob's thirteenth birthday really hit home. After a Japanese submarine had fired on an oil facility near Santa Barbara, a popular coastal retreat located eighty miles north of Los Angeles, rumors of an invasion spread like a Santa Ana wind–whipped wildfire. The next day, a Tuesday, families throughout the L.A. Basin (the coastal plain incorporating most of Los Angeles and Orange counties) prepared for an attack. As night fell, air raid sirens blared and people took cover. Warned to extinguish all lights, cars crashed into each other as drivers with headlights off attempted to navigate darkened streets. With windows covered and house lights off, the Moores huddled around the radio, anxiously listening to news reports. The tension escalated when about midnight it was announced enemy planes had been spotted over Los Angeles. Anyone living on the coastal heights who had fallen asleep was jolted awake by the sound of anti-aircraft guns blaring. Searchlights lit up the sky. Spent shells fell on houses, cars, and streets. The communities of Long Beach and Santa Monica experienced the most damage. But none of it was caused by enemy fire. It had been a false report.

For two hours, the so-called "Battle of Los Angeles" raged on. There were phantom sightings of planes, parachutes, and bombs. There were reports one of the enemy planes had crashed near the intersection of 185th and Vermont, not far from the Moores' darkened house. There were rumors parts of the city were on fire. Even the editors of the *L.A. Times* fell victim to the made-up story. The front-page headline on February 25, 1942, screamed "L.A Area Raided."

The Japanese didn't drop bombs on Los Angeles, but just knowing they could kept Southern Californians on edge. It was a tumultuous time. War production kept Ken Moore extremely busy. Now that he was in charge of sales for the industrial division, he was traveling more. And selling on the road meant drinking more. A heavy smoker, too, he was up to three packs a day. There was pressure on the job, and there was added responsibility at home. On March 16, 1943, Doris gave birth to a girl and they named her Jeannie. Throughout the pregnancy, Bob's dad was adamant the new addition to the family would be a girl, and he teased that he had already picked out her name. She would be called Roberta. Bob was so excited his little sister would be named after him. It was a Tuesday morning and he was sitting in Mrs. Zoig's social studies class at John Muir Junior High when he got called to the principal's office. Told by the assembled office staff that his mom had just given birth, they asked what her name would be. "Roberta," he proudly stated. "I'm Robert, so she's named after me." It wasn't until his dad arrived to pick him up from school that he learned old Pop had just been kidding about the Roberta thing.

In a letter he wrote to Jeannie on her fiftieth birthday, Bob reminisced, "as I went through the rest of my classes, it was really a fun day. I had the most wonderful feeling inside that something very special had just happened to me, and, of course, everyone thought it was a big deal I had a new sister at fourteen. I was very proud. I've always been impressed with how certain dad was that you would be a girl and I'm still proud to be the brother of such a wonderful sister. I love you very much."

That night, Bob wanted desperately to see his mom and meet his baby sister, but Methodist Hospital's policy was you had to be at least sixteen years old to visit patients. So, his dad dressed him up in one of his suits and put a fancy tie on him to make him look more mature. It worked. Bob had just turned fourteen the month before, an age difference with his newborn sister that was significant in their relationship. By the time her older brother was graduating from high school and going into the Army, Jeannie was barely four years old.

CHAPTER 6

LESSONS LEARNED

Wᴵᵀᴴ ʜɪꜱ ᴅᴀᴅ ᴛʀᴀᴠᴇʟɪɴɢ ᴀ ʟᴏᴛ ᴀɴᴅ ʜɪꜱ ᴍᴏᴍ ꜰᴏᴄᴜꜱᴇᴅ ᴏɴ ᴀ ɴᴇᴡ baby sister, the undivided attention Bob enjoyed as an only child was changing. He knew his parents loved him deeply. And his love for them never waned. Ever.

"It brings tears to my eyes when I think about it," he says of his love for his parents. "I don't know about everybody else, but I miss my mom and dad every day of my life."

With the confidence and security of knowing he was a much-loved son, Bob's transition from boyhood to young man was comfortable. He knew what he liked and he knew what he didn't like. Cub Scout days were over, but he wasn't interested in Boy Scouts. His passion for music endured, so he preferred playing the violin and piano over sports. He still didn't care for school that much, but he was attracted to the girls in his seventh-grade class, so he tolerated it. In a scheme to get close to one of the girls he found particularly attractive, he signed up for a typing class she was in. He was the only boy in the class. And he loved it.

All those piano and violin lessons were paying off. When he sat down in front of that typewriter, his fingers started flying across the keys, just like they did when he played the boogie-woogie blues. He was fast and nimble-fingered. But he typed too fast, according to Miss Miller. She wore her hair in a bun and would scold him because he made too many mistakes. "If you would just slow down a little bit, you could be the best typist in the class," she admonished him. "You could type one hundred words a minute, if you would just slow down and cut out the mistakes."

But Bob wouldn't slow down. He was determined to find out just how many words per minute he could type. He didn't care that for every mistake he would be docked four words per minute off his timed score. He would make up for it by typing faster, a choice that totally wound Miss Miller's bun tighter. In his second semester, Bob set a goal to score one hundred words per minute, which would earn him a certificate. To Miss Miller's total exasperation, he did it. "I know it just killed her to award me that certificate. She wanted to strangle me, but I got the biggest kick out of it. I carried that certificate in my wallet for years until it finally fell to pieces."

Typing was about the only class Bob took seriously in junior high and high school. He was a terrible writer, so that hampered his learning. He got by, mostly with C's and D's. Some of his teachers, like Miss Jones, would take him aside and tell him he had a great deal of promise, lots of potential, if he would just apply himself. To others, he had a reputation of being rambunctious, and they tolerated him.

"By the time I turned eighteen, I realized I was really stupid. Really stupid. I knew enough to realize I had just passed by where all the knowledge was. Everything I needed I just passed it up. I mean, I would have been a lot better off if at ages thirteen and fourteen I had taken my studies more seriously."

He would get the school work done (he did graduate from high school, but only because he took summer school classes to make up for some failed grades), but it usually meant last-minute cramming. Instead of bringing his books home and studying like he was supposed to do, Bob would invariably wait until the day before a report on South America or Abraham Lincoln was due, and then copy entire sections of an encyclopedia. He would stay up all night, fueled by graham crackers, peanut butter, and a bottle of milk. And in the morning he would deliver his report, neatly typed. In the process, he did at least learn it was impossible for a teenage boy to not drink milk from the container in front of an open icebox. Later, when he had three teenagers of his own, he marveled that that fact still held true.

"I remember my English teacher trying to explain to me the importance of applying myself, but my attitude was 'What do I need this for? I do not need any of this. This is a waste of time.'" It was only later in life, after his military service, that Bob realized what a mistake he had made. It cost him time and money, because he had to go back to school for remedial training.

But classes like Latin, Literature, Spanish, and Social Studies at Manual Arts High School? He rejected them all. He was more interested in cars, girls, and making money.

Jobs were plentiful for junior high and high schoolers at that time because most able-bodied men were off fighting the Germans and Japanese. Schools would allow young men with work permits to start classes at 7 a.m. instead of 9 a.m. and be done by 2 p.m. And they let you skip study hall classes (not that Bob needed another incentive to forego his studies so he could earn money, but it was nice).

His very first job was tearing down furniture that was to be reupholstered – using special tools to pull staples, tacks, and old upholstery – at Carson's Furniture. He and his friend Billy Short got fifty cents an hour (plus all the loose change they could find in old couches and chairs) ripping stuff up. He also got a splinter under his fingernail about the size of a Popsicle stick, which one of the upholsterers had to pull out with a pair of pliers. Bob, wincing, says he never had anything hurt so bad. But it was worth it.

"Getting money you totally earned yourself when you're thirteen, fourteen years old makes a real big difference in how you think about your world, about yourself, everything. I mean it really makes a difference. It's not the same as getting a quarter a week or something from your mom. There is a transition in your life when you get a little envelope handed to you with some money folded up in it. You never go back."

Billy Short quit after a couple of months. The work was too much for him. Bob stayed a year. As a young teenager, he started buying his own underwear at Sears.

At fifteen, Bob parlayed his experience at Carson's and went to work for the May Company in their warehouse at Jefferson and Grand in downtown Los Angeles. He made sixty-five cents an hour as a general laborer unloading furniture from boxcars that rolled in on the rail line adjacent to the warehouse. For three hours every weeknight and eight hours on Saturday he did manual labor. He got strong, holding his own with the adults and enjoying the camaraderie and banter with older men. The experience also provided a key character-building moment that awakened his entrepreneurial spirit.

He worked in "Department One," the order-filling unit that got a specific piece of furniture to the right floor of the nearby department store. He and his supervisor (everybody called him "Shorty") would review the paperwork and then go in search of the armoire, dining room table, or couch that was stored in one of the boxcars. With pry bar in hand, Bob would force open the steel doors that always seemed to be stuck, and then start pulling out the heavy paper-wrapped freight stacked inside the airless enclosed railroad car. It was hard work, even for a strapping fifteen-year-old. Without exception, it seemed the item they were searching for would be in the back, so they had to unload the entire shipment to get to it. It became a running joke between the two of them: "I must have heard Shorty say it a hundred times," Bob recalls. *"Well, here it is, the 'ONE' we've been looking for – the LAST one.'"*

After he'd been on the job a few months, Shorty came to him and said, "The big boss wants to see you." Bob was petrified. He'd only seen the man a few times, maybe gotten one "hello." The boss always wore a suit and a fedora. Smoked a cigar. His office was on one of the upper floors, in the back behind a wooden partition with large panes of glass. It wasn't the office one went into to interview for a job, but Bob surmised that's where you went to get fired. He thought he had seen the head guy watching him a time or two, but now he was convinced he had done something wrong and was about to hear the bad news.

A secretary ushered him into the nicely appointed office. He was scared, trembling actually. But then he remembered his dad's words: "If you ever meet the boss, stand up straight, look him in the eye, and give him a firm handshake." So the son did as he had been told. Then he sat down in front of the big desk with the very staid businessman sitting behind it. The boss made some small talk, asked how he was doing. Bob was about to turn sixteen, and for the life of him, he couldn't fathom why the top guy would be chatting it up with a sixteen-year-old underling. And then came the question, "Do you think you could handle Department One by yourself?"

Bob almost passed out. He had been expecting to hear he had screwed up, that he was a failure, and they were letting him go. Instead, he was being asked if he thought he could run the department.

"If he'd have asked me if I could run the whole place, I would have told him yes. Yes, sir! I'll do a good job for you." When told the promotion would pay him one dollar an hour, Bob couldn't believe it. That was almost double what he had been earning. What an emotional roller-coaster. He had walked into the boss's office expecting to be terminated, and he walked out a department manager. He crossed the threshold scared and intimidated, and walked out the door with a pat on the back and a "job well done." It was a defining moment in his young life. He discovered he had abilities. He had earned the respect not only of his elders, but of his employer. He had proved his responsibility and he was rewarded for it. And, most of all, he had made his dad proud.

Recalling that pivotal experience of sixty-five years earlier, Bob marvels at the significance and amazing circumstances of that day. He is sitting in his CEO office at Bob's Red Mill Natural Foods, which is located at 13521 SE Pheasant Court in Milwaukie, just off Highway 224 in Clackamas County. The company's "World Headquarters," as the huge billboard with Bob's picture on it atop the 325,000-square-foot building bills it, sits on a seventeen-acre site once housing Meier & Frank Company's master warehouse. The facility was the department store's warehouse for its Oregon operations. In 1966 the May Company acquired Meier & Frank. So, Bob is sitting in the boss's office of the May Company (now Macy's) warehouse, just as he was doing in Los Angeles in 1944. Only now he is the boss.

The promotion meant more money, and that was nice, but it was the affirmation of who he was as a young man and the recognition of the potential of what he could become that "was one of the things in my life that kind of made me who I am," Bob pointed out. It was character development, motivation, and pride all rolled into one life-changing instant. He walked into that big boss's office, all sweaty and scared, and he emerged standing tall, confident, and anxious to prove he was a man. He was the Manager of Department One! He was making one dollar an hour, which was a very good wage in 1945. So what if it was the most miserable department in the entire warehouse, and they couldn't find anyone else who wanted to work in those stifling conditions (as Bob later learned). He was in management. And he liked the feel.

He really liked the money, too. Because now he could afford to buy a car. He wasn't old enough to drive a car, but that didn't matter. He knew as soon as he turned sixteen his parents would let him drive. It was something he had been dreaming about forever. He talked about cars with his dad all the time. He coveted the freedom those four wheels would bring. And he fantasized about driving around town with a pretty girl sitting next to him.

Two major milestones in his young life happened in February of 1945. He plunked down $300 for a 1933 Chevy three-window coupe. And two weeks later on his sixteenth birthday he drove that beautiful blue machine all by himself. The car was parked in front of their house, teasing its new owner as those fourteen days dragged on. He got his driver's license and his dad taught him how to use the clutch. They drove around the block a couple of times, but the wait was killing him. Early on the morning of February 15, Bob got up and his mom was waiting for him in the kitchen with breakfast and birthday wishes. "So, what are you going to do today?" she asked, of course knowing it was a Thursday and her son was supposed to be going to school. Right then, the birthday boy knew it. His wonderful mother was giving him the best birthday present ever – permission to skip school and take his car for a drive. Dad had already left for work, and Bob knew if he were home he would have told him to bite the bullet and go to school ("He would have called it a character-building moment," Bob knew). But his mom even wrote him a note for the teacher, saying he had a headache and wouldn't be in class today.

Keys in hand, Bob bounded out the door and settled into the driver's seat of his '33 Chevy coupe. He fired it up and with a couple of obligatory grinds of the transmission by the newbie clutch/gearshift operator he pointed his little blue bomber east toward the familiar back roads of San Bernardino. There were no freeways, so his meandering trip that terminated atop Mount Wilson thirty-four miles, as the crow flies, from Los Angeles took half the day. No worries. He was enjoying every second of it. Every mile he put on the odometer felt like another badge of freedom. "It's still one of the biggest days of my life," Bob remembers.

He made a point of stopping at Mount Wilson Observatory, which at the time was home to two of the world's largest telescopes – the 60-inch Hale telescope and the 100-inch Hooker telescope – as well as a resort hotel. Founded in 1904 by George Ellery Hale, the Mount Wilson Observatory with its pioneering instruments and brilliant scientists dominated the world of astronomy. Its facilities for studying the sun were the most powerful in existence. It could have been the reflection from those incredible mirrors and glass, but Bob was literally beaming from his mountain-top adventure. He floated over to the swimming pool behind the resort hotel and imagined himself one of the beautiful people. Past the tanned men and women lounging in big comfortable chairs, he stopped in the gift shop located next to the restaurant. He needed something, a memento, to memorialize this high point in his life. He found one of those touristy postcards that read "Having fun at Mount Wilson Observatory, wish you were here!" He signed it "Your son Bob" and mailed it to his mom. He would have loved to stay longer, looking down from his vantage point of 5,715 feet on the rest of the San Gabriel Mountains with a panoramic view of Pasadena and the valley floor below, but it was time to get his head out of the clouds and drive *(he loved that concept)* to work. He kept his birthday destination a secret from his parents, privately enjoying the thrill of driving out to San Bernardino and back, until the postcard arrived a day or so later. They were astounded. He had driven more than one hundred miles – through Los Angeles at high elevations and over mountain passes to desert roads – in a car he had just learned to drive and on the first day the state of California allowed him to legally operate a vehicle.

Having a car and driver's license afforded Bob the luxury of pursuing his other favorite teenage pastime – girls. He had a series of girlfriends, none serious, but it was the combustible combination of a girl and a car that steered Bob Moore's life in a whole new direction. It was prom night, and he and his date, Jane, had had a wonderful time. On the drive to her house, the young lady in the pretty dress had his full attention, and that's undoubtedly why the accident occurred. It was about 11 p.m. and he was navigating south on Normandie Avenue. With his right arm around his prom date, he had to reach through the steering wheel with his left hand to shift. It wasn't that difficult a maneuver, especially if you had lots of practice, but it took quite a coordinated effort. He was getting close to Jane's house and was paying more attention to her than the traffic on the dark road ahead. He didn't see the car making a left turn onto Normandie from a side street until it was too late. Slamming on the brakes to avoid hitting her, his car veered to the left, just missing nipping her back bumper. But now he was facing oncoming traffic, and the guy driving the 1942 Plymouth couldn't stop in time. They collided head-on.

The impact totaled Bob's car and smashed in the front end of the Plymouth. No one was hurt, but the loud crash in the middle of the night drew people out of their homes. Someone called Jane's dad and he drove over from the couple blocks away and picked her up. Whether it was the accident or her dad's insistence, the incident ended Jane's relationship with Bob. But he had bigger issues to deal with. For one, he was technically at fault, even though to this day he blames the lady for her bad decision to turn in front of him ("I should have hit her – at least they would have called it a draw," he maintains). The guy he hit was reasonable; he just wanted the damages paid for. The problem was Bob had no insurance. And now he had no car. Some of the assembled neighbors helped push his ruined Chevy coupe to the side of the street. After a tow truck hauled the other guy's car away, Bob began the five-mile walk home. He was devastated. Lost the girl. Lost the car. And he knew enough about cars that even though this was 1946, the 1942 Plymouth was the newest model on the road and sold for about $800.[3] Later, when he got the estimate of the damages, he realized he had to pay more than half what the car cost new to get it fixed. $447 to be exact.

It was after two in the morning when he got home. His dad was still awake, but he didn't press when his son avoided the question of what had happened. They would talk in the morning. So Bob went to bed, more depressed than he had ever been. His life, for the foreseeable future, was ruined. He had no transportation and no money saved up. He would have to walk to school and take the bus or walk to work. And who knew how long it would take him to earn the money to pay off his new debt. He fell asleep in a cloud of despair.

In the morning at the breakfast table, his dad asked his obviously distraught son to come clean. Something had surely happened to make him so upset. When Bob confessed he had been in a wreck, his mom reacted with an explosion of questions: "Was anyone hurt? How is Jane? Where's your car? Did you call the police? What about the car you hit?"

His dad was much calmer, approaching the subject in search of a teachable moment. "Son, sounds to me that you weren't paying attention to the cars in front of you; maybe speeding a bit. And you made the wrong choice to turn the steering wheel left when you should have steered

---

3 Production came to a halt early in 1942 as Plymouth converted one hundred percent to the war effort. They didn't start building them again until 1946.

to the right. But, you know what, these things won't happen when you're older. You'll gain a sixth sense about how to react in situations like this. Given the same circumstances in the future, you might have perceived that she was going to turn in front of you."

"My dad was very reasonable," Bob says, recounting the episodes of his youth when he didn't always make the best decisions. "I tried to be reasonable with my three boys, too, but I was a little more on the explosive side like my mom. And, of course, my dad only had one son…

Later that morning, dad and son drove over to where the mangled car ended up. They had brought some tools and were able to get the wheels straightened enough so they could tow it with a rope. They got it home, and for days Bob just stared at the wreck. To the seventeen-year-old, it seemed to be a mirror commenting on the state of his life. Those were dark days, and unbeknownst to him at the time, he would face many more disasters in his life. But he dealt with it in much the same way he would overcome life's challenges in the future – with resiliency and creativity. He needed wheels to get to school, work, and home. He couldn't afford four wheels, so maybe two would get him by. He needed a bicycle, and it just so happened his friend from band, Allen Smart, said he could borrow his. It was a huge step backward for the independent, car-loving student and warehouseman, but he was willing to do whatever it took to finish school and keep earning a paycheck. Little did he know that in less than two weeks after his accident, that "whatever" would become a much steeper hill to climb.

It was Normandie Avenue again, one of Los Angeles's longest north-south streets, dissecting the city and stretching more than twenty-two miles, all the way to the Pacific Coast Highway. This time Bob was riding his borrowed bike home from work. It was getting dark and he was worn out from hauling furniture around the May Company warehouse. He was pedaling along, thinking about the backlog of homework and make-up classes he owed, when all of a sudden, *WHAM!* A car turned suddenly in front of him into a driveway between two parked cars. Unable to stop or even slow down, Bob and Allen's bike smashed into the guy (he'd apparently driven past his house and was going to turn around in the neighbor's driveway; Bob doesn't remember smelling alcohol on the errant driver's breath, but he wondered how he could have missed his own driveway), catapulting Bob over the hood and into the front fender of one of the parked cars.

When Bob came to, he was sprawled on the sidewalk, looking up at people from the neighborhood who were staring down at him in horror. He didn't realize it right away, but there was a big gash on the top of his head. All he could think of as he lay there dazed next to Allen's twisted and mangled bicycle was "What am I going to do now?" His thoughts were a jumbled mess, mostly from the scrambling his brain had just endured, but the realities of his situation kept turning over in his mind – no car, no girlfriend, no insurance, no money, no bike. Yes, he was in shock, but it was the double dose of a busted skull and a crumbling life that had his head spinning. He came to his senses long enough to tell the man whose car had hit him where he lived, and mumbled something about an emergency hospital located near his house. Shooting nervous glances at the boy he thought he might have killed, the guy drove Bob to the hospital and turned him over to the nurses. By this time, blood was dripping down his face, so they wrapped his head in a towel and laid him on a gurney. They called his parents and Bob remembers his dad showed up in just a few minutes. He was scared now, not knowing how badly he was hurt, afraid his parents would be mad at him, worried how Allen would react, concerned about his future.

"I thought this was the end of the world for me. Was I dying? Was I a complete failure? It was a very low moment. And then my dad walked in. He was so good. I remember reaching out and holding his hand. I wanted to hold his hand. It was probably the first and only time I held my dad's hand."

Bob wasn't dying. In fact, he would recover with just some stitches and an embarrassing bald spot on the top of his head where they shaved his hair off so they could sew up the wound. He still has the school picture where an artist touched up the photo by painting in the bare spot.

And his life wasn't over. But it did change dramatically. Without transportation, he couldn't figure out a way to get to school every morning and to his job at the May Company every afternoon. He needed money to pay for the car accident, so he couldn't simply quit working. That $447 was another added pressure he didn't need, but he knew he had to deal with it somehow. He was committed to paying the man off, and he knew for sure his dad would hold him to that commitment. It was the right thing to do and another one of those difficult life lessons he knew his dad wanted him to learn. What he wasn't prepared for was the demonstration of love his parents showed him when they went to Household Finance Company and took out a personal loan for the amount their son owed.

Doris and Ken Moore didn't ask their son if that's what he wanted. And they didn't threaten him with a strict repayment plan. They just did it. Out of love.

"As I look back, that was really an amazing thing they did for me, uncalled for actually," Bob says, remembering the day the Household Finance loan officer showed up at their home and proceeded to take an inventory of all their possessions. "With interest, that loan was well over $500, which was a lot of money in 1946. I remember the guy getting out of the car. He comes out and has a clipboard. He gives Mom and Dad his business card and then he walks through the house and inventories everything they owned. That's why it was called Household Finance. That's how it worked. One couch – eighteen dollars. All the things in the house – radio, dining room set, stove, refrigerator, beds. I look back at that now and it was the most demeaning thing that could ever happen. *And they did it for me!* They didn't have any money, yet they took out a personally guaranteed loan and paid the guy off. All for me."

So, no, he couldn't quit his job at the May Company without the assurance he could get work somewhere else. Fortunately for him – the guy without any means of transportation – that "somewhere else" turned out to be a machine shop two blocks away from where he lived, right in the same building where Tom's Market had been.

"Here I was, almost eighteen years old, and I was very discouraged.

Nothing seemed to be going right for me. But now, more than sixty years later, I can look back on that period of my life and see how all of these experiences were like building blocks, like puzzle pieces. It's as if a picture of your life is the entire surface of a table, and someone hands you a big box with all the shapes and pieces that represent your life's journey, and you spend eighty-one years taking those things out of the box and putting them together. As you assemble it, you kind of look back and ask yourself 'Why did you do this?' and 'Why did this happen to you?' and 'What did you learn from this experience?' Eventually, it all comes together and it makes sense."

The war had ended in 1945 with the surrender of the Germans and Japanese, but in 1946 there were still lots of jobs available for ambitious young men. So, when Bob walked into the neighborhood auto electric shop and asked the owner if he had any job openings, Mr. Boyer said "yes" and hired him on the spot. It was Bob's fascination with cars and motors that drove him to Boyer Auto Electric. But in his big picture approach to life, he believes it was a higher power that steered him to a job that inspired his lifelong pursuit of working with motors and machinery. If he were to trace backwards on a map from the finish line that is CEO of Bob's Red Mill Natural Foods, the starting point would be apprentice at Boyer Auto Electric.

After he quit his job at the May Company, Bob worked for Mr. Boyer every day after school and all day Saturday. He loved every minute of it. The smell of oil and grease. The sound of whining motors and whirring generators. The feel of hot metal casings and coiled copper strands. The mystery of measuring voltage, amps, resistance, and ohms. The satisfaction of taking worn-out starters and generators and rebuilding them. And he got to be around cars.

Mr. Boyer was a shop guy – he always wore a blue shop coat and he smoked a pipe. But when he went to Pep Boys to pick up used starters and generators that needed rebuilding, he drove his fancy car.

"Oh, that car was lovely. A classic. A 1940 Cadillac Fleetwood four-door hardtop. It had the sweeping fenders, twin side mount spare tires, big solid doors – just a dandy, fantastic car. And he drove it like a truck."

Even before he started working for Mr. Boyer, Bob was very familiar with Pep Boys. It was a popular destination for young do-it-yourselfer boys in need of bicycle tires, repairs, and accessories. And as they graduated to getting around town in cars, they frequented Manny, Moe & Jack's place, a nickname for the automotive aftermarket chain, for batteries, filters, wiper blades, fuses, and other automotive parts and accessories.

Because of his burgeoning passion for working on cars, Bob would spend extra hours with Mr. Boyer, learning how to operate a lathe, rewind armatures, and meter voltage regulators. Within months, he mastered engine tune-ups, alignments, and brake installations. He could overhaul a car now. So, why not his own? "By then, I figured out that I liked working on cars. I could tell it was becoming part of the fabric of my life."

The '33 Chevy Coupe, in all its mangled glory, was still parked in front of his house. With his newfound knowledge and passion, he took on the challenge of replacing the crumpled body parts and rebuilding the damaged engine. It took many trips to the junk yard, some late nights at Boyer's, and a healthy chunk of his meager savings, but he did it. He got the car running and street legal. He was proud of his accomplishment, but disappointed with the immediate outcome of his efforts. As soon as it was ready to roll, his dad sold it. Most car companies hadn't begun making new cars yet due to the wartime hold on manufacturing, so used cars were valuable. The thirteen-year-old Chevy sold for what Bob paid for it. The $300 went into the bank, leaving Bob with some spending money, but the debt of $447 plus interest still hung over his head. Although he didn't have a girlfriend or car to spend his money on, that didn't mean he didn't go out and have any fun.

He loved music and was a pretty good dancer, so he could usually get a date, especially for the Wednesday student night dances at the Trianon Ballroom in nearby Southgate when tickets were cheap (fifty cents per couple) and Cokes were a nickel. But the entertainment was first class. Bob and two of his buddies would invite three gals along, and they would all squeeze into one of their cars for the drive over to the dance hall at 2800 Firestone Blvd. It was the big band era and owner/band leader Horace Heidt brought in big names like the Dorsey Brothers, Benny Goodman, and Glenn Miller. Heidt, who was a contemporary of Lawrence Welk, hosted national radio broadcasts at the Trianon on the Mutual Broadcasting system during World War II. He also created a radio and later television talent contest where famous entertainers like Art Carney, Gordon MacRae, the King Sisters, Al Hirt, and Frank DeVol were discovered.

High school was winding down and Bob couldn't wait to put that phase of his life in the rearview mirror. His senior year was a bust. He didn't flunk out of any classes, but he was barely getting by with C's and D's. If he hadn't gone to summer school for some make-up classes, he wouldn't have graduated. He hated spending his July and August free time in a classroom, and the extracurricular experience essentially sealed the deal that he would not be going on to college.

Most seniors would cherish their final year of high school, with scholastic achievements, sports accomplishments, social outings, and fun times captured in the annual yearbook, forever documenting one of the best times in their lives. Bob simply didn't appreciate the experience. To him, school was a distraction. It got in the way of his personal interests. He would later regret not applying himself, not taking advantage of all the learning opportunities that were available to him. All his teachers told him he had great potential, that he could achieve much more in life if he studied harder. But he had dismissed school as unimportant, a waste of time. Ultimately, he realized how wrong he was. In fact, later in life he would demonstrate how much he valued education by donating millions of dollars to schools. He became a huge advocate for higher education and sponsored numerous scholarships. Nearly a high school dropout, he became a champion for scholastic pursuits.

"I might not have deserved it, but I have a certificate proving I graduated from high school," Bob says with a laugh. "I really had no interest in school. I got by, especially that last year. All the different things that happened to me – the car wreck, busting my head open, ruining my friend's bike, finding a new job, fixing my car, going to summer school, which I hated – that year was very difficult. I had a very serious job that I ended up having to quit because of transportation difficulties, and I still owed my folks a lot of money. Anyway, my life was really screwed up."

Getting his high school diploma was like "letting the air out of a hot air balloon," he admits. "I needed to get out of there."

CHAPTER 7

THE CURSE

So, Bob joined the Army. He graduated on a Wednesday, and Thursday morning he and four of his friends took the streetcar to the downtown Los Angeles recruiting office. He had told his mom and dad what he wanted to do – his mom was definitely against it, but his dad thought it was a good idea. It was January, 1947, and the war had been over for nearly eighteen months, but the draft was still on, so there was a good chance he would be going into the military anyway. By signing up for three years, you had more flexibility to choose an area of specialization. Bob chose accounting. It was a crazy choice, but he was so profoundly concerned about his inability to write that he chose to work with numbers.

After the swearing-in ceremony, a bus took them to nearby San Pedro for a physical exam. They were all standing around in their skivvies when Bob heard his name called. He went up to the front and stood before the man with the clipboard.

"Kid," he said, "you're not eighteen. We need to have your parents give their okay on this form before you can enlist."

He was just weeks away from his eighteenth birthday, but he knew there was no wiggle room in the Army's black and white regulations. He would have to go back home and get his mom and dad to sign the papers. He knew his dad wouldn't be a problem, but he was worried about his mom's reaction. She had already told him she thought he was nuts to volunteer.

Watching his four buddies board a bus bound for the Army post at Fort Ord, Bob wondered what else could go wrong. Nothing seemed to be working in his favor. Oh well, he thought, just get home, sign the papers, and come back tomorrow. In twenty-four hours, he would be with his friends on beautiful Monterey Bay. Only problem was he didn't have any money for bus fare. He approached one of the recruiters, but the guy said "Can't you call someone?" He considered calling his dad, but opted not to. His dad had bailed him out enough. So he hitchhiked home.

His mother was overjoyed to see him, hopeful that the Army thing hadn't worked out. When she learned it was just a technicality, that her son still wanted to go, she was disappointed. Bob doesn't know how long into the night his parents discussed his situation, but in the morning they signed. His dad maintained that this was the best thing for his son.

"My dad always had a million things to tell me about stuff," Bob says. "He had me all tuned to being obedient, doing what you're told, all those 'Dale Carnegie' type of things."[4]

Now, with signed paperwork in hand, Bob boarded the number eight car once again, 54th Street all the way to Spring. He told the recruiters his story and they ushered him straight through to San Pedro, where he passed his physical. They put him on the next bus to Fort Ord. As they headed north with Long Beach and Los Angeles now behind him, Bob could feel the change happening within him. Things were finally working out. He knew he would do fine in the Army. He didn't have to worry about himself. He would just do what was expected and they would treat him right. He wasn't the rebellious type. He just had to stay focused, keep

---

4 Dale Carnegie was the author of *How to Win Friends and Influence People*. First published in 1937, it has been recognized as one of the first self-help books. A consummate salesman, Ken Moore had undoubtedly read the book and probably flagged sections that promised the reader they would *get you out of a mental rut, give you new thoughts, new visions, and new ambitions.*

his nose clean, and come out the other end more mature and with some money in the bank.

Arriving at Fort Ord, he reported in: Moore, Robert G., RA 19300973. He was Regular Army. A recruit, who made it through private, private first class, corporal, and then sergeant in his three years. A few weeks into basic training, Private Moore discovered he really liked being in the Army. "I did good at everything, got along fine with everybody. I was in excellent physical condition – I loved all the running, the obstacle courses, the guns. I was determined I was going to be up in the front of the class. That was the world I was in, that's what I thought. And when you think that way, it's amazing that it sort of is that way. You can be disappointed, but you forgive easy. You find the world about the way you look at it."

In Bob's observation, everything was working out better than he had expected – except his job.

"I don't know why I picked the finance office. When you signed up for three years you got to pick any job you wanted. I picked finance. Even today I can't figure why I picked that. I really didn't have any interest in it. And I just wasn't qualified."

The woman he worked for had no patience for an eighteen-year-old kid who could barely write. Like most accounting types, she was very

Moore, Robert G., RA 19300973, proud of making Tec 5 in the Army, Fort Worden, Washington (1948)

strict about what was written in her log books. She wasn't happy with Bob's writing abilities and she let him know about his poor performance.

"I developed kind of an inferiority complex because everyone around me was writing like crazy. They could spell. Sure, I had a pretty good gift of gab and what not, but this was my first real job and I was discovering my inadequacy – I could not write."

But he could type. And it so happened he was the only one in a couple hundred soldiers who could. One day when the troops were lined up, the sergeant announced the company clerk had washed out. Were there any volunteers – *who could type* – that might be interested? Well, he knew you were never supposed to volunteer for anything in the military, but hey, he was failing in his current job and he knew he could be successful typing. And, besides, company clerks got out of certain duties like twenty-mile forced marches.

Bob regained his confidence as company clerk, banging away at the typewriter every day ("Everything in the Army is eight pages, so I had to type real hard because there's carbon paper in between each one."). He still kicked himself for being dumb enough to not know how to write, and he swore he would someday go back to school and learn what he should have learned a long time ago. It wasn't the only mistake he ever made. In fact, he was about to make another bonehead decision, starting a bad habit that would haunt him for seventeen years.

With basic training over, Bob was assigned to the Second Engineers Special Brigade at Fort Worden, an Army base located on a bluff near the Washington town of Port Townsend. Nowadays the fort's claim to fame is that *An Officer and a Gentleman* (the 1982 movie starring Richard Gere) was filmed there, but in wartime its strategic purpose was to protect the Puget Sound Naval Shipyard and the cities of Seattle, Tacoma, and Everett from any invasion attempt by sea.

"They didn't exactly tell you as a recruit where you were going to go or what you were going to do next. You just followed the guy in front of you." Bob had no idea that path would lead him overseas to a tiny island in the Pacific Ocean where the military set off atomic bombs as part of a nuclear weapons testing program. Forty-three in all. Three when Corporal Moore was stationed there.

Soldiering at Fort Worden was fun for Bob. He was settling in to Army life and he enjoyed the experience. He was outgoing, talkative, and he made friends easily. His musical abilities contributed to his popularity, as he would often entertain the guys at night by playing boogie-woogie and jazz on the piano in the dayroom. But there were also long periods of boredom and tedium as the men trained for their secret mission. Soldiers got set in their routines. One of them was the ubiquitous cigarette break. And Bob succumbed to the peer pressure. He started smoking.

"I did a very foolish thing," he says, thinking back to that first puff. "Everybody in the Army smoked. They tell you to take a cigarette break, and if you don't smoke you just stand around with your hands hanging out. So, I got started on the habit. They tasted terrible, just awful, made me cough. But then, you take another one; pretty soon you buy one. About two weeks into it, you wake up in the morning and that's all you want."

So, Bob went from a household where everybody smoked to the Army where everybody smoked. And the cigarette companies made it easy for him – they were almost free in the military. He remembers paying maybe seventy cents a carton. But the cost to his health was high. He thought it was the wet Pacific Northwest weather, but looking back he realized it was the tobacco that caused him to be sick. It seemed the entire time he was at Fort Worden he had a cold. He also caught pneumonia while he was there.

"Years later when I quit smoking, all those health problems went away. So I know it was the cigarettes. That's part of the reason why I have such a hatred for the tobacco companies and anybody that has anything to do with tobacco. It's a terrible thing. It's awful. And my dad – three packs a day. Forty-nine years old. I'd have been dead long ago, too, if I hadn't quit smoking. Tobacco is just a curse."

It would take five years of desperately trying to kick the habit, but at age thirty-four he finally quit smoking. The anger wells up even today when the subject comes up.

"When people ask me about cigarettes and tobacco and I tell them how strongly I feel about the subject, they say 'Well, what are you so upset about?' I tell them 'You have no idea why I'm so upset about tobacco. Here, sit down for about two days and I'll tell you why I'm so upset about tobacco. Then I think of farmers back there growing this stuff, and factories making these cigarettes, and then I think of companies, advertising companies, knocking themselves out to figure out ways to get tobacco advertising around seventeen-year old kids in 7 Eleven and stuff. That's why I hate the tobacco industry."

Further reflection uncovers a not-so-subtle connection between his nicotine addiction, his hatred of the tobacco companies that market to kids, and the death of his father and his present-day evangelistic and unconditional commitment to providing healthy whole grain foods to people throughout the world.

"You know, every one of my life experiences has had an effect on the person I am today. They are little pieces in that picture of my life that have made me what I am; pieces that changed my life a little bit and moved me a little closer to, say, what I'm doing here and now in the health food business."

Another one of those life experiences that scared Bob straight happened when he was on duty at the Fort Worden guardhouse. He only had to do it once, because he shipped out shortly afterward, but standing guard over those incarcerated soldiers had a profound effect on his life. He determined he would never, ever go to jail because of what he observed that night. Some of the men he was charged with watching over were behind bars because they had been arrested for being drunk and disorderly. A minor offense compared to others who had been charged with more serious acts like assault or rape. But Corporal Moore noticed in each of them a certain attitude that, regardless of the severity of their crime, permeated their being. It was like a fog that settled on them – once they were escorted through that prison door, that dark covering never left them. Even when they got out, the stain of incarceration marked them for life. They were never the same.

"I hated having to pull guard duty that weekend, but I'm grateful for the important lesson it taught me. I watched what happened to those soldiers when they walked through those big doors. They changed. They were broken men. They had awful attitudes. It was a totally different mindset than I had. But I realized once you were broken like that, you would never come back the same. You would think different. You would say things different. You would never get away from it as long as you lived."

Bob wasn't a religious man, but he admits God must have been in charge of his life all along. "I think He allowed me to drift in and out of some of those things a little bit to see that is not where you want to be." Years later when the mere prospect of having to go to jail was waved in front of him if he got one more traffic ticket in a year, Bob refused to drive a car for 365 days, just so there would be zero chance he would spend one minute behind bars.

Corporal Moore never went back to that Fort Worden guardhouse, and that was just fine with him. The Second Engineers Special Brigade was reassigned to Eniwetok, a tiny atoll in the Marshall Islands, about 2,200 miles southwest of Hawaii. His outfit was going to build bridges, roads, and huge cement embankments. Then the military blew everything up with atomic bombs, just to see what kind of damage nuclear weapons could do.

CHAPTER 8

ATOMIC PORK CHOP

T HEY HAD NO CLUE AS TO THE PURPOSE OF THEIR MISSION, BUT THE
Second Engineers Special Brigade was transporting some major
earthmoving equipment across the Pacific Ocean. U.S. Navy LSMs
(Landing Ship Medium) loaded gigantic cranes, D7 Caterpillars, bull-
dozers, and dump trucks, and they set sail for Eniwetok Atoll. Just a
speck in the North Pacific – its land area totaled less than three square
miles – the coral island was a strategic airfield and harbor for military
operations. It was one of hundreds of islands the Japanese had invaded
and claimed in the early 1940s, but they lost it to the Americans in the
five-day Battle of Eniwetok in February, 1944. By the time Private First
Class Moore arrived there in September of 1947, the island with its deep
protected lagoon was being used as a forward base for Navy operations.
But that was all about to change.

With the establishment of the Pacific Proving Grounds on July 23,
1947, the United States Atomic Energy Commission had determined
the Marshall Islands would be one of the sites the military would use for
nuclear weapons testing. Two tests had already been conducted at Bikini
Atoll, 190 miles to the east of where Bob was standing when he landed

on the shore of Eniwetok. The first, called "Able," was detonated above ground, and "Baker" exploded underwater. "Operation Crossroads" was the first nuclear testing done after the atomic bombs were dropped on Hiroshima and Nagasaki. Both tests used small boats and decommissioned vessels to determine the effects of atomic weapons on naval fleets. The nuclear bombs exploded on Eniwetok while Bob was there showed the military what kind of damage they could do to buildings.

"Here we were halfway around the world, on this beautiful island with coconut palm trees everywhere, and we didn't have any idea what was going to happen," Bob remembers. "I guess the fact we weren't allowed to bring a camera or take any pictures should have told us something."

It seemed pointless, as so much of Army life did, but the troops started building towers. Three of them, each about three hundred feet tall. Metal structures like the Eiffel Tower. The exercise in futility also involved the pouring of concrete to build cement blocks of varying sizes. They built hundreds of them, from small to incredibly large, each with a hole through the middle that a pipe fit in. And every one of them had to be oriented just so to face one of the towers. It felt like six months of hard labor, especially with the intolerable heat.

Fortunately for Corporal Moore, he wasn't one of those sweating grunts in their shorts and no shirts, digging holes and mixing concrete. The company clerk had gotten a promotion. He was only a few weeks into his cushy office job, where his responsibilities included typing up the morning reports for First Sergeant Norman Bayes and writing letters for Captain Gordon L. Eastwood, who was seeking retirement after a lengthy service record. The barracks, Quonset huts, and storage tents had all been erected, and now the officers had one more item to check off on their list. They needed a PX (Post Exchange) and someone to run it. Captain Eastwood looked over at his company clerk and asked, "Do you think you can do that, *Corporal* Moore?" It hadn't taken him long to decide whether he could handle May Company's Department One, but this *"Yes, sir!"* came firing back with much enthusiasm.

So, the eighteen-year-old corporal would run the company store. He had to set it up; order the beer, soft drinks, cigarettes, candy, magazines, personal care items and the like; take inventory; re-stock the shelves; balance the books; provide security; and take responsibility for the entire operation. It was good practice for the future flour mill operator – Bob always had a retail store in his mills.

One afternoon as he was getting ready to open the PX for the first time, Sergeant Bayes stopped by and said, "You know, with all this beer and cigarettes here, this place is going to be a sitting duck. I think you better move your bunk over here."

Corporal Moore could hardly believe what he heard. Move out of the barracks and sleep at the PX? By himself? No formations or regular duty? It was a dream come true for any soldier – privacy, autonomy, freedom. And then it struck him. Why the sergeant was giving him this special treatment. It was Bayes' way of making up for the humiliation he had heaped upon PFC Moore days before. Yes, it had been Bob's fault, but the punishment was not commensurate with the minor infraction, in his opinion. But, again, looking back, it was a significant attitude adjustment that forever altered his DNA. Or at least the genetic code that suggests it's a good idea to be on time.

First Sergeant Norman Bayes had been through many campaigns in World War II and he was as tough as nails. He commanded your respect, even though his red hair and freckles seemed to soften his countenance. Bob thought he was a great guy and they got along fine. Maybe a bit too chummy. He never called him "Rusty" or "Norm," but admittedly, the atmosphere in the headquarters office was rather casual. It was always "Yes, sir" and "No, sir," but in between there were some lax moments. Especially when it came to reveille every morning.

"At six o'clock in the morning we always had to meet in formation, everybody. The captain was there; the first sergeant was there. We always fell out, and after we fell out and had roll call we would break for breakfast; go back to the mess hall and eat. Well, I got so I wasn't making that little gathering. I was sleeping."

While Bob had come to appreciate Sergeant Bayes' sense of humor and their witty banter back and forth, he felt the officer had gone too far after the punishment for his misdemeanor had been levied.

"Well, I just don't know what we're going to have to do with Corporal Moore to induce him to come to our little 6 a.m. meetings," Bayes said one morning after his company clerk had overslept again. "But we are going to have to find something."

Well, the deal had already been made with Pork Chop – the chubby, sloppy mess cook everybody liked because he was a good chef. Corporal Moore was ordered to report to the kitchen for a meeting with the cook and the sergeant. Again, the set-up: "Well now, Pork Chop, what can we find for Corporal Moore to do to impress upon him the need for early rising and meeting with the rest of us in the morning?"

They had obviously already rehearsed the conversation: "Well," Pork Chop said, scratching his two-day stubble, "it has been a long time since the grease traps have been cleaned out and that really does need to be done."

"Well, fine," Bayes replied in his practiced tone. "Would you proceed to find the necessary equipment for Corporal Moore to perform that duty?"

So it came to pass that Corporal Moore reported to Pork Chop, and with shovel in hand and wheelbarrow at the ready, he started scooping the stinky slop out of the grease traps. "I do not think there is anything in the world more foul-smelling than a military kitchen's grease trap," Bob says, his face scrunched from the recollection. "Especially if it has been there for a while, because it just really ferments and smells horrible. Oh, it was awful."

Wheelbarrow load after wheelbarrow load, he sloshed his way out the back of the kitchen. He wheeled the glorpy goo all the way to the dump area. It kind of oozed out the front when he tipped the wheelbarrow, so he had to use the shovel to scrape out the slimy residue. It was gross. He almost lost his breakfast. Covered with yellowish-brownish grease from digging deep into the traps, he was on his way back to the kitchen for his final load when he saw them. The entire company. Marching right past him. With Sergeant Bayes in the lead.

"He was making fun of me in front of all the men. I wanted to just throw down that shovel and walk off. But, I mean, you didn't do that. I knew you did not do anything like that, but that doesn't mean you don't feel like doing it. That would have made it serious. It was tough enough as it was. Here you have your entire company, probably a few hundred guys, and he marches them by me while I was shoveling that awful stuff. It really, really hurt my pride."

He got through it, but it humbled him. He was also never late to another meeting. To this day, he still tries to get to meetings early. The smell of the grease and the smirks of the troops compel him.

"I thought I knew Sergeant Bayes well enough that I could miss the meetings. What didn't impress me at the time was the fact that *he* made the meetings, so he was only expecting me to do what he did every morning. Oh I tell you, sometimes life's lessons, they just have depths, after depths, after depths, and you can just plummet, you know. It took me a while to get over that. I mean, I was a pretty quiet guy for awhile."

He did get over it. And he realized shortly thereafter he really needed to learn a lesson. Whether it was the voice of his dad or the voice of God, he truly felt convinced this was one of those lifetime lessons he must pay attention to – no sweeping this one under the rug.

"That experience really did make an impression on me and I never wanted to go through anything like that again. Bayes knew it had really made an impression on me; he could tell I was very embarrassed. But, you know what? I made the best of it. I really did. I was going to run a grocery store! I just always kind of felt like it was Sergeant Bayes kind of making up to me about that very embarrassing moment. I liken it a little bit to falling into that grease trap and coming out smelling like a rose."

Even though it was punishment, one of the good things that came from that unpleasant clean-up duty was a friendship with the company cook. Bob ran the store and Pork Chop ran the kitchen, and each benefited from the other's privileges. Sunday mornings Bob would sneak into the kitchen early and find a nice thick steak Pork Chop had left for him. He was living the good life with steak and eggs for breakfast. And since Bob had the key to the beer closet, Pork Chop usually finished his night shift duties with a cold brew in his hand. They even teamed up for a special treat that involved a bit of creative engineering.

With no potable water on the island, sea water had to be pumped through four-inch pipes into large canvas tanks that were erected atop wooden platforms. Twenty-four hours a day a series of Buda diesel engines powered the water purification operation, providing clean water for drinking, cooking, showering, and shaving. The water treatment plant with its constant "thumpa-thumpa-thumpa" engine noise was located out past the PX and mess hall, on the other side of the camp from where the barracks were. The seclusion provided the ideal setting for the middle-of-the-night ritual Corporal Moore and Pork Chop hosted.

The problem with the water was that by the time it got pumped over to the showers by the barracks, it was cold. So, everybody took cold showers. Except for Corporal Moore and Pork Chop.

Every day after he had closed up the PX, Bob would grab a bite to eat and hustle over to the tent that had been designated as the company theater. With his stage crew class experience from high school, he had volunteered to run the projector and show movies, making a dollar an hour more than his regular pay because the Army deemed the duty "special services." He added the extra two to three dollars a night to his fifty-five dollars monthly pay – and because there was really no place on the tiny atoll to spend it – he would send half home to his dad to pay off his debt. It took nearly his entire stint in the Army, but by the time Bob got out, he had paid the $447 from the auto accident, plus the interest from the Household Finance Company loan.

"I have never not paid a bill," Bob points out. "Never left a bill unpaid. I'm sure it's a principle I got from my dad, and it's stuck with me my entire life."

The movie set-up, showing, and take-down usually took about three hours, and while the men retired afterwards to their bunks, it was rendezvous time for Corporal Moore and Pork Chop. The cook brought the fresh-baked bread – warm and with a slab of butter. The grocer stopped at his store to pick up the beer. They would meet under the water storage tank – the one whose inlet pipe had been retrofitted with a shower head. Warm bread, cold beer, and a hot shower. It didn't get much better than that on Eniwetok Atoll in 1947.

As the calendar turned to 1948, activity on the base was picking up. The hundreds of concrete blocks had been laid out just so in relation to the three towers. All the trees on the atoll had been cut down and burned. The men were antsy, wondering what this was all leading to and guessing something big was about to happen. They got their answer one day in early April when teams of scientists from the Atomic Energy Commission arrived. The men watched as dozens of odd-shaped boxes were unloaded from the ships and transported to the towers. With that, their mission was made clear. And then came the orders. Move out. Pack up everything and get ready to leave. Once everyone was off the atoll, atomic weapons would be tested to see what kind of damage the blasts would produce.

Bob figures he was one of about 10,000 men who early one mid-April morning boarded a ship that took them about fifteen miles out to sea. Dark glasses were distributed as the soldiers lined up on all levels of the ship to watch the explosion. It was just becoming dawn – kind of dark, kind of light – and Bob wanted to make sure he didn't miss anything, so he didn't put on the glasses. He remembers seeing the big mushroom cloud, but he was transfixed more by the B-17 drones that were flown right into the radioactive cloud, apparently to collect atmospheric samples.

They detonated two more atomic bombs on Eniwetok as part of Operation Sandstone. The third and final one Corporal Moore witnessed exploded on May 14, 1948. None of the soldiers went back to the atoll, but AEC personnel did. They examined the air, the sand, and how far the concrete blocks moved. Bob ended up flying over the atoll in a helicopter – one of the perks from his close association with Captain Eastwood. He saw the devastation. The total annihilation of all that was beautiful on that tiny island. He sums it all up with this understatement: "Atomic endeavors are not very pleasant, but we really didn't know what we were doing. We were just soldiers."

"It was crazy, a big joke," he adds. "We knew how the atomic bombs worked on Hiroshima and Nagasaki, so I don't understand why we did all that. To me it seemed like playtime, like a bunch of kids playing in a sandlot with firecrackers on July the Fourth."

After the fireworks, the Second Engineers Special Brigade returned to Fort Worden. In addition to the memories of embarrassing moments, lessons learned, and some fun times, Bob came away from his experience on Eniwetok Atoll with a commendation from Joint Task Force Seven. It read:

> This Certificate of Achievement is Hereby Presented to Tec 5 Robert G. Moore, RA 19300973, Company "D" 532nd Engineer Boat and Shore Regiment for your outstanding performance of duty in the operation of the Post Exchange during the testing of atomic weapons at the Eniwetok Proving Grounds.

It was dated May 22, 1948, and signed by Army Task Group Commander David A. Ogden and Joint Task Force Seven Commander J.E. Hull.

Back on the base in Port Townsend, Washington, Bob served out the rest of his three-year term, not knowing exactly what he wanted to do when he got out of the military. Captain Eastwood thought he would make a fine leader and tried to talk him into staying and attending Officer Candidate School (OCS). In his letter of recommendation, Eastwood wrote:

> Corporal Robert G. Moore has proved to be an exceptionally valuable man to the company. I would be glad to have him in any organization commanded by me at any time, as he is of increasing value to the service and his attention to duty is that which is desired by all unit commanders in the service.

So, Bob got all the paperwork ready and started prepping for Officer Candidate School. There weren't a lot of other activities to keep him busy, so he filled his free time playing piano. "I could type like the dickens; just go like a streak. Same with the piano. I would go to the day room at lunchtime to pound out a little boogie and stuff. They were always asking me to play. It was fun."

Music, dancing, and girls. Those were the thoughts that filled the heads of most twenty-year-olds, who like Bob, had just returned from duty on an island with no women. Seattle was just a ferry ride away, and the city had an active USO (United Service Organization). Committed to "lifting the spirits of America's troops and their families," the USO organized dances and hosted other entertainment events for men and women in the military. Every available weekend, Bob and his buddies would spend Friday and Saturday nights dancing with the pretty girls to the sound of live big band music. More than once, when the band members would take a break, the men would egg Bob on and push him up to the stage to play some boogie-woogie on the piano.

"So I got up there and started playing some of my boogie – the 'St. Louis Blues,' Freddie Slack, and maybe 'Bumble Boogie' by Freddy Martin & his Orchestra – and, of course, all the girls came over. Here is this soldier playing pretty good. And pretty soon the band begins filing back in. The drummer is back there tapping away, and then there is a horn and what not. I played a long time. Everybody was getting a real kick out of it. So finally the band leader would have the full band accompany me because those guys could play anything. It doesn't make any difference what key you are playing in or anything of the kind. Those guys just pick it right up and pretty soon you are hearing some of your stuff paired in by the clarinet and different things like that. I tell you, when you've got a band behind you like that and they are getting a kick out of you, it is fun. I mean it is really FUN! Finally the band leader comes over and puts his hand on my shoulder and says 'That's really great kid. Now I think we better get back to earning a living.' So I ended it and I got such a hand. It is hard to shy away from stuff like that. Those are nice moments, really nice moments."

It was his dad who brought him back to reality. Ken Moore didn't want his son to spend the rest of his life in the military. It had been a time of peace from January, 1947, when Bob went into the Army until January, 1950, when he was to be discharged, but the Korean War was right around the corner. Maybe his dad had a premonition.

"Was he predicting that we would go to war in Korea? I don't know, but I could have been killed, maybe not. Anyway, I took his advice and withdrew my OCS application."

CHAPTER 9

TAKE A HIKE

B OB WAS THREE WEEKS SHY OF HIS TWENTY-FIRST BIRTHDAY WHEN HE got out of the Army. And he was lost. He had moved back in with his parents and seven-year-old sister. He had applied for several jobs and all he got were rejection letters. He couldn't even get a date – and that had never happened! Something had to be wrong. Here he was – an Army veteran with a G.I. Bill, a musician, a good dancer, a nice guy. And he couldn't find employment or get a girl to go out with him!

He finally got an indication why he was striking out in the dating game. He had reconnected with Jeanie, one of the gals he used to dance with on Wednesday nights at the Trianon Ballroom. But as soon as she saw him light up a cigarette, she didn't want to have anything more to do with him. Same story with cute little Shirley Baker. Bob knew her from high school band and she agreed to meet him at her house. Walking up to the Baker residence with cigarette in hand, he was met at the door by Shirley's mom. They were a very religious family, and, certainly, no smoking was allowed in the house. "I do not think Shirley wants to have anything to do with you," she let him know. He was 0-for-two.

"I was really depressed," he remembers. "Coming out of the Army,

I knew a few things – I could type, I could play the piano, I could run a projector, I could manage a store. But that was about it."

Through a job placement service, he finally got hired on with the Arrowhead and Puritas Water Company. It was a dead-end job working in the mailroom. And it didn't last long. Still looking for direction in his life, Bob accepted an invitation from an old high school buddy to leave Los Angeles and join him in Phoenix. His friend, Phil Henry, worked for Wilber-Ellis Grain Company, and had learned from friends about a job opening at Davis Bros. Body & Fender Shop. Remembering Bob as a stand-up guy and pretty handy around cars, he had mentioned to owner Floyd Davis his friend would be a reliable employee. So, with limited prospects and no real ties to the L.A. area, Bob loaded his meager possessions into the 1934 Chevy he had bought with his Army savings in Port Townsend and left his parents' house – he thought for good.

He and Phil moved into an apartment and for the next twelve months lived a fairly carefree life in Arizona. Bob had experienced limited freedom in the military, and he felt cooped up in Southern California with all the traffic, smog, and dead-end relationships and jobs. In the wide open desert surrounding Phoenix, which in 1950 had a population of 100,000, the twenty-one-year-old finally felt free. No commanding officers to tell him what to do, no parents to ask him where he was going, and no old girlfriends whose mothers told him to take a hike. Living with Phil was easy. Bob liked working on cars. He was good at it. He would put in his eight hours at Davis Bros. Body Shop, and then the two pals in their early twenties with few responsibilities would take off and go have some fun. Bob had bought a Cushman Motor Scooter – kind of looked like a poor man's motorcycle – for fifty bucks, and with a gallon jug of gasoline on the floorboard between his legs and Phil sitting in the back, they would ride that thing all over town. Sometimes they would head straight out into the desert, going fifty miles an hour or so until the whiny engine sputtered and quit on them. Then they would fill the tank again, turn the scooter around, and head back to Phoenix. They never got into any real trouble, though they did push the limits a few times. Like the time they could have gotten killed climbing a 400-foot chimney at an abandoned copper mine.

"It was the tallest chimney I have ever seen in my life – it was absolutely incredible," Bob describes the site in Bisbee, Arizona. "And, of course, we had to climb it."

It was on one of their weekend exploratory trips around the state in Phil's 1940 Plymouth Club Coupe that they discovered the Queen Mine, about two hundred miles southeast of Phoenix. It was one of the richest mineral sites in the world, having produced nearly three million ounces of gold and more than eight billion pounds of copper. But when Bob and Phil stumbled across the open-pit mining camp, the place was deserted. It had been running at full capacity to meet the heavy copper demands of the war, but by 1950 the boom time had ended and the mine had been abandoned. So, the two interlopers sauntered into the empty offices of the Copper Queen Consolidated Mining Company, rifled through some open drawers, read documents that looked like they had just been left on the desk the day before, and wandered around as if they owned the joint. Then one of them challenged the other to climb to the top of that ominous-looking chimney that was located in the middle of the mining camp. They were already a mile above sea level in Arizona's Mule Mountains, and looking up, Bob had the feeling it would be like climbing up another mile to get to the top. But, hey, they were young and stupid. So they jumped on the ladder affixed to the side of the chimney and started climbing. It seemed to take forever, but they made it to the top. And holding onto the top rung of the ladder, they took a step onto the very top of that brick chimney.

"Here we were standing on top of this incredibly tall chimney, and the wind is doing this," he says as he stands up and sways back and forth and back and forth. "I never saw or felt anything like it in my life. You get yourself into a predicament like that…and then you realize you have to go back through it again. You had to get yourself down."

Obviously, they made it. But the episodes of pushing the limits and taking risks were starting to take a toll on him. Not that he ever really felt a sense of danger or looming doom, but the end-of-the-line scooter rides and chimney-top climbs made him think. About his future. About the direction in his life. Was there a purpose to what he was doing and were there good enough reasons to make a go of it in Phoenix?

He pondered these things on the five-hour drives back and forth between Phoenix and L.A. He had started making the weekend drives to see family and friends a little more often, and every trip brought him closer to the realization that he needed to move back home. When his car threw a rod halfway back to Phoenix late one Sunday night, that about clinched it. There he was, on his back in the sand under his twenty-year-old beat-up Chevy, with a flashlight in his mouth, trying to yank that rod back into place. He wrestled with it until two in the morning, ultimately using a piece of his leather belt to tie the thing back together. Covered in grease and sand and oil, he limped along at twenty-seven miles per hour (the only speed he found that didn't shake the car to pieces) until he finally made it downtown.

"It was about four-thirty in the morning and here I am, a greasy, sandy mess, driving through the middle of town, no one else on the road, and my car is making this awful knocking noise – bangity, bangity, bangity, bangity, bangity – the sound ricocheting off the sides of the buildings. I tell you, that was a lonely moment."

He parked the noise maker at the body shop and got cleaned up in time for work, but all he could think about was what was he going to do with the car. He ended up taking it to a mechanic who fixed it and suggested he dump it quick. Bob traded it in for a very neat yellow 1940 Oldsmobile Club Coupe – the car he drove when he courted his future wife.

He had had it with Phoenix. It all seemed so temporary. Like the patch job he did on his broken-down Chevy. There was no redeeming, lasting reason to stay. So he moved back into his parents' home almost a year to the day after he had left.

"It wasn't a vacant time in my life," Bob points out. "I've never really had any vacancies in my life; I mean I really haven't."

He had had fun and all with Phil, but now it was time to get serious.

He wanted a real job. He wanted a lasting relationship with a woman. And he wanted to go back to school to get more education.

He found them all at U.S. Electrical Motors.

CHAPTER 10

A GIRL NAMED CHUCK

"MAYBE HERE IS WHERE PROVIDENCE – A STRONGER SENSE OF
direction – sets in in my life," Bob reminisces. "I don't know;
I never really had any close sense of God in my life or anything like that
at that time. But a couple of things happened."

Driving down Slauson Avenue one afternoon on his way home, Bob
noticed a "Help Wanted" sign posted in front of an industrial-looking
building. He pulled into the parking lot of U.S. Electrical Motors,
thinking "I've got experience working for Boyer Electric; maybe that will
get me an interview." Sure enough, shortly after he filled out the application they hired him on the spot.

In business since 1908, U.S. Electrical Motors provided the global
market with electric motors, gear, and drive products. During the five
years Bob worked there, the industry leader introduced the Right Angle
Syncrogear motor and the Holloshaft Right Angle Gear drives for deep
well pumping.

They started him in the model department, which for the kid who
liked building model airplanes seemed more like fun than work. His job
was building scaled-down versions of large factory motors the salesmen

would haul around in their cars for demonstrations. They drove specially outfitted 1950 Mercury station wagons with the model motors built into a four-foot by eight-foot wooden platform that slid out the back. The motors were cut in half from top to bottom with the internal machinery covered with a clear plastic plate so prospective buyers could see how they operated. The cast aluminum motors, glossy in their lacquer-painted company colors ran off an extra car battery powered by a second generator. Pretty high-tech stuff for its day.

The work was fun, easy, and so were his living conditions. His folks had added a covered patio to the back of their house, and when Bob moved home again, he and his dad enclosed it, and the room became Bob's bedroom. He was settling into a comfortable routine with lots of

Bob's handiwork – building lightweight models for
salesmen at U.S. Electrical Motors (1951)

time on his hands. He still didn't have a girlfriend, but he enjoyed sitting in the backyard with his parents, basking in the Southern California sunshine, smoking cigarettes, and having a beer or two. But six months into his model-building job at U.S. Electrical Motors, he decided now was the time to keep his promise to himself and go back to school. His boss, the aptly named Mr. Steele, supported the notion, as long as the education fit into the scope of job training. Bob had always enjoyed working with motors and machinery and was more than happy to further his knowledge in those areas, especially since his G.I. Bill covered the cost. So he enrolled in an eighteen-month program at National Schools, a local trade school, taking courses in electronics and mechanical engineering. Mr. Steele allowed him to move to swing shift so he could attend the eight-hours-a-day, five-days-a-week school. They gave him a new job, too, working in the mechanical and electrical testing department. Here he was, studying industrial electronics and mechanical engineering from seven in the morning to three in the afternoon; and going to work from four to midnight alongside professional electrical and mechanical engineers.

"This was the beginning of my stepping out and learning a skill that stayed with me for the rest of my life. That year-and-a-half was the most mentally lucrative eighteen months of my life. I came out of that with a wonderful knowledge of industrial electronics."

With days and nights filled with school, work, and homework, there wasn't a lot of time left for socializing, or even sleep. But Bob didn't need much sleep. Never has. It's kind of been a trademark of his – and well known by his peers – that he runs around the clock. Even in his "resting times," he admits his mind is going full tilt. Coming up with ideas. How the plant can run more efficiently. Ways to motivate his employees. Product innovations. His mind literally never quits operating.

He did have some free time on weekends, so what did he do? He took a part-time job pumping gas at the local Shell station.

"I was just wound up. And even though I went to school full-time, and had a full-time and part-time job, I don't think I ever missed work. That was a thing with me, and my dad…," he trails off.

For all of 1951 and the first part of 1952 his single-minded approach to life was school and work, but when he finished trade school, his focus changed. He had heard about a single woman with the nickname "Chuck" who worked days in the company's drafting department. With his school and work schedule, he had never seen her, but his swing shift buddy Gordon Demeraux was dating Georgeanne, who also worked days, and she said the young lady was very pretty. Would he be interested in a blind date, they asked him. Of course, he replied. So Georgeanne queried her day-shift friend. Bob Moore from the mechanical and electrical testing department wanted to go out with her. Would she be interested? No, she would not, the answer came back. Gordon delivered the rejection message to Bob, but he didn't give up. Two weeks later he asked Gordon to relay another request via Georgeanne: How about a double date with Georgeanne and Gordon? Just dinner and a movie.

This time Chuck said "yes." That's what the draftsmen at U.S Electrical Motors called her. Her real name was Charlee, named after her dad Charles Coote. Her middle name was a much more feminine "Lucille." To family and friends, she has always been "Charlee Lu." The twenty-four-year-old brunette was tall, with an athletic build. She had played tennis in high school and was a cheerleader for the football team.

Charlee was one of a dozen young women who supported thirty-seven draftsmen. She would make copies of their drawings of motors and gears and distribute them to the various departments. More reserved than shy, she kept to herself, quietly going about her business.

She attributes her quiet demeanor to her English heritage and its stiff upper lip reputation for exercising self-restraint. Her dad's dad, who was also named Charles, was born in England. The Cootes eventually migrated to the United States, settling in Kansas. That's where Charles II met and married Cora Triplett. They moved to Colorado in the 1920s and started a family in the town of Inglewood. Their first child, a girl, died ten days after she was born. Three years later, on March 11, 1928, Charlee was born.

While it was her grandfather on her dad's side who influenced her behavioral traits, it was her grandmother on her mom's side who had the greatest impact on the person she became. Gertrude Triplett lived with her daughter and family for several years – from the time Charlee was about five to thirteen. Her husband, Guy, who worked on the railroad, had died in the flu epidemic of 1918. Like most of the estimated fifty million people who died worldwide, he was a healthy young man until he contracted the deadly virus. The pandemic, which lasted from June, 1918, to December, 1920, killed an estimated 675,000 Americans.

A widow at age thirty-five, Gertrude raised two daughters by herself, cleaning people's homes to pay the bills. When she was about fifty-two, "Donno," as everyone called her (but Charlee can't remember why), moved in with the Cootes after they had relocated to the Los Angeles area. Cora had a bad heart, and her doctor had told her the high altitude in Colorado would put a strain on it and that Southern California with its lower elevation would be a better place to live for someone in her condition. Whether it was her daughter's health issues or her deceased husband's susceptibility to the deadly H1N1 virus, Donno preached a healthy-eating lifestyle. She did a lot of research on the kinds of nutrients the body needed and read all the books she could find on the subject. She became a devotee of author Adelle Davis, who was one of America's best known nutritionists in the 1940s, '50s, and '60s. A pioneer in the movement toward healthier eating whose views were not readily accepted by the scientific community at the time, Davis concluded that adding vitamins and essential minerals to the diet could alleviate certain sicknesses, even diseases thought to be incurable. Donno read all of Davis's *Let's* best sellers, including *Let's Have Healthy Children, Let's Get Well,* and *Let's Eat Right To Keep Fit,* and she would prepare meals for the Coote family using recipes from Davis's cookbook *Let's Cook It Right.*

Charlee remembers her grandma espousing the virtues of whole unprocessed food and denigrating food additives. She favored eating fresh fruit and vegetables, whole grain cereals, and whole wheat bread. This philosophy had a profound effect on Charlee's future husband, too, who not only devoted his life to manufacturing whole grain foods, but wholeheartedly agreed with Davis's viewpoint about who has been the instigator behind our nation's unhealthy eating habits and obesity issues. Bob Moore couldn't agree more with the statement Adelle Davis is said to have made at the ninth annual convention of the International Association of Cancer Victims and Friends at the Ambassador Hotel in Los Angeles in the early 1970s. Citing U.S. Department of Agriculture statistics about tens of millions of people in the United States suffering from afflictions such as arthritis, allergies, heart disease, and cancer, she stated, "This is what's happening to us, to America, because there is a $125 billion food industry who cares nothing about health."

When Donno passed away at age eighty-eight, Charlee inherited the books her grandmother had collected. Looking back through the worn pages, she marvels at the detailed notes written in the margins. "These are the words that inspired me and my husband to prepare healthy food for our children, and ultimately to go into business making whole grain foods for everyone to enjoy."

Growing up in Huntington Park, a suburb southeast of Los Angeles, Charlee Lu enjoyed a pleasantly spoiled upbringing as an only child. Her mom never worked, never even learned how to drive a car. Dad was in charge of the janitorial staff at Huntington Park High, the school Charlee Lu graduated from. Her grandma lived with them for about eight years while she was in grade school, and her Aunt Babe (her real name was Gertrude, named after her mom, but everyone called her Babe) was a regular visitor. In fact, Babe was with them on one of the more memorable experiences Charlee remembers growing up.

"It was a Friday, March 10, 1933 – the day before my fifth birthday – and my parents were out shopping for my presents. I was home with Grandma and my Aunt Babe, having something to eat, when the ground started to shake. Donno yelled "Earthquake!" and told us to run outside. It felt like an ocean wave under the house – a weird, weird feeling. As I was scrambling out the front door, I tripped and fell on the fork that was still in my hand. I still have the scar on my lip."

The 6.4 magnitude earthquake that struck just off the coast of

Newport Beach at 5:54 p.m. was Southern California's deadliest seismic disaster. The ground shook for only about ten seconds, but the damage in the cities of Huntington Park, Compton, and Long Beach was extensive. More than 120 people died in the quake, most from falling bricks and building ornaments when they ran outside, and there was an estimated $50 million (in 1933 dollars) in damage.

"I was afraid to go back into the house because I thought it might collapse on us from all the aftershocks. I slept in my clothes that night, and every few hours Donno would wake me up and we would have to run outside because there was another aftershock. It was really rough, something you remember your whole life even though you were only five years old."

Neither will she ever forget the harrowing story her mom and dad told when they finally got home that fateful night. They had barely escaped disaster on their shopping trip, as a building they were leaving collapsed, and a woman walking right in front of them was hit and killed by falling debris. She also learned the earthquake had destroyed Huntington Park High School, putting her dad out of work for an extended period of time. Even as a five-year-old, Charlee Lu remembers it was only through the grace of an understanding landlord that the family was able to stay in their home for a year without paying rent.

They lived in that house on Middleton Street for twenty years, with Charles supporting the family on his janitor's salary, Cora at home, and Charlee Lu attending Pacific Boulevard Grammar School, Gauge Avenue Junior High, and playing tennis and cheering for the Huntington Park Spartans grades nine through twelve. Like many of their neighbors, the Cootes lived paycheck to paycheck, so their high school daughter helped support the family by working part-time at the local Sears, Roebuck and Co. store.

"Coming out of the Depression and through the war, we were really used to having nothing," Charlee recalls. "So I worked weekends and summers making enough money to buy my own clothes and things like that. I remember feeling that I'm a grown young woman and I need to help my father and mother, who are not well-to-do people."

She graduated early – the winter class of 1947 – and went to work full time as a cashier for the Veterans Administration. At twenty-two years old, she was still living at home when the family moved to the nearby city of Cudahy. So Charlee Lu went looking for work closer to their new neighborhood. She got the job at U.S. Electrical Motors and became fast friends with Georgeanne, her workmate in the dialing department. Both were single, but Georgeanne was dating a guy who worked the swing shift.

Charlee Lu didn't have a steady in her life at the time, and she wasn't in a hurry to date. She passed on the first request to go out on a blind date with Georgeanne's boyfriend's friend, but the second time with some urging by Georgeanne and Gordon, she thought "Oh well, I might as well." So she did.

The double date was March 25, 1952. After dinner the two couples went to the theater to see Cecil B. DeMille's *The Greatest Show on Earth,* the Academy Award-winning tribute to circuses starring Charlton Heston, Jimmy Stewart, Dorothy Lamour, and Betty Hutton.

"My mom asked me what I thought of her," Bob says about that first date, "and I told her, 'Well, I don't know; she didn't talk any, so I guess I'm going to have to have another date with her to maybe find out what she is like.' I knew one thing for sure – she was a very pretty girl. Soft-spoken. A nice Christian girl."

Bob asked Charlee out a few weeks later, initiating a year-long courtship filled with dinners, dancing, music, and goofy stuff young lovers do. "Our second date we went out for fried chicken at a nice eatery in L.A., called the Southern Plantation or something like that. They brought these little bowls of water out and they had a rose in each one, and neither one of us knew what they were. I asked the waitress what they were and she said they were finger bowls. Here we were, just young as heck and kind of attracted to each other, and for some reason or another we thought that finger bowl was the funniest thing that had ever come down the pike, and we got to laughing about this crazy rose in the finger bowl and what we were supposed to do with it. I don't know, we must have laughed for an hour over it. Just funny stuff. I think we wanted to laugh, and it was very pleasant. Very pleasant."

Bob never went out with anyone else. But Charlee did. Well, technically it was a date, but it was with Bob's dad.

"It sounds bizarre, but there was nothing bizarre about it. He took her to a real nice restaurant for dinner and dancing. That's crazy. My girlfriend! That will really stick in a son's craw, I tell you. Anyway, she really liked my dad. He was a cool guy."

The verdict came back: "She's a keeper. You ought to marry that girl," Bob's dad told him. Ken and Doris Moore adored Charlee. Thought she was a sweetheart. A lovely girl.

Bob was in love, and he lavished Charlee with his time, his attention, and his money. On the weekends he would take her to piano bars to listen to music and dance. On Sundays it was always dinner at his mom and dad's. They would see each other every weekday at work, too, although they worked different shifts. Sometimes when she finished hers and he was starting his, she would take his car and be there waiting for him when he was done. "She loved driving that little yellow Club Coupe. I can still see my car with her going down the street. I'd be thinking 'That's my car. That's my girl.'"

Bob describes their courtship as "just a fun time, real nice. Real nice stuff. I took her to a lot of places. I spent all my money courting her, and I was always talking about getting married. She would say 'I don't want to talk about that right now,' and she'd change the subject.'"

"I knew he was the guy for me," Charlee admits, "but it just took me a long time to say yes."

She finally told Mr. Persistent she would think about marriage and have an answer for him when she returned from a two-week vacation to visit her family in Colorado. She wanted to be sure, and by the time that train arrived in Denver, she knew. She couldn't wait to tell her Aunt Lola,

Uncle Ward, and the rest of her dad's family that she was going to marry Bob Moore.

Bob figured he had two weeks to get everything ready. He wanted their reunion – and the moment of his proposal – to be perfect. He had scoped out a nice new tract home he could get with his G.I. loan. He couldn't afford a new car, so he took his twelve-year-old Oldsmobile in to get the inside all re-upholstered. He put on his best suit and got to the train depot early.

"I was really in love with that girl, and I really wanted her to marry me. I felt that same kind of Providential pressure that I've felt before – like after the fire, to keep going. To get that mill in the first place. Somehow I just kind of knew that marrying Charlee was the next big thing in my life. I guess I just conned her into it. I don't know, it's been nearly sixty years, so I guess it must have lasted a little bit."

Stepping off that train, Charlee looked more beautiful to him than ever before. They both had that glow about them that lovers reconnecting exude. Walking up to the car, he popped the question: "Well, did you?" Charlee knew he was asking whether she had been thinking about "it," as promised. "Well," she answered, "I have been thinking about it, and I will marry you."

CHAPTER 11

AN AWAKENING MOMENT

Now that the engagement was official, Bob could get serious about buying a house. Since they both worked at the same place, they wanted to find an affordable home as close to U.S. Electrical Motors as possible. That meant about fourteen miles away, in a nice new neighborhood in the city of Hawthorne. They were able to finance the $10,000 mortgage through a VA Loan program with a very low interest rate and just four hundred dollars down, which Charlee furnished from her savings because Bob had spent all his money courting her.

The wedding was an intimate, justice-of-the-peace kind of a ceremony at Bob's grandmother's house. Ethel "Monnie" Moore coordinated all the weddings at Vermont Square Methodist Church, and she and Grandpa Frank were more than happy to host the nuptials. They even convinced Dr. Crist, a retired minister, who had christened six-month-old Robert Gene Moore in 1929, to officiate.

"I have such great memories of my grandmother's home," Bob remembers. "It was a lovely big house, close to where I grew up. I used to stop there both on the way to school and on the way back, and Monnie would fix me scratch biscuits."

Bob and Charlee got married on March 14, 1953, just less than a year from the day they met. Their new home wasn't quite ready, so Bob moved into the small house Charlee rented on her parents' property. She continued working days, and he nights – because it paid fifteen cents an hour more. "It's funny looking back on that, but those extra few pennies were significant to me at the time. Plus, I actually liked working nights. You didn't have all the management fuss and all that kind of stuff."

It was a busy, crazy couple of weeks. When Charlee left for work, Bob would head over to their new house to oversee the final construction touches. They would see each other briefly at the shift change, and then Charlee would drive over and tidy up the new place. After midnight, they would sit and talk about the day's activities. They spent all their spare time – and money – buying furniture, setting up the kitchen, and stocking the pantry. Bob describes it as "a madhouse for a while, but the whole thing was a big ball. Lots of fun. I think back on all those moments

Bob and Charlee on their wedding day (March 14, 1953), with Dr. Crist officiating at Bob's grandmother's house

as being pretty special. She got pregnant right away, and then we had three kids just about as fast as we could. Then I got this kid thing figured out."

Well, it was actually a visit to his family physician, Dr. Shipley, that put an end to the baby parade. With a little incentive administered by Charlee's dad.

After Ken and Robert, Charlee was pregnant with David. The cramped quarters caused Bob to consider moving their old wringer washing machine out of the kitchen and into the garage. That, and he also flooded the kitchen floor one time when he let the darn thing run over.

"So I poked around a little bit, and I figured there was plenty of room in the attached garage. I crawled underneath the house and looked around and thought there was nothing to it. The drain is right there, the bathrooms are over here, the side of the wall is there; and I thought, well heck, I could just easily run pipes over here and a drain right there. I will just go buy one of those automatic washers, which were getting popular. It was one of the best washers we ever had. Sears and Roebuck. We had it for twenty years, I think. Anyhow, Charlee's dad stops over. Charlie was his name. Good guy. Real sweet man. He didn't talk too much, but that morning he kind of had a funny look on his face, and he said 'If you make sure you will not get my daughter pregnant again I will help you put in the new washer and I will buy a dryer to match it.' I guess he thought three kids were enough. I had been thinking about it, anyway, so I said, 'Charlie, you got a deal.'"

After the procedure, the good Dr. Shipley handed Bob the evidence in a little plastic container. Seeing the proof, Charlie went down to the Sears and Roebuck and plunked down $350 for a new dryer. He even helped Bob install it.

Moving into a new house and starting a family produced some of the best memories for the young married couple. But tragedy struck twice within about a year. Eight months after they were married, Charlee's mom died. The next year Bob's dad died. They were two crushing blows that tore at the fabric of their lives.

"We had just gotten home after a Sunday visit at Charlee's parents' house, and a police officer knocked on the door. He said he had a death notice concerning Cora Coote. We didn't have a telephone, so I guess Charlee's dad had called the police and they sent someone over. I couldn't believe it! We had just been with them and now she was dead. Poor Charlee. She cried and cried and cried. It was terrible, just terrible."

They immediately drove back to where they had just been sitting down for dinner. Her mom, just fifty-three years old, lay dead in the bed. She had had a heart attack.

"I can remember Charlee laying over her mother, just sobbing and sobbing, and I thought, 'Are we going to live through this?' It was just so profound and so heavy. I can't believe how heavy it is. Even now, it just grabs me. It is just so…incredible. It just tore her apart. But somehow we got through it."

And then the man Bob loved with all his being died. The dad who dreamed with his son about going into business together suddenly dropped dead of a heart attack at age forty-nine. The future Bob and Ken Moore had been planning for years came to an end on February 23, 1955.

> When I lost my dad it felt like my right arm got torn off and then my left ear got torn off, and then my middle toe got cut off, and I am running around like half a person. Sometimes there are things that are so difficult you just break them up into seconds or half a minute, and you think, "I'll get from this half minute to that half minute, and if I do that then I can get to the next half minute." You just sit there and think, "This is the most uncomfortable, difficult, disagreeable moment of my life; I'm never going to experience anything like this again." It was crazy. Just crazy. A moment of awesome pain.
>
> Charlee and I, I think we kind of both fell back into a fog. I did that after the fire, too, when I just came to work every day and did what I knew I had to do and then went home and then came to work and then went home and came to work and then went home. I got to thinking about that one time

and I thought, "You know you think you aren't making any progress, you are just kind of moving in a fog," but I fashioned a little phrase that says in essence, *Progress sometimes is just being there.* That was something I pinned up on my mirror at home and I put it on my telephone. It is still on my phone today: *Progress sometimes is just being there.* Because you just don't feel like you are making any headway, yet you are still going there. Still going there.

So that was one of those moments in life where I definitely would not want to go back and live through it again. I really would not want to go back and live it again. Charlee and I, we were very close and sometimes we just didn't know what to say. It was just such a loss. I was very close to my dad and he died so suddenly. When I lost Dad I thought, "we are never going to go into business together," because that is what we had talked about – going into business together. It was always *when* we go into business together. This thought of going into business together, it permeated things. We didn't even have to talk about it sometimes. It was just an important ingredient in our relationship. Now I do not have that.

Thinking back to the lifestyle his dad had, the typical salesman's life in the mid-1950s as glorified in the popular TV show *Mad Men* – the martinis all afternoon, smoking three packs of cigarettes a day – he admits it probably wasn't all that surprising he would die at an early age.

"I'd have been the same way, but the example my dad set that cost him his life made it just out of the question for me to do anything like that. Those are awakening moments in one's life. Really, really awakening moments. My life changed after he died. I realized I was waiting for something until he died. Waiting to go into business with him. I just didn't even think of life without my father. I still can't really. Dad and I were so close right up until then. And then it was over."

As devastating as it was, it caused a major shift in Bob's thinking (although in his actions he stayed with the cigarettes), a definitive change in life direction that propelled him into a future to which he had not given much thought. There was no father to wait for to tell him now was the time to go into business together. There was no one else he could depend on to lead him in the planning of what that business would look like. He was on his own now. Coming out of the sharp pangs of his loss, he realized the desire his dad had instilled in his heart – to have a company of his own, to be his own boss, to be in charge of his own destiny – had not diminished. In fact, as he mulled over the circumstances of the past few cloudy days since his dad's passing, the picture in his mind about his future came into sharper focus. What remained was the burning desire to go into business. That moment he thought the chance for entrepreneurship had evaporated on the news of his dad's death that Wednesday afternoon in February became a rallying point for Bob to strike out on his own. He shared that the feeling was "pretty strong – not as strong as my desire to marry my wife – but pretty strong."

The assumption all along had been he would stay with U.S. Electrical Motors permanently. But now, following the burial of his dad just days after his own twenty-sixth birthday, his mind was consumed with the notion of going into business for himself. The big question was what line of work could he find that would support a family of five on his own. Charlee had quit working when she started having babies, and Bob had moved to days with a new position. With four years' experience building model motors and then working in the testing departments, he knew all the ins and outs of the products U.S. Electrical Motors sold. Management had recognized his unique skill set and had created a new position for him. Anytime and anywhere there was a problem with an installation, Bob would show up, assess the problem, and make a recommendation. Most of the time, he would discover the salesman had sold the wrong motor, so he would write up the specs for the right motor and make arrangements for the re-install. The company was happy with the work he was doing, but it was Charlee who wasn't so thrilled her husband had a job that forced him to travel so much. They were flying him all around the country at a moment's notice, which wasn't that conducive to a happy home life with three baby boys and a stay-at-home mom.

Plus, Bob was still working just about every free weekend at the Shell station down the street from their house. He was bringing home a little extra money, but with all the work and travel he was pretty much gone all the time. One Saturday at the gas station, Bob was sharing his conflicting feelings about being on the road so much and missing the opportunity to go into business with his dad when owner Ed Neeland asked if he had ever thought about getting his own gas station to operate.

"Of course, I had never considered running my own station because up until then I just knew my dad and I were going to go into our own business together. But I loved working at the gas station. I liked being around cars. I liked raising the hood and looking at the motors. I loved talking to the people. Pumping gas, washing windows, checking their oil and tires – all that kind of stuff. I don't know, maybe it's just a guy thing, but that's how I felt."

The wheels were turning now. He pressed on, asking Ed how much cash he would have to come up with to get started. When he heard "maybe three or four thousand," his enthusiasm waned. He didn't have any savings. Undeterred, he queried Ed about operating costs, and was encouraged to learn pretty much everything sold at a gas station was done so on consignment. That made it easier for a cash-strapped operator – payment for gasoline, tires, fan belts, batteries, accessories, etc., would be due only when the goods were sold. It boiled down to being pretty cheap to set oneself up as a gas station operator. But that still didn't resolve the fact the Moores had no extra money lying around. Hmmm, where could he get three or four thousand bucks? There was no equity in the home, so a loan against the house was out of the question. Well, there just happened to be a real estate company located on the same lot as Neeland's Shell Station. Maybe it wouldn't hurt to ask what houses were selling for. So, with much trepidation, Bob walked next door to ask the realtors if the local G.I. houses were selling and how much they were going for.

"They said they were selling like hotcakes, that I could get maybe

$14,000. So I immediately went to talk to Charlee. I never kept any secrets from her. We talked about it and ultimately made the decision to put our house on the market. I'm confident she was right with me all the time, even though I knew how much she loved that first home of ours."

Bob did get his gas station. But it wasn't a Shell like he and Ed had talked about. Right about the time the "For Sale" sign went up at their house, another sign appeared a few blocks from Neeland's Shell Station. There was a McMahan's Furniture store on one corner, a bank on the other, a Foster's Freeze on another, and a vacant lot with a big sign that announced *Coming soon – Mobil Gas Station,* and then *Dealers Wanted,* with a phone number listed below.

While Ed Neeland was negotiating to get him a Shell station, Bob pursued the Mobil opportunity. Convinced he had the experience, his rep, Milo Trumble, told him he would have to pay $3,200 to buy into a Mobil dealership.

"About this time I remember feeling like I was slowly creeping out into deep water. And every few steps or so I could look back and tell myself, 'Let's see now, I could turn back now and make it to the shore,' and then I would walk out a little farther into deeper water; and then I would see the shore farther away and I would think, 'Okay, I guess I can still make it back safely,' and then…"

Bob took the plunge. As soon as their house sold, he took the four thousand dollars they had made on the sale and wrote out a check for $3,200 to Mobil. He deposited the $800 of profit into his savings account, knowing that small amount of money would have to tide them over once he quit his job at U.S. Electrical Motors. Of course, he wouldn't leave until the station was up and running. They were living paycheck to paycheck and certainly couldn't survive very long on eight hundred bucks.

The Mobil station on the corner of 147th and Crenshaw went up fast. Bob would come by every day after work to see the amazing progress. It seemed everywhere around him a new housing tract was going in or a new retail development was opening up. He was right in the middle of the post–World War II boom when subdivision housing became a mass-production industry.

Boys returning from the war were now men with young families. The population of Los Angeles had swelled to nearly one million in 1955, and with the public opening of Disneyland on July 18 it seemed all of Southern California that summer was the Happiest Place on Earth. Except in the tiny apartment where Bob and Charlee had moved with their three boys after selling the house.

"Oh, it was awful. We hated it. People rattling around late at night, and then there was a big fight down in the street one Saturday night with a bunch of drunks down there beating up on each other. Poor Charlee. Poor Charlee. How did we make it through that? I do not know. That was my own making. It's one thing to fall in a river or have your house burn down or have a car wreck or something. You can always say 'Well, it wasn't my fault.' But this, this was ten thousand percent my doing. Charlee didn't do it. My mother didn't do it. Her dad didn't do it. I did it."

Even though the gas station seemed to be flying together, it couldn't open soon enough for the cramped couple. When the construction crew told him they were two weeks out from completion, Bob put his plan into action. He walked into his boss's office at U.S. Electrical Motors and handed him his two-week notice. Herb was floored.

"*What?* Bob, you've got to be kidding," he countered. When he realized Bob wasn't kidding, Herb tried a different tack. "You've been with us for five years; we have great plans for you. Are you sure you're not making a mistake?"

Bob assured him he wasn't making a mistake. And since the company not long afterwards was sold and moved to Milford, Connecticut, where he was certain he would have never wanted to move, he was sure he had made the right decision. But what he didn't know almost ruined him.

It was just days before the station was supposed to open. The gasoline storage tanks were neatly covered over in concrete. The two bays with their shiny new lifts were primed and ready to start bench pressing cars. The pumps painted red and white stood at attention, ready to start dispensing the consigned gasoline that had been delivered. The all-metal building decorated with creamy white porcelain was gleaming in the sunshine. Out front riding atop a tall shiny pole was the bright red Mobil logo Pegasus, the winged horse that was a divine fantastical creature in Greek mythology. And most impressive, at least to the proprietor, was the sign that read "Bob Moore Mobil Service."

"I was so excited. I mean *my* station was days away from opening. I remember standing in front of that dirt-covered lot – pouring the asphalt was the last thing they had to do – and looking down Crenshaw this way and up 147th that way. All the streets were white, concrete. When they planted trees along the road it looked like paradise. All of L.A. looked that way, at least it did to me. It felt like a dream."

The dream turned into a nightmare when the asphalt workers went on strike. Nobody's driveway was getting paved. No blacktop going down on any parking lot in the city. A work stoppage literally hours before Bob Moore Mobil Service was supposed to open. Certainly this was just a temporary glitch, Bob thought, although he did do a quick assessment of his finances. After cashing his final check from U.S. Electrical Motors, paying the realtor's commission on the sale of the house, and calculating the moving expenses to get into that lousy apartment, his checking account was empty. All he had was the eight hundred dollars in savings. He projected his living expenses – rent, utilities, food – would be running him about two-fifty a month.

Well, they would just have to hold on, hang in there until the strike was over. Every day Bob would be there, re-setting displays, re-organizing racks and shelves with product, sweeping the dirt out of the garage, getting ready. Days stretched into weeks. Still no resolution to the asphalt workers' labor dispute. With dwindling resources, frayed nerves, thinning patience, and less-than-satisfactory living conditions, most families might have disintegrated. But the Moores persevered. With a little bit of help from Charlee's dad, who loaned them a thousand bucks when their bank account finally ran dry.

"It was a tough time. I was just sick about it. I wonder how we got through it; how Charlee got through some of that. I do know I have a very devoted wife. I realize people have a lot of trouble with this equality thing, but Charlee is perfectly equal. I don't know what makes it work, what makes it not work. I don't know. This is what I have. I don't know what everyone else has, but this is what I have."

They held on for two months. And then the strike ended. With freshly poured asphalt covering the block-long by half-a-block-deep lot, Bob Moore Mobil Service opened. It was a glorious thing.

"When the station opened, my life just shone. If I ever knew I was cut out to do anything, it was to be in business for myself with a white uniform on. It's kind of like you have this board in front of you, and it has holes – squares and triangles. You are whatever you are, and you look over the whole thing – the holes are all the things people can do. You try to fit the peg into different ones, and then all of a sudden it just drops right into one, and it is tight and it just slides slowly down, and then there it is. That is what I'm supposed to do! To me, it was being in my own business. Having my own customers. I feel the same way today

**One of his first days as an entrepreneur, Bob (on right)
with an employee at Bob Moore Mobil Service gas station
at 147ᵗʰ and Crenshaw in Gardena, California (1955)**

at eighty-one as I felt at twenty-six. I loved it. I was good at it. I opened every morning. I closed every night. I worked seven days a week."

He worked for 365 days straight. And then he took one day off. The reward for the family was a trip to Santa's Village, a year-round Christmas wonderland located at Lake Arrowhead in the San Bernardino Mountains. The elfin theme park, which entertained young and old from 1955 to 1998, was a popular day-trip destination that featured life-size gingerbread and doll houses, live reindeer, a petting zoo, monorail, and, of course, visits with Santa Claus himself. It was a fantastical experience for Robert, Ken, and David, who sailed down the bobsled run together, traipsed through the maze of snow-covered trails, and leap-frogged over the large and brightly colored concrete mushrooms and toadstools that dotted the mountainside. It was an other-worldly event for Dad, whose head and hands had been steeped in gasoline, motor oil, and brake fluid for twelve hours of each of the past 365 days. And for Mom, it was a proud moment. She was finally able to treat her kids to a fun outing and spend a little extra to buy them some candy and toys. She also took great pride in celebrating with her husband the one-year anniversary of owning their own business together.

CHAPTER 12

ON THEIR OWN

"**I** WASN'T STUPID OR BLIND OR DUMB, BUT I WASN'T INTIMIDATED BY business," Bob explains about his start as an entrepreneur. "Does that make me different than most guys? You would have to take a poll of people who voluntarily saved their money, borrowed from a relative, then went into business, and ask them, 'Were you intimidated by this venture?' and see if it's normal to worry about it or not. I didn't worry about it. There were gas stations all over the city. If they could make it, I could make it. I knew I could make it. There was a kind of underlying confidence that this was going to work."

He admits it was a love-hate relationship. He loved the independence of being in business for himself. He loved the customers. He loved the challenge of lifting the hood and trying to figure out what was wrong with someone's car.

But he hated the rules and regulations; the "dos and don'ts." Still does today. He figures Bob's Red Mill spends a third of its energy, time, money, and personnel on state and federal programs like HACCP (Hazard Analysis and Critical Control Points) and other mandates dictated by the Food and Drug Administration and the U.S. Department of

Agriculture. Some might call them necessary evils, but to Bob they're not the fun part of the business.

While Mobil allowed a certain level of autonomy to its franchisees, it carried a big club. Continuing education was required. There were unannounced spot checks to see if the restrooms were clean. The "secret shoppers" of that era would drive in and report back about the level of customer service. Did the attendant check the air in the tires, the oil? Did they wash all the windows? Were they wearing a clean uniform? "It wasn't a gas station in those days – it was a service station," Bob points out. He didn't mind, actually. He ran a tight ship and was proud of his station's performance.

The only glitch was figuring out cash flow. The money that came in wasn't necessarily yours because you always had to pay the piper. When he started the business, his pockets would be stuffed with cash and he thought he was rich. He learned quick enough that in the consignment business, that paper money wasn't actually his. He pumped the gas, collected payment, and held onto the money…until Mobil replenished the underground tanks and re-stocked the accessories, and expected immediate payment of five or six thousand dollars for its products that had been sold.

One day early on when the Mobil truck pulled in, Bob realized he didn't have the cash on hand to pay the bill. So he ran across the street to the Citizen's Bank where he had his checking account, which by the way didn't have the required five or six thousand dollars. He pled his case to Joe Roberts, the manager whose daughter, Marian, Bob happened to date in high school, and was surprised at the answer.

"He knew I didn't have enough money in my account to cover the check I needed to write, but he said, 'Just write a check to yourself for the amount you're short and I'll deposit it in your account.' In those days, it took a couple of days for checks to clear. Joe knew I brought in a lot of cash and was good for the money. It was kind of funny – my banker taught me how to kite checks."

Banker Joe's "favor" to float some cash that allowed Bob to get out of a sticky financial situation was only a one-time occurrence, but the lesson

Bob learned that day was profound. For the next fifty-five years as a businessman, he made it a point to have a strong relationship with his banker. Even if he didn't think at the time there was a remote chance he would need a loan, line of credit, or a favorable interest rate, he invested the time and energy into staying on very good terms with the bank manager.

"Once you got in their good graces, they could make things a lot easier for you," he says of the numerous bankers he's dealt with over the years. "I've loved to borrow money. It's just part of doing business for me. And it's been imperative to me to have a relationship with a more powerful institution than I am."

He was certainly influenced by watching his dad's and granddad's family business go down the tubes. And he remembered the sting of the unfavorable interest rates slapped on his parents' loan at Household Finance Company. On the other hand, he experienced the very kind G.I. Bill financing that allowed him to get into his first home.

"Dad was a nice contrast – this had nothing to do with good or bad. He came out of a Depression. I don't know his inner thoughts and I can't ask him, so I don't have any idea about some of the things that pushed him this way or that. But I formed a plan in my life, in a sense, that my dad did this and I am going to do this. And one of those life-changing decisions for me was to have an excellent relationship with the banking system."

Once the cash flow issue was figured out, Bob Moore Mobil Service thrived. Of course, as with most start-ups, it wasn't easy. There were long stretches with no days off. By this time, he had John, Jerry, Bob and a few other guys working for him, so there was payroll to make. And the margins were very small – four-and-a-half cents on regular gas and five cents on ethyl. That equated to making fifty cents or less on every ten-gallon fill-up.

"You get weary because you're not making the money you should make for the amount of time you put in and how hard you work. But I've never been, like, wishing I didn't have to go to work or something like that. I guess there are some people who don't have the energy to do stuff like that, but that never was an issue with me. I've got more energy now than I had then, I think."

While it was his dad's untimely death that propelled him into a lifelong pursuit of owning his own business, his success and satisfaction with running the service station in the mid-1950s convinced him he was on the right track. He never looked back. But along the way, the challenges of entrepreneurship taught him several lessons that forged his character and made him the happy and content man he would become.

"What I did was jump into something I didn't know anything about," he says of his owner/operator status with Mobil. He would later say the same thing when he ventured into the milling business. "But I just knew it was the right thing for me to do. Of course, there were rules I had to play by that got me through: Pay your bills. Save your money. Be conservative. Be frugal. Don't spend money just because you've got a whole pocketful of it. Do it yourself. Do without if you have to. I've always done it that way. Definitely. Definitely. Definitely. You have to play by the rules. That's all there is to it."

Appreciating your customers and providing great service were more like philosophies than rules, but those attitudes have dominated Bob's approach to business throughout his entire life.

"I've always loved my customers. They came to my 'service' station – service! I had a little desk in the back of the garage, but you weren't in the office very often. If you were, you weren't going to make any money. You were doing tune-ups or brake jobs. You would lube cars, change oil, pump gas. And you were always looking for business. Of course, you had people coming in for gasoline, which they had to, but that was just an opportunity to impress them with how friendly you are and what a great place it is to bring your car and have it serviced."

About midway into his second year, he was very organized and pretty much had it figured out, even though he admits dealing with the money at the end of the day "put a serious look" on his face. But what he couldn't control was the stuff of life – and death. First, it was her mom; then his dad; and then in September of 1956 Charlee's dad had a massive stroke and died. He was only sixty-two.

Charlie Coote had been a heavy smoker most of his life. He rolled his own cigarettes, which transfixed his three grandsons. They used to gather around him and watch him take out his pouch of Genuine Durham Smoking Tobacco, sprinkle some onto the paper, lick it, and light it up. Bob remembers it was cute to see his boys huddled around their grandpa that way, even though he ultimately came to despise cigarette smoking.

"Charlee's father smoked like a furnace in the house, which my dad and mom both did around me. And then I started smoking. Man, oh man! The cards were really stacked! Really stacked against us all. That and the nefarious tobacco just gets me going, I can't hardly believe anyone could grow tobacco or manufacture cigarettes, and then on top of it all, have massive advertising to promote smoking. That's crazy! I just can't believe it! In the '50s and '60s – I don't know when they stopped all of that stuff – you were just inundated with tobacco ads on everything. They sponsored half the shows on television. Everywhere you went they were promoting cigarettes. In the Army, they were, like, seven cents a pack. Anyone could afford to smoke; they made sure of that. That's just terrible."

With the money from Charlie Coote's estate and the first-year profits from the business, Bob and Charlee were able to build their own house. They had moved out of that cramped and noisy apartment after a few depressing months and into a rental house just down the street from the station. It was tolerable – like most young married couples of the day it seemed they were living out of boxes stacked in the garage – but Bob was driven to "give Charlee her house back." He still felt bad he was the instigator behind selling their first house to finance the gas station. But he would make it up to her by giving her total control to customize their new home and buy everything new.

Charlee reveled in the opportunity. The Colonial-style house had three bedrooms, two bathrooms, a double car garage, and a lot of amenities like forced-air heat. They had paid $19,500 – about double what their first house cost – and, to them, everything seemed twice as good. It had a huge yard for the boys to play in. There was a nice fireplace and carpet throughout. A designer came in and hung all the curtains and drapes. Charlee had all the furniture custom made in maple, the popular style at that time in California – couches, overstuffed chairs, coffee tables, end tables, etc. She went to the May Company to buy all the bedding, towels, silverware, and dishes. Everything was first class, including a brand new Kimball piano. It was all exactly as Charlee wanted it. Including the white picket fence.

"I just know it was one of the nicest times of her life," Bob says about all the dream house planning, decorating, and entertaining Charlee did. "It was so much fun for both of us actually. When we moved into that house – we called it the Torrance house because that was the city where we settled in; only about three miles down Crenshaw from the station – it was really a nice moment in time. Sometimes it's good to stop the clock. And you look at that moment in time. You snap a picture of it. You have this nice home. You have a pretty good station. You have a nice customer base by that time. Of course, it cost you all of your family. I mean in a sense, I would have never gone into the gas station business if my dad hadn't died. I just wouldn't. We'd have done something together. Probably something in advertising or something like that."

While this was the most fun and exciting time of their young married lives together, there was an element of sadness and emptiness they couldn't shake. They both terribly missed the parents they had lost, and it pained them that their boys would grow up never knowing three of their four grandparents. Bob still had his mom and sister, but Charlee's closest relatives were all gone. They had their friends, as well as some aunts, uncles, and cousins, and because they had the nicest house in their combined family, they regularly hosted dinners and holiday parties. Of course, they had each other, and it was that bond, their strong love for one another, that held them together through their losses. They also found strength in reading the Bible and attending the local Baptist church.

"When we moved in, it was just like we had moved into a new world.

It was one of those really pleasant moments in my life. Everything new – house, furniture, dishes; even the towels, sheets, and blankets."

They sealed the new chapter in their lives when they called Goodwill and had them haul away all their possessions that were left behind in the rental. Everything old was gone. They were starting a new phase in life where all was shiny and new. The past was behind them. It looked to be a bright future ahead.

CHAPTER 13

A LOW POINT

THE PLEASANT MOMENT BOB HAD EXPERIENCED WHEN THEY MOVED into the Torrance house was fleeting. He wasn't happy.

He loved Charlee. Adored his growing sons Ken, Robert, and David. The business was thriving. The house was perfect. Money wasn't a problem. So, what was wrong with this picture?

A snapshot of Los Angeles in the mid to late 1950s would make it clear. Well, actually the picture wouldn't be that clear. And that was the problem.

"The smog in LA, it was driving me nuts," Bob recalls. "My eyes were watering all the time."

Bob wasn't the only one who suffered from air pollution in the form of smog (a word cleverly derived from combining "smoke" and "fog") that hung over the Los Angeles basin. Millions of Southern California residents dealt with the eye irritation, sore throats, and blackened lungs that were a result of breathing in the exhaust that spewed from cars, trains, airplanes, and manufacturing. Due to its unique geography and atmospheric conditions, those toxic fumes blanketed the L.A. area in what is known as an inversion layer, which basically traps the smog close to the ground. The air quality was so bad you couldn't see the buildings in downtown Los Angeles, even though they were just a few miles from where the Moores lived. On a good day, you could make out the form of the San Bernardino mountains that towered over the basin, but too often "the haze" (as many Angelenos liked to downplay it) obliterated the sight of anything more than ten miles away. One October, heavy smog conditions shut down industry and schools in Los Angeles for most of the month.

Measures were taken to try to reduce emissions, but there was such a heavy reliance on automobiles (actually a blessing and a curse for Bob Moore and his livelihood), that the air seemed to get dirtier and dirtier. In their book *Smogtown: The Lung-Burning History of Pollution in Los Angeles,* Chip Jacobs and William Kelly described the losing battle this way:

> When smog collared the city in the early 1940s, local government assessed it a moderate nuisance as fixable as a pothole-chewed boulevard. Los Angeles – America's newest industrial powerhouse, not just its redoubt of Hollywood cool – had, after all, a military to arm and a neon future. After the first batch of rule-making accomplished little, a troupe of politicians from Bowman to eventually Ronald Reagan enacted progressively tougher rules that they expected would give the people back their sky. Smog, though, had a knack for dragging these expectations into exasperation, for inverting cheery promises into broken ones. As the years passed, the chemical air humbled many of the countermeasures against it with tenacity and guile, sowing discord among its victims, be they aggrieved family men or scapegoated industrialists. They knew smog would have its say into whether Southern California represented a land of the future or a civic flash-in-the-pan, and influence it would. Just when you thought it had lifted, it would strike harder, smudging the West Coast dream with a vapory char.

Just months after moving into their dream home, Bob and Charlee began to have second thoughts about planting roots in Southern California.

"We weren't having any ill health or anything like that, but we were very concerned about the health of the boys and everything else. To me, L.A. was a big dirty, sinful city, and it began to take some dominance over our thinking. I'm not quite sure where all of that came from, except that it probably is a big, dirty, evil city."

He was trying to make sense of it all. His wife, a devout Christian, put her faith in God and believed everything happened for a purpose, even if it meant walking away from the beautiful home they had just built. But Bob was still searching. He began reading the Bible every day and going to Bible study. He was reading about the "end of the age" and was struggling to figure out what that meant to him and his family.

"I remember reading the Bible and thinking, 'None of this makes any sense at all. What's the point of all of this? I thought it was a foreign language.'"

That didn't stop him from digging deeper into the Scriptures, and ultimately he says, "It took me awhile to get it figured out; not to say I've got it all figured out now."

But he still couldn't determine what the driving force was behind his desire to leave L.A. Turns out it was a combination of factors.

"If I were to stand back and look at my life then, I would think 'How could anyone ask for anything more?' and yet I wasn't happy. I wasn't happy about the smog every morning. I wasn't happy about all the crime on TV. It was partly what I was reading in the Scriptures about the end of the age, but everything just kind of lost its spark."

The ties that had bound Bob and Charlee to Southern California were loosening. Sure, they enjoyed Sunday dinners at his mom's place, but without his dad and her parents, life just wasn't the same. They liked the local Baptist church, but their attendance had more to do with convenience than a strong bond with the denomination or its members.

Oldest son Ken had started elementary school, but the two youngest at four and two were still at home.

Bob doesn't remember if it was one specific incident, but the wincing at the crime stories he read in the newspaper every day, the exposure to the dirtiness of the city, and the stinging redness from the smog finally opened his eyes to what he must do.

"For some crazy reason, I said, 'Well hon, we've got the boys, we've got each other, and we have the Lord. I can make a living anywhere with a gas station, so why don't we take some time and look around."

Charlee concurred. Partly driven by the physical elements of smog and crime, but more by their protective feelings for the boys, Bob and his wife began planning their escape from L.A. It became more of an adventure, really, as they enjoyed their forays into the small towns of Central and Northern California. They would pile the kids into their 1951 Pontiac and head north. Lancaster, seventy-two miles away was too hot, like a furnace. There was a Texaco station available in Susanville, but it had been closed for a while and at 578 miles away it seemed too far. The family loved spending a night in motels along picturesque Highway 395, with the small towns of Lone Pine, Independence, Big Pine, and Bishop growing on them on each successive trip. When Bob heard about a Chevron station in Mammoth Lakes that had recently come on the market, they made the 252-mile drive up through the gorgeous Sierra Nevada Mountains, and fell in love with the area. It felt just right.

How could one not fall in love with this remote burgeoning resort town, especially if you were looking for a safe place to raise kids and a captive audience to buy your gasoline? There was only one other gas station in that twenty-five-square-mile area, a Shell station on the other end of the minuscule downtown. With the post office on one side and a restaurant on the other, it was a better location than the dormant Chevron. But Bob was somewhat blinded by the beauty. And by the buzz among the locals that this was to be the breakout year for Mammoth Mountain Ski Area. Operator Dave McCoy had invested in a new chair lift, and the expectation was skiers would be flocking to the mountain come

October when the snow usually started to fall. The townspeople were gearing up for a banner year, many planning to keep their businesses open that winter instead of heading to warmer climes like they usually did. And Bob landed right in the middle of it. The opportunity seemed almost too good to be true.

"The restaurant people, the motel people, the people up at the ski lodge, they were all telling me this would be the year everyone would be coming from L.A. to ski on the new lift. This was going to be 'The Year of Mammoth Lakes!' LA-DI-DA. A big, big, big deal. Boy! Everything was just humming, really humming."

And Bob bit. It was an intoxicating time. Even though the economy had shrunk 3.7% from October, 1957, to March, 1958 (the largest six-month decline since 1947), everyone in Mammoth Lakes was optimistic the 1958–59 ski season would be the best ever. And, yes, breathing in the fresh air in this high-alpine playground (9,000 feet above sea level at Mammoth Mountain's Main Lodge) was heavenly compared to the choking smog of the city he was about to leave, but to Bob it was the smell of opportunity that was the biggest draw. Like the gold miners that had come before him to these mountains, he figured he could tap into the area's bountiful natural resources and strike it rich. After all, the year-round resort at Mammoth averaged 385 inches of annual snowfall and 300 days of glorious California sunshine.

To a savvy gas station operator, those heady numbers translated into a steady stream of fall hunters, winter skiers, and summer hikers and fishermen, all driving vehicles that would need what he would have to sell – gallons of gasoline and quarts of oil. Was it a gamble? Bob didn't think so. So he bet it all.

He made a deal for the Chevron in Mammoth Lakes and walked away from Bob Moore Mobil Service. They sold Charlee's dream house and put all of her custom-built furniture and personal items in storage. They pocketed $17,000 from the sale of the home and cash-out of the business, loaded the kids into the car, and headed north.

"Everyone experiences high points at certain times in their lives, and,

for us, the Torrance house was certainly one of those high points," Bob
mused as he thought back to the highs and lows of his experiences in
California. "It was just dandy because we had enough money, so going
out to buy something and not having to worry about putting it on credit
was very nice. I've had a few moments where things were pretty tight, but
that time was one of the really pleasant ones."

The almost two years they spent in the new home marked an important turning point in their lives. Bob and Charlee realized they wanted
something better – for their kids.

"I've always felt strongly protective about the boys," Bob says of Ken,
Bobby, and David. "And we had a strong desire to have the three of them
in our life, all of our life. I mean, build a life to where they can be a part
of it. It was very important to me. It was fundamental, fundamental. So,
after we got settled out there in the new home, our life's goals kind of
took over, and, technically, I guess we started getting ourselves geared up
to leave."

The Moores arrived in Mammoth Lakes in September of 1958, wide-
eyed and expectant in their new picturesque surroundings. The oldest
two boys would soon be attending a new school, and all three of them –
in fact, the entire family – had the High Sierras as their backyard playground. The thin air didn't stop them from climbing mountains, fishing
in the twin lakes, descending into deserted gold mines, hiking in the
woods, soaking in the natural hot springs, and driving on every local road
just to see where it ended. They spent all their free time exploring postcard places like Devil's Postpile National Monument, Minaret Summit,
and the Ansel Adams Wilderness. Because, as it turned out, Bob had *a
lot* of free time on his hands. As in, if you don't have much business to
occupy your day, there's nothing else to do but stare at the sights…and
wait for the customers to arrive. And wait. And wait. And wait.

"I could have made it, if the weather had cooperated," he laments.
But Mother Nature didn't cooperate. She turned her back on the High
Sierras that season, making the winter of 1958–59 one of the worst
droughts in the history of that mountainous region.

Everyone in Mammoth Lakes – the chamber of commerce, restaurant owners. hoteliers, ski lift operators, service providers – had the welcome mats out. But when October rolled around and the expected snowfall didn't drive the deer and antelope down into the valleys, the hunters stayed away. "Not to worry," the locals told Bob. "We always have snow by Thanksgiving."

But Bob was worried. Unlike his Mobil dealership where everything was on consignment, the Chevron station was more of a franchise operation where he had to pay the owner up front for all of the gasoline in the storage tank, all the equipment in the garage, and all the parts and accessories in the shop. Plus, he had to pay $500 a month on the three-year lease he signed for the property. That was just to get everything under his control so he could start operating the station. Then there was the small detail of their living arrangement. There weren't a lot of affordable rentals available for a family of five in the resort town, and he couldn't afford to buy a house, so Bob, liking the convenience of living close to where he worked as he did in L.A., did the next best thing. He bought a ten-foot by fifty-foot trailer and moved it onto the gas station property.

"Poor Charlee," Bob remembers thinking, but actually not at that moment. "I was so enamored with this whole concept that I'm sure I was oblivious to her feelings."

In less than four years and at just thirty years old, his wife had set up and moved out of two new homes. And in between had lived in that dreadful apartment. Now, with all of her beautiful furniture and personal items in storage, she was back in a cramped environment raising three boys while her husband once again rolled the dice on a new venture.

"I certainly didn't have a very good track record, and it looked like I was going backwards. Most wives probably would have left their husbands, but there was never anything like that. Never, ever, ever anything like that. I still marvel at the relationship between two people and how it works. I mean, it's a mystery. We've never had a relationship where either of us has said, 'I'm putting my foot down; I'm not going to do that!' I've never even given that any thought and I don't think Charlee has either. We were together and that was it. We loved each other."

As they settled into their brand new top-of-the-line trailer, Bob began to take inventory of his situation. He had paid out $7,000 cash and financed the other half of the $14,000 trailer (a dumb move, he later realized as he became more and more strapped for cash). He had purchased a pickup truck (which he said was stupid because he should have gotten along without it), and he had to buy "that dumb tow truck" from the gas station owner. He got a little money renting out one of the station's three garage bays to a guy who ran the local ambulance service. Bob has long since forgotten the man's real name, but they called him Digger O'Dell after the undertaker character Digby (Digger) O'Dell on the TV show *Life of Riley*. Digger had an arrangement with Bob to store the ambulance in one of the bays, and earned the nickname after picking up a dead body shortly after the Moore family arrived. The kids got a kick out of asking Digger "How's business?" And they would chuckle at his answer, "It's a little dead tonight."

But there was nothing funny about Bob's current state of affairs. He was beginning to think he had been sold a bill of goods. There were "all kinds of surprises" he didn't expect. The promise of hordes of people flocking to the mountain paradise wasn't materializing. The few hunters that did show up were regulars who went down the street to get all their gas and automotive work from the Shell operator who kept his station open year round. Turns out the Shell guy had grown up in Mammoth Lakes and was a friend to all. Plus, his location between the post office and the most popular coffee shop in town was the prime traffic area. But probably most telling of all – and this shouldn't have been a surprise – was the fact the Chevron guy closed his station every year for the winter. He only operated in the summer and boarded the place up as soon as the snow started falling. Nobody went to the Chevron station, except in the summer. And here it was November. And still not a single flake of snow.

"I just kind of pulled the blind over my eyes and told myself, 'I'm going to do this no matter how bad it sounds,'" Bob says of his somewhat irrational decision to try to make a year-round business out of what had been a part-time operation. Standard Oil Company had been pushing to have twelve-month representation in Mammoth, and, according to Bob, "They were looking for a patsy; someone who would use their own money on the gamble of staying open year-round." At the time, he felt confident, and figured he was the man to make it happen. "I just kind of backed into the whole thing, telling myself, 'I can make it, I can make it.' Well, I found out you can be pretty cocksure of yourself and not make it. There was no justification for being that sure of myself, really."

One thing that was for sure was Mammoth Lakes was in the middle of an historic drought. The old-timers told Bob they had never seen anything like it – no snow the entire month of November.

"I remember that Thanksgiving – it should have been a super busy week, but we just did nothing. I actually walked out onto the highway in front of my station and stood there. I turned one way and looked. I

No snow for months – then fourteen feet fell at Mammoth Lakes (Bob Moore on the left with Bob Wyler, an associate of his at the gas station)

turned around and looked the other way. There were no cars. No cars. I'm thinking, 'this is crazy, this is crazy! I'm using up all my money.' But I still thought things were going to be okay, that I was going to make it. Until one day I looked in my checkbook and the money was all gone."

That realization came about the following August. He made it through that record-setting winter, because the snow finally did fall. Boy, did it ever. Mammoth experienced one of its first and only non-white Christmases, but right before the end of the year it began to snow. And it snowed and snowed and snowed. When it finally stopped, Bob shoveled his way out of the trailer and measured snowdrifts fourteen feet tall. Now, no cars could get to Mammoth Mountain.

It was days before the highway got plowed. And then the skiers started trickling in. But they didn't buy enough gas to pay the bills. Fortunately, though, the city slickers also didn't know how to drive in icy conditions, so Bob stayed busy hauling cars out of ditches and towing vehicles illegally parked overnight in certain public parking lots. The towing business wasn't very fun, because a lot of the calls came in the middle of the night and most were from angry and annoyed people, but it sustained them through the lean months.

That season of 1958–59 was devastating to a lot of businesses in Mammoth Lakes. As Bob says not altogether wistfully, "That mountain is so beautiful, it just takes your breath away. But it can break people; more people go broke up there in that crazy place than you can shake a stick at."

And "that mountain" finally got to Bob. Rating the Mammoth experience on a scale of one to ten, "as far as finances are concerned, it turned out to be below a one," he admits. "It was pretty bad, pretty bad. I can hardly describe it – when I realized after not quite a year I wasn't making it. This is a *serious* matter. I'm here, my mobile home is up here, my wife, my kids, two more years of commitment on the lease, *and I'm not making it.*"

Other men might have freaked out. Lost it. Given up or walked out. Maybe gone on welfare. But Bob persevered. He couldn't fail because failure meant losing the most important thing in his life – his family. It was definitely a low time in his life, as far as his financial situation was concerned. But, remarkably, he wasn't worried.

"It's a funny thing, the gut feeling I had," he remembers about the inner peace he felt. "There was no anguish, no cursing. Nothing like that. It was, 'Okay, here is what we're going to do: I'll start packing, let's go.' That was it."

The confidence was there, but so was the realism. Bob knew they were in trouble. Charlee knew it, too. There was no dancing around the stark reality of a meager bank balance. But her husband exuded a kind of strength she was able to grab onto, and it carried her through the difficult moment. They shared a resolve that, no matter what, they were in this together and they were going to make it.

"We were a team, a unit; we always thought of it that way," he says about the trying times. "She knew I was going to make it, that she wasn't going to have to give the kids up to the Welfare Department or go out and find a job. There was never even a remote question about that."

But they both got the message loud and clear: *Get out! Leave Mammoth Lakes now!!* Out of money and out of options, he found someone to take over the remaining two years on his lease. Nearly one year to the day they arrived in Mammoth, the Moores prepared to leave. But first, Bob had to find a job. With no cushion, he couldn't afford to be without steady income. At a minimum, he had to make the payments on the trailer and their L.A. storage unit, or else he would lose everything.

He heard there might be work in Spokane, Washington, so he hustled up there and scoured the city for three days. No luck. He scrambled back to Mammoth Lakes. He spent a few hours with the family, and several long minutes on a strategy. He would start looking in cities where he could drive there and back in one day. He didn't like leaving Charlee and the boys alone for extended periods of time, especially now that someone else was running the gas station where their trailer was parked. His first choice was Sacramento and he left immediately.

Five hours later he was head down in the classified section of the *Sacramento Bee*. But a day spent filling out applications and driving around the city looking for work did not produce the needed result: a job that started tomorrow. Discouraged, he headed for home. On the way out of town, a familiar sight caught his attention: a Sears, Roebuck and Company sign. He and Charlee loved Sears. Bought most everything they owned from Sears. Thinking a visit to this big, new store would cheer him up, Bob circled back and went in. As he was walking around, checking out all the fancy displays and sharply dressed employees, he thought to himself, "Wait a minute, I'm a good salesman. I bet I could talk my way into a job here." And he did. With his experience selling motors and fixing cars, the personnel manager figured he would do fine in the hardware department. The position paid seventy-five dollars a week and he could start right away.

It was better than nothing, which is what he was dealing with, but what a huge fall from just over a year ago when clearing seventy-five bucks would have been a decent *day*. But he couldn't dwell on that right now. Like a struggling swimmer, all he was focusing on was keeping his head above water. He knew he would survive, although he had calculated he needed at least $100 a week to make it. He found an available pad at a mobile home park in Citrus Heights near the Sears that cost him $150 a month, and his top priority now was to get that fifty-foot long trailer over the High Sierras and park it in Sacramento. He drove the 237 miles back to Mammoth as fast as he could and rushed to share the good news with Charlee: he had found a job at Sears and they were moving to Sacramento *now*. Grabbing the kids and what clothes they would need for the next few days, they jumped into the car and left that bust of an experience in their rearview mirror. He put them up in a Sacramento motel across the street from a hamburger stand, and split up the last bit of cash he had so Charlee and the kids could eat and he could pay for the gas and help to haul the trailer. He made arrangements with a guy from Citrus Heights who specialized in towing mobile homes to follow him back to Mammoth, and then he was back on the highway again. Bob's memory of all those miles he drove that week is blurry, but he would remember forever the deep conversations he had with the guy who towed his trailer.

"He was a Christian fellow, a nice lad, and as we were hooking up my mobile home and getting ready to drive back over the High Sierras again, he said, 'Let's pray we have a safe journey,' so we did."

Whether it was answered prayer or not, the blown tire coming down the mountain could have been catastrophic. Looking back, Bob considered it more of a blessing because they got to spend several more hours together, driving all the way to Reno and back because they didn't have a spare.

"I was really at a low point in my life, and just talking to this guy was very comforting. It was just what I needed at that moment in time. I was curious about his Christianity because it seemed to be a living thing, something that was a part of him, which is different than what I felt at the time."

Once they got settled in Sacramento, Bob stayed in touch with his new friend, and even began attending the Nazarene church the man invited the Moores to attend. It turned out to be a little too "Pentecostal" and demonstrative for Bob's liking, so they eventually switched to an independent evangelical church run by George and Millie Staples. That transition and relationship with the Staples turned out to be a godsend in more ways than one.

With a salary of seventy-five dollars a week, Bob wasn't able to pay for his family's living expenses and keep up the payments on the trailer and their storage facility. It was only twenty-four dollars a month, but when he fell three months behind, Lyon Van & Storage cleared out their L.A. unit and sold their belongings at auction. The less-than-two-year-old furniture Charlee had custom-made for her dream home? Gone. All of Bob's books, schoolwork, music? Gone, gone, gone. All the family's personal stuff in boxes sold for a few bucks per unopened box.

It got worse. Bob had to put the mobile home up for sale. He was asking for $500 down and the buyer could just take over the payments. The best he could find was someone who agreed to take over the payments with no money down. Soon they would be homeless.

"Financially, I was a total failure. I lost everything. And my family was this close to being on the street. But I still had my wife, still had my family, and I had a relationship that was growing in the Lord. This whole downward slide was really humbling me."

As he was going downhill, he admits his bleak situation was getting to him emotionally. "It's kind of like once they start beating you, you just kind of bend over and let them beat. You don't fight back. You don't do anything. All of the different things I thought about later – like, I could have gotten a part-time job at a gas station. I mean, I'm a gas station operator! I could have easily gotten a job at a gas station and worked nights or something. I could have done that, but I didn't. I just kind of kept letting them beat me. I think the Lord had a plan for me. The plan was to start all over at the bottom. I mean, really start at the bottom, and, believe me, I did."

Beaten down, but not defeated, Bob needed a break. He had to move the family out of the mobile home, and he had nowhere to go but the streets. A leaky shower became their saving grace. The shower actually belonged to their pastor, George Staples. George and Millie lived on the main floor of a two-story house and had converted the upstairs into two apartments they rented out. The larger one was occupied, but because of a leaky shower in the smaller apartment that he wasn't prepared to fix anytime soon, George couldn't rent it out. But if Bob, Charlee, and the three boys wanted to live in that small apartment rent free, he would let them use his shower on the main floor.

With no other place to go, and no money to pay rent, anyway, the Moores moved in. Charlee must have the patience of Job, Bob figured. Here she was, back in a tiny, cramped apartment with only a living room, kitchen, bedroom, and a bathroom with no tub or shower. Mom and Dad slept on a mattress on the floor. Two of the boys slept on a cot, heads on opposite ends and feet constantly fighting. The other one had a sleeping bag on the floor. When Bob or Charlee wanted a shower, they had to go downstairs, go outside, walk around the house, and knock on the door to see if George and Millie's shower was available. To keep interruptions to a minimum, Charlee just washed the boys in the sink.

"That was the lowest point in my entire life," Bob reveals. "Relying on a rent-free landlord and needing to use his bathroom; losing all of the possessions Charlee and I had accumulated; having a job, yet knowing it wasn't enough to sustain us. That feeling, when you're not going to make it, it's a very distinct feeling in an entrepreneur's body, very distinct. I had that feeling only one other time in my life, and that was after the fire in 1988."

But, like after the fire that destroyed his mill, Bob didn't wallow in his misery. He didn't feel sorry for himself. Yes, he was mad. He was upset with the storage company that wouldn't let his mom come over and salvage their personal belongings before getting rid of them. He was offended by what he felt were misleading promises from his Mammoth debacle. And, worst of all, he was disappointed in himself for letting his family down. His wife and kids were counting on him to be the provider, and he was doing a poor job of it.

With nowhere to go but up, that's where Bob finally found salvation. In the heavens. At his landlord/minister's invitation, Bob joined a handful of others from George's flock for a baptismal ceremony in the Sacramento River. There were about a hundred witnesses from the church, everyone singing and crying tears of joy, as Bob was dipped into that cold river water.

"It wasn't so cold that I didn't have the most marvelous awakening," he says. "I really felt the Lord respond to my humble request to accept Him, the Lord Jesus, as my Savior. It was a great experience, a real experience, a very real experience for me."

Outwardly, little changed in his life after his baptism, but on the inside Bob was a new man. He continued to read the Bible feverishly and tried to incorporate what the Scriptures were teaching him. His challenges were still the same, and the most pressing was the family's financial situation. Whether it was his "awakening" experience or sheer desperation, it seemed his eyes were finally opened to what he needed to do. What he should have done when he first got to Sacramento.

"I can't believe I didn't think of it before, but one day I opened the phone book and looked up the local U.S. Electrical Motors dealer, which was Sacramento Engineering and Machine Works. I went over there and showed this guy my old business card from when I worked at U.S. Electrical Motors in L.A. He couldn't believe I walked in the door with all those years' experience at one of their sister companies. He said I was just the perfect guy for them."

When they offered him a sales job that came with a company car, Bob told them he needed to make at least $100 a week. He about flipped when they told him his starting salary would be $200 a week.

Talk about a change of fortune. His salary more than doubled. He got a car in the deal. And he would be doing a job he loved and had excelled at a few years back.

CHAPTER 14

SOUL SEARCHING

I N HIS WEAKEST MOMENTS, BOB FELT LIKE A COMPLETE FAILURE. FINAN-
cially, he had hit the bottom of the barrel. There was nothing in the
bank account. And certainly nothing in reserve. He had lost his mobile
home. The storage company had taken all his possessions. And while
he considered it a blessing to live rent-free in George and Millie's apartment, he still didn't have enough money to care for his family, who were
sleeping on the floor of that one-bedroom upstairs unit that didn't have
a working shower.

His financial situation couldn't get any worse, he thought, because
with a new job he would soon be able to start digging himself out of that
deep hole. But just about the time he began to claw his way back up,
the Internal Revenue Service got their talons into him and dragged him
down again.

The notice arrived in the mail innocently enough: *Dear Mr. Moore, We
are in receipt of your tax form filed April 15, 1961 for the 1960 tax year. However, payment of the taxes owed was not included in your filing. Please contact us
immediately. Failure to remit payment will result in further IRS action.*

It wasn't a mistake that he hadn't included a check with the tax filing.

For one thing, Bob couldn't believe that after a year of not making any money, he would owe taxes. But he did. And he didn't have the $750 or whatever it was anyway. So he had sent the tax form without the required payment. The IRS didn't like that, he would learn. In fact, that first notice he received in the summer of 1961 was just the start of an ugly relationship between Bob Moore and the government. It was like a dark cloud hanging over his head, and it followed him for months.

"Good grief! I was a failure. But I don't think I *felt* like a failure. Charlee didn't think so; oh, heavens no. Our thoughts were 'We have a problem and we need to work through it. There's a storm in our life; the waves are splashing over on us; and we've got to bail to keep this boat afloat. And then eventually we look out into the clouds, and we see the shore, and we start paddling towards the shore, until we finally make it to dry land.' We finally made it, but, oh my gosh, I couldn't go through that again if my life depended on it. I think I would just have a heart attack and die right there. "

His outlook on life was much sunnier when he started his new job at Sacramento Engineering and Machine Works. Bob got along great with his new boss, Bob Brosmer, and he shined once again in his role of selling machinery, this time to the vast agricultural community that dominated the Sacramento valley.

"I sold chains, sprockets, belts, and all kinds of stuff; but the biggest thing we sold was the capabilities of our machine shop and our fab shop. I would bring them the plans and we would figure out how to make stuff. This was just right down my alley. I look back on that time in my life with great joy – the opportunity to work with machinists. Even now, some fifty years later, I'm doing exactly the same thing I was doing then – talking to my guys in the shop, looking at plans, and seeing whether what we are building is going to work or not. I do it right now. That is who I am. That is who I became, working with Brosmer and the machinists at Sacramento Engineering and Machine Works."

Happy at work, but not content whatsoever with his living conditions, Bob focused on saving money so they could move into their own place. On Sundays, he would get up early and head down to the local drug store to scan the *Sacramento Bee* classified section for places to rent. One particular Sunday, after not finding anything to his liking, he folded the newspaper, set it on the counter, and was about to leave when something caught his eye. It was a small column on the back page titled "Too Late to Classify." Among the few listings was the heading, *Five-acre dairy goat farm for rent*, and below that a phone number.

Intrigued, Bob dialed the number and told the man who answered that he was interested in the rental. The guy was surprised because he had checked the paper that morning to look for his ad, and not finding it in the "For Rent" section of the classifieds, he thought it hadn't run. "Well, you're the first to call, so come on out and I'll meet you at the farmhouse."

Farmhouse. On a five-acre goat farm. That sounded so "country" to a guy who grew up in L.A. But when he drove out Highway 99 a few miles outside of Sacramento and turned down that dirt road, he had to smile. *The boys are going to love this*, he predicted.

And Charlee did, too. Even though it was quite rustic and very humble, the Moores thrived in their new open space surroundings. The old farmhouse was square, with a very narrow kitchen, small living room, and one sparse bathroom with a toilet, sink, and an industrial-type metal shower. Someone had moved a chicken shed next to the house, and it became two bedrooms for the boys. Everything was built on a foundation of various lengths of old telephone poles, so if you dropped a pencil on the floor it would roll clear across the room. Drop a marble on another section of floor and it would take a different path to the other side of the room.

Their furnishings were just as humble as the crooked structure they inhabited for the next five years. Old worn-out couches, hand-me-down chairs, mismatched dinnerware, cobbled dining room set – all courtesy of the generous folks from their church. No bedroom furniture for the kids, but they were having so much fun playing in the barn, raising chickens, and running amok on the dusty acreage they didn't seem to care where they crash-landed at night.

Meager surroundings or not, the IRS didn't care. They wanted their money. The Moores had been living on the farm just a few weeks when the government agent came calling. He demanded a payment plan for the back taxes they owed, and for good measure, he took an inventory of all their possessions – just in case.

"I had just started working for Brosmer, and this IRS guy starts hounding me," Bob says, the distaste still evident after all these years. "He wants an accounting of everything: 'How much money do you have in the bank? How much cash? How much do you spend on food? On gas? Utilities?' When he got done filling out all these forms that told him how much money we should have left over at the end of the month, he ended up taking most of it; at least half!"

Bob felt he had no other choice, so he took a second job at a nearby 24-hour truck stop. He would change out of his business suit when he got home from his sales calls, grab a bite to eat, and then hustle over to his $2.50 an hour job pumping gas. He worked there from seven at night until three in the morning. He would sleep a couple of hours, shower off the smell of diesel fuel, put on his business suit, and be back on the road selling for Sacramento Engineering and Machine Works.

"Those stories about the IRS are absolutely true. Once they get you in their sights, they don't leave you alone. I remember getting home from work one evening and Charlee telling me the IRS had called and they wanted to come over for another evaluation. It was awful!"

Bob worked almost around the clock to get the IRS off his back. He took every dime he made at the truck stop and paid down his debt. What a relief it was to make that final payment and quit the night job. But the nightmare wasn't over.

He didn't discover it until months later when he tried to use his Sears credit card to buy Charlee a washing machine. They were finally in a much better financial situation now, and it was time to start replacing all the things – like appliances – they had lost. Plus, it was time to buy a car.

So Bob was quite disturbed when the sales clerk at Sears told him he would have to pay cash for the washing machine, and, by the way, he would have to confiscate his Sears card. When Bob asked why, the man would only say, "Your name is on the list." Same thing when Bob tried to finance a car. They refused his application for credit, and no one would tell him why. Finally, Bob went back to the Sears store and approached the credit department manager. Here he was, a Sears cardholder since he was sixteen years old, and a former Sears employee; couldn't someone please tell him what was going on.

"She finally says, 'I'm not supposed to tell you this, but you have a lien against you, and it's a government lien, and there is nothing in the world I can do.'

"I was beside myself! I had cleared everything up with the IRS. And I have always paid my bills. So, I went down to the county courthouse and inquired about myself, and they said, 'Well, you have a government lien against your name.' *How is a person ever supposed to know this?* And I told this guy, I said, I have been trying to get my credit back and no one will talk to me because this is a federal government lien. Nobody seems to know anything, except that the federal government has got their thumb on me and the credit companies want nothing to do with me."

It took a while, but Bob gradually got his credit back, and his name cleared. He had to make several trips to the courthouse, and just when he thought he was done with that unpleasantness, another, even more dramatic, court appearance smashed his world apart. Just when he thought he had put all the pieces back together, another day in court would fracture his future.

He was driving a lot for work – at least eight hours a day, but sometimes ten or twelve when he had to make sales calls late in the afternoon in Truckee or Stockton. He often wouldn't get home until six or seven o'clock in the evening, after having logged a couple hundred miles on the company car.

One night he got home a little later because he was delayed by the police officer who wrote him a ticket for going forty-five in a thirty-five-miles-per-hour speed zone. No big deal. He'd been driving for Sacramento Engineering and Machine Works for nearly eighteen months and this was his first moving violation. An acceptable job hazard.

It was the second ticket two months later that caused the very *unacceptable* situation. Bob was driving down a one-way street, and after stopping at a red light, turned left onto another one-way street. No problem, he did it all the time. Well, yes, problem, said the police officer who wrote him up for making an illegal turn. According to the current California Driver Handbook, it *is* legal to make a left hand turn from a one-way street to another one-way street against a red light, as long as there isn't a sign specifically prohibiting the maneuver. But, apparently on *that* day in 1963 and according to *that* Sacramento cop, Bob had made an illegal turn. So, like he had had to do a few months prior, he brought the ticket with him to the courthouse on the specified day to pay his fine. He doesn't recall what day of the week it was, but he has a vivid memory of every detail once he stepped into that county building.

It was a hot summer day, probably one-hundred-plus degrees, and there was no air conditioning in the courtroom. All the windows and the two big doors at either end of the room were open. Along the front left side of the room behind a railing with a swinging door sat a couple dozen men, criminals, Bob assumed, waiting for the traffic court proceedings to finish up before the more serious crimes and punishments would be debated. He later learned they had all been bused over from the county jail. The bailiff was seated up front at a large table, and above all loomed the judge behind a fortress-looking wooden dais. There were lots of uncomfortable chairs where people sat until their names were called. Bob sat in one of them for most of the morning, listening to people plead their cases and complain when they lost. More often than not, the rather stern-looking judge would cut them off and boom his decision.

When it was his turn, he tried to explain the left turn thing from a one way to another one way, but the judge was pre-occupied.

"This is your second moving violation in two months," he accused.

"I'm looking at him, thinking, 'Yeah, so what?' But I say, 'Yes, sir. I drive eight to ten hours a day, and...'"

The judge abruptly cut him off, and what he proclaimed shook Bob's world.

"Mr. Moore, California state law decrees that if you get a third moving violation within the next twelve months, you will go to jail for five days."

"Boy, that really stopped me. I said, 'Your honor, I am a local businessman, and I drive all day long. I have three lovely children. My wife and I are active in church. If I go to jail for five days, *it would destroy my life.*' In fact, I said, 'I think I would leave the country if you told me I had to go to jail for five days.' I told him, 'This is a very serious thing you are telling me.' I was almost in tears. Really, almost in tears."

He was thirty-four years old, and he truly believed his life would be over if he went to jail. To most men, the thought of being cooped up with those gnarly-looking, hardened characters off to the side of the room would be reason enough not to want to go to jail. Yeah, they wouldn't want to experience the shame and embarrassment of being locked up, but most men might have rolled the dice and taken the chance they wouldn't get another ticket in a year. Especially if their job depended on it. And, so what, five days in the slammer couldn't be all that bad.

But to Bob, even the remote chance, just the mention of the possibility, penetrated his inner being with a resolve that, no matter what, he would never, ever step foot in a jail. *Bob Moore* and *going to jail* were mutually exclusive concepts. They were beyond incompatible. In his mind, they simply did not compute. It was impossible.

"It would have destroyed me; destroyed me to go to jail," he says today, as adamantly as he said it then. "*No, no, I wasn't going to go to jail.*"

He had plenty of time to think about how he was going to get through this potentially devastating dilemma. The judge, with another harsh admonishment about the consequences of another infraction, ordered Bob to pay a forty-dollar fine. The problem was Bob thought the fine would be thirty bucks and that's all he had. The bailiff didn't care he was short ten bucks and stubbornly refused Bob's request to use a phone in the hallway just outside the courtroom to call a friend who worked downtown. He said he could use a phone back at the jailhouse, and directed him to join the prisoners awaiting their hearings. They would all be bused back to the jail at the end of the day.

"This guy was being impossible! Once you get caught up in the legal system, you give up all personal autonomy and freedom. You just go where they tell you to go. It is a terrible feeling. A terrible feeling!"

Sitting there, anxiously gazing up and down the row of prisoners and feeling like he wasn't even a person anymore, Bob says, was the most uncomfortable experience in his life. Here he was, dressed in a business suit with a tie and his hair combed, and he's being viewed by everyone in the room as just another common criminal. He wanted more than anything to get out of there. So, after suffering through a couple of hours wedged in with these sweaty, angry men, he approached the bailiff again with a compromise. If he could just use the pay phone in the lobby, he promised to come right back. The bailiff looked him over, craned his neck around to see the available pay phone through the open door, and relented, but not without two or three threats he hung over his detainee's head.

Bob got his friend to come right over and loan him the balance of his fine. He paid it in a hurry and scurried out of that hellhole. He never wanted to go back. And he knew what he had to do to make sure of it.

"To me, it was as if there was this big boiling cauldron of oil in front of me, and somebody said, 'I want you to voluntarily jump into it; now just stand there until you get into the right state of mind and then jump in.' I wasn't about to jump in because I didn't have to. And I wasn't going to go to jail because I didn't have to…if I didn't drive a car for the next 365 days, nobody could put me in jail."

Resolute in what he needed to do, Bob drove over (very carefully) to Sacramento Engineering and Machine Works. He parked the company car, brought the keys, and handed them to Bob Brosmer. He briefly gave him an overview of the three-tickets scenario, and announced, "So, I'm quitting."

Brosmer thought the story was the craziest thing he had ever heard. He thought Bob was nuts! While his former employee waited there for his wife to come pick him up, Brosmer tried everything to convince his star producer to stay. He tried reasoning with him. He tried scaring him

(*How would he put food on the table for his family?*). He tried mocking him (*You're scared; just drive like a normal person and you'll be fine.*). He told him how much he was letting him down. Nothing worked. Bob had made up his mind. He was leaving the car. Leaving the job, He would not drive for an entire year.

Brosmer kept pressing. He couldn't believe anyone would walk away from a good-paying job when there was a high likelihood a guy who hadn't gotten a ticket in almost two years could go one year without blowing it. He kept asking Bob why he was making such a foolish decision.

"I kept telling him, 'For the foolishness of getting a traffic ticket, to go to jail for five days would take precedent over everything in my life.' I just wouldn't do anything that might affect my record. Because whatever you want to do, the rest of your life is going to be determined by those five days you spent in jail. If it had happened, I don't think I would have ever gotten over it. That's how I feel. That's how I reacted. And that is how I live. I don't think I have changed any either."

On the drive home that day, Bob told Charlee how seriously he was going to take this lifestyle change over the next year. He would ride a bicycle. He would not drive a car. She would drive the family to church, to buy groceries, to get the kids to their activities. They would have to cut back on living expenses as much as possible.

Bob remembers that period of his life as "being devastated by the stuff that was happening to me," while "going through all of these experiences as a Christian with a strong sense of Providential guidance."

"I was going through one of the toughest, most soul-searching moments of my life," he bares. "I mean, just thinking about the whole experience ties me in knots. To think about that court and the meanness in the whole situation there with the bailiff, and the judge, and the prisoners. And at the same time in my life, how much I loved my wife and my kids, and how much life means to me, and how the progress of life would be stopped if there was even a chance of me going to jail. I was willing to give up anything and everything to maintain my sense of fairness and lawfulness; my dreams and aspirations. That's how I felt. Plain and simple. I feel that way right now."

The course had been set, at least for the next year. He had just walked away from a lucrative sales job, and probably wasn't going to find another (that didn't require driving) anytime soon. He could go back to the truck stop, but he definitely needed something that paid better. And he wanted something close to home, so he could walk or bike to work. A Firestone tire center about five blocks away fit the bill. He got hired on as a "tire buster," someone who changed tires, balanced wheels, checked brakes, washed whitewalls, and did safety inspections. It was kind of mindless work, certainly less stressful than driving around selling machines, but, most of all, Bob enjoyed the service aspect. He ended up staying with Firestone three years.

With more time to spend at home, Bob dedicated himself to raising three young boys and helping Charlee around the place. Whether it was trying to keep up with a trio of rambunctious farmboys, or his wife's gentle nudging, Bob finally quit smoking. He had been hooked on cigarettes for seventeen years. This period of time in their lives was also significant because it was at the dairy goat farm that Charlee embarked on a mission to establish a healthier lifestyle for her family. It became her lifetime passion to feed children natural foods, and it was the inspiration that ultimately led to the creation of a business called Bob's Red Mill Natural Foods. In Mammoth Lakes she didn't have access to a natural foods store, and in the Staples' apartment she certainly didn't have an accommodating kitchen, but ever since her grandmother Donno had introduced her to a world of whole unprocessed foods, she had wanted to incorporate more fruit, vegetables, and whole grains in her family's diet. Good thing she hadn't left Adelle Davis's books in storage back in L.A., because they would have been tossed with all of her other personal belongings.

Charlee harvested fresh produce from the large garden she had planted, and the kids helped her gather eggs the chickens blessed them with daily. She shopped at Elliott's, a local health food store (as they were known in the counterculture era of the sixties and seventies) where she bought her whole wheat flour, whole grain cereals, seeds, and other natural ingredients. With one of Davis's books – like *Let's Have Healthy Children* – open on her kitchen counter, she would teach herself how to bake healthy bread and cookies, prepare vegetable stir-fry, make granola, blend breakfast cereals, and cook delicious dinners without meat.

Bob loved coming home for lunch, especially after Day 365. It was exactly one year after that day in court where he had learned about the consequences of getting a third ticket when he finally felt comfortable enough to jump into the driver's seat of the 1954 Pontiac station wagon he had bought a year earlier.

By this time, Firestone had recognized their tire buster had a lot more potential than most of the other guys in the shop and they had bumped him up to foreman, where he regularly had to report to Fred Weller, the district manager. Revered as "a big shot in the company," Weller was tall, thin, and intimidating. He never smiled. Didn't pass the time of day with anyone.

"He was hyper-critical about everything, and when he came around I would just shake in my boots," the former Firestone foreman remembers. "This one day, Fred comes over to my desk, I was kind of busy, and he just starts going through my paperwork. He doesn't say anything. He just kind of towers over me, with this stern, unfriendly look on his face. Finally, I say, 'Fred, can you see me here? I'm just scared to death of you. My hands are shaking. Is this the way you want people to react to you when you come around?' He just looked at me and said, 'Come with me.'"

Bob thought his career at Firestone was about to come to an end. The big boss escorted him outside and around the corner to Zim's Restaurant. He told Bob where to sit. He ordered them coffee. Then what came out of his downturned mouth surprised the heck out of Bob.

"Is that what I do"? he asked, the stern countenance gone. He looked more like a sad little boy.

"I really thought for a few minutes that Fred was going to cry. He just kind of melted in front of me. He wanted to know how I felt about him as a boss, how others reacted to him. I told him that I had worked for a lot of people, but around none of my bosses did I feel so frightened, so threatened. I asked him, 'Is that the policy of the company, to intimidate everybody?'"

Fred, apologetic now, assured him that was not Firestone's policy. They talked some more, and by the time they shook hands and Bob walked back to work, he had a totally different point of view. Fred was actually a decent guy. The district manager apparently had a new appreciation for his shop foreman, too, because next thing Bob knew he was promoted to assistant store manager. Not only that, but Fred wanted to give him his own store.

"He must have had an epiphany or something, because, after that, Fred was the friendliest guy I ever knew in my life. He would come over to my desk, put his arm around me, and ask me how things were going."

Friendly Fred had Bob on the fast track at Firestone. He sent him downtown for more training. He told him he had a brand new store he wanted him to take over. It was in Lodi, about half an hour's drive south on Highway 99. Bob and Charlee took a drive down there and liked what they saw. The small agricultural town looked like a good place to work and possibly live. All indications were that when the tire center opened in the Fall of 1965, Bob would be the new manager and they might be moving.

As Bob spent the rest of the summer preparing for this new phase in his life, he looked back on the family's six years in Sacramento as a great time of learning. Charlee taught herself how to cook with whole grains, which revolutionized the way she and the kids ate ("She went 'all natural,'" Bob describes. "She did; I didn't."). The boys blossomed in their outdoor adventure on the dairy goat farm, learning how to raise chickens and eat stuff they grew in the garden. Bob studied the Bible, got saved, was tried and tested, and says he came out of the ordeal feeling blessed. He was attracted to the goodness of the Christian fellow who towed their trailer, and to the giving nature of the Staples who shared their home and asked for nothing in return. It led to his baptism.

On the other hand, the "tried and tested" experiences made a lasting impression on him as well – especially the uncaring IRS guy and what he perceived as a mean court system. "I felt the love of unselfish people, but I also witnessed man's inhumanity to man. It taught me to be the kind of person who if I can help someone who is in a tight spot, it's my responsibility to do so. I came away from there believing I am my brother's keeper. I don't care what people think about the Bible or anything else, but you are your brother's keeper. Period. That is the basis of every relationship everywhere – in your personal life or in business."

Yep, as Bob evidenced, you're even your boss's keeper. Fred appreciated that.

A JC PENNEY MAN

"**B**UT BOB, YOU'RE A JC PENNEY MAN."
      That's what the manager of the next-door JC Penney store would tell Bob every time he brought his car to the Firestone for service.

"Bob, I can tell just by the way you greet people, the way you treat your customers, you're a JC Penney man," the manager would repeat.

Bob was flattered. He knew a little about James Cash Penney, and he respected him. For instance, he had heard Mr. Penney originally called his stores "The Golden Rule," because it was his personal and business philosophy to treat others the way he himself would want to be treated. Bob felt he could be a good fit for JC Penney because he shared the same principles and belief system with the company's founder. But, since he initially thought JC Penney was just a department store, he dismissed the idea. He didn't want to sell clothes. He liked working on cars.

He didn't necessarily like Firestone's aggressive upselling strategy, because he felt he had a moral obligation not to sell things people didn't need. But since the company offered spiffs on a regular basis for selling certain items – shock absorbers, for example – most of the guys would tell customers they needed new shocks, whether they truly did or not.

The neighboring manager would tell him, "You're not like these other guys; you're a JC Penney man. Let me at least get you an interview at one of our new JC Penney Auto Centers."

So, figuring he had nothing to lose, Bob took his JC Penney fan up on the offer. The manager went right to work on it. Because he was in management, he knew a lot of the right people to call. Bob got a kick out of hearing him say to someone on the other end of the phone, "Hey, I've got a guy. He's running a Firestone store, but he's a JC Penney man."

The manager told Bob about a job opening in Santa Cruz, a beach community about seventy miles south of San Francisco. He took a vacation day to drive over there, and in the interview was disappointed to learn the position had already been filled. But the manager didn't give up. He told Bob JC Penney was opening up auto centers all over the country, and within a month, he had him lined up for an opportunity at a JC Penney Auto Center that was about to open in Redding.

This time, Bob brought Charlee, and they took the boys out of school for the day so they could come, too. They even brought Patty, their beagle, and they all rattled around in the big 1954 Pontiac station wagon on the three-hour drive north. They had friends from church who had moved to Redding, and Brosmer had sent him up there on a couple of sales calls, so Bob was somewhat familiar with the area. They traveled on Old Highway 99, which took them right through the middle of town, through downtown with its diagonal parking spaces, prompting Charlee to exclaim, "Oh, this is *so* nice; such a quaint community," Bob remembers.

The manager had set Bob up with Les Vira, who was doing all the hiring for the new auto center. They drove around the small town – it had a population of about 15,000 at the time – until the interview, and then Charlee took the car and drove the boys over to the Sacramento River. It was over one hundred degrees on that typical summer day in Shasta County, so a couple of hours swimming in the cool water sounded pretty good to Ken, Bobby, and David. On the way back to pick Bob up, Charlee swung through a quiet residential area a few blocks from the JC Penney. She spotted a guy painting one of the cute homes, and curious, she parked the car and walked into the empty house to inquire whether it was being fixed up to rent or sell. She talked to the man awhile, his name was Joe Hill, and then she came out, got in the car, and drove up Pine Street to where Bob was waiting.

As she got out of the station wagon, she asked, "Well, how did you do?"

"Well, I got the job," Bob answered.

"Wow," she replied, "I got us a house!"

"Those couple of hours were so exciting, just a joyous experience," Bob remembers. "First, Les Vira offered me the job as manager of the auto center, and then we went back and rented the house from the guy Charlee had just talked to. It was one of those moments in life where you need to say, 'Okay, somebody get a camera and take a picture so I can play this over and over again.'"

His starting wage was six dollars an hour, which equated to about what he was making in salary at Firestone. The good news was he was working five eight-hour days instead of six ten-hour days. Compared to the demanding work environment at Firestone, JC Penney was lenient. Maybe a bit too easy-going for Bob's liking. He loved his job, his crew, and the friendly customers from small-town Redding. But he didn't get along with Mike Charles (not his real name), his department manager who oversaw the JC Penney hardware store, which was connected to the auto center. Charles didn't like Moore, and Moore didn't like Charles as his immediate supervisor. Bob was convinced Charles was an alcoholic, and felt he regularly crossed the line between what was personal and what was business. He had Bob's guys work on converting an old Volkswagen in the shop into a brush buggy "whenever they weren't busy helping customers."

"He expected me to work on his cars, which didn't set well with me at all. In fact, it doesn't set well with me now, much less then. I mean, it was against the rules of the company, but he was running that part of the show. We did some things I was really ashamed of, but in that kind of situation, when you're way out in the sticks, you can't just walk out and quit. You have to come to work and say 'I've got to make this work. I have a family. I have responsibilities.' I hear guys – and even some of the women who work for me whose husbands have walked out on their jobs – say, 'I can't stand my job, I'm going to quit.' So I ask them, 'Well, what are you going to do then?' and they say, 'Well, nothing. My wife can get a job someplace.' I hate to tell you, down deep inside, what I think of a person that does that. I don't think much of them, I can tell you. It's totally lacking in responsibility. If you're the head of the household, and God says that you are, then you better take that responsibility seriously. That's how I feel about it. That's how I've lived my life, always. It precludes you from doing really stupid things, like getting on your high horse and quitting, and going home and telling your wife who is in tears that you don't know how you are going to pay the bills."

Bob endured Charles' inappropriate activities, but he made sure he let him know he was compromising himself and he wasn't comfortable with it. Maybe that's why Charles didn't care much for Bob. Maybe he was jealous that Bob's employees respected him so much, that his customers really liked him, that Bob seemed to be so damn happy all the time (Bob did have a habit of saying his job was swell). Charles did eventually get his comeuppance. He was high up in the High Sierras with a bunch of his brush buggy buddies when he crashed. The stories Bob heard were consistent with what one might expect about a heavy drinker. The buggy tipped over and Charles' body was crushed underneath. Bob heard when they operated on him they found his body full of alcohol.

He was in the hospital a long time, but he did come back to work. Bob remembers how enjoyable his job was without him around, and then how stressed out he was when Charles returned. He came back "skinnier than a rail" and more unpleasant than before. It was about that time in his career Bob realized to be truly happy in his work, he needed to be in business for himself. No working for somebody he didn't respect. No moral compromising forced on him by a rule-breaking boss. No company man's personal agenda that could trump the conscience of his employees. No making his customers suffer because some higher-up stepped all over company policy.

There was another challenge Bob faced working for somebody's company other than his own: being forced to deal with unions.

With lots of jobs in manufacturing, industrial, and lumber companies, Redding was known as a union town. Even the employees of the JC Penney Co. in Redding were union members, one of the only unionized JC Penney stores in the country. As part of management, Bob wasn't in the union; never had been in a union. But the seven guys who worked for him were, including shop steward Tom Parker. And just two years into his job, the union went on strike because of a wage issue.

"The next thing I know is here are all these nice people I knew from over at the store and my guys, they're all out walking the picket line. And because this was a small town, a small *union* town, my business dried up to nothing."

The work stoppage lasted about ninety days, with the members finally voting to disband the union and go back to work. But the damage was already done. Relationships, like the one with shop steward Tom Parker, changed forever. When Bob and Charlee went to the Parkers' home one night during the strike, Mrs. Parker wouldn't even let them in the house. For years, they had socialized together, gone to parties as couples, enjoyed each other's company. The strike ended all that. Tom Parker never spoke to Bob again.

But some bonds grew stronger. Just a week after they had walked out, all of Bob's guys – including Kenny, Alex, Ronnie, and Andy; everyone except Tom – crossed the picket line and got their jobs back. Of course, there weren't many customers and not a lot to do, so they swept floors, drank coffee, and talked a lot. They became "one happy family," Bob remembers fondly, that stayed together a long time.

As a result of that contentious employer/worker incident in 1967, the lasting imprint on Bob was a strong belief a company should be sufficiently benevolent to its workers so there would never be a reason a third party would have to come in and protect the people. And that employees should have total access to information and a true working relationship with ownership.

"If my people were to unionize, then I'm off limits to them if an issue were ever to arise. I could not take that. I would consider myself a total failure if that were to happen. In all my years in business, I've felt the same way about my employees – they should be part of the company in every way. I know with confidence that you must bring your employees into an open environment where your financial information is transparent. I've done that for years and years now. And it has worked. Every tiny piece of it has worked, every piece."

It was a tumultuous three months for the Moores. Not only were some of their personal relationships ruined, the strike affected their normal routine at home, too. Shortly after the walkout, Les Vira called Bob and told him he needed Charlee to come down to the store the next day. In fact, all the managers' wives were asked, pretty insistently, to fill in for the workers who went out on strike. That meant crossing the picket line every day. And seeing the angry faces of friends and acquaintances, who now scowled at them and shouted "scab" and other derogatory words.

When the strike finally ended, Charlee decided she liked working. Besides, the boys were in school most of the day. So she went over to Sears and got a job. The extra money came in handy, because it was time to become homeowners again. There were a bunch of new tract homes going up in Enterprise, a nice section of Redding about four miles from JC Penney, and Bob qualified for the CalVet (VA loans for California military veterans) lending program. With a much-needed $600 gift from Donno, and for the second time in their young married life, they built a brand new home.

The plans for the house on Wheeler Street called for three bedrooms and a single-car garage, but with three growing boys, Bob and Charlee wanted a fourth bedroom and a two-car garage with room for a workshop.

"Because I had boys, I needed a shop. You need to work together on stuff, which we did. I was so excited about that." In fact, it was the workshop that got them the boat. Well, indirectly.

CHAPTER 16

BOBBY DID IT

I T WASN'T LIKE STARTING OVER FROM SCRATCH, BUT WITH A NEW HOME and both Mom and Dad making good money, the Moores spent the latter part of the '60s working hard to replace the tangible assets they had forfeited in the Mammoth experiment. And Redding turned out to be a wonderful place in which to settle down and rebuild. The city is surrounded by mountains to the north, east, and west; and with Lake Shasta and Whiskeytown and Keswick dams close by, that northern part of the Sacramento Valley is a mecca for camping and water enthusiasts. And with an average possible sunshine eighty-eight percent of the time, the second-highest percentage of any U.S. city (after Yuma, Arizona), what wasn't to like about the area?

While Bob was very contented with his job, every week he looked forward to Sundays and Wednesdays, his days off. Charlee had a flexible schedule at Sears that allowed her the same days off, and they cherished their time together. On the weekend they had a dedicated family day, and mid-week they had twenty-four hours all to themselves.

Every Wednesday, the boys knew they had to fix their own breakfast and get to school on time. Mom and Dad would sleep in sometimes, or more than likely, they were already down the highway on one of their favorite pastimes – a driving adventure. They would be gone all day. Bob figures he's driven on every single road in Shasta County.

"Sometimes we would get in the station wagon and just drive, drive all day. Other times we would just lollygag around the house and be together. Wednesdays – they were always a special day!"

One of those Wednesdays coincided with Bob and Charlee's wedding anniversary, and it was a special day, indeed. They left early, drove out to Lassen Volcanic National Park, and got home late. When they turned onto their street, they noticed some neighbors anxiously gathered near their house. Middle son Robert (they called him Bobby) was standing out front in the street with a silly grin on his face. Maybe they're going to surprise us with an anniversary party, they thought. It was a surprise, all right. As he turned down the driveway, Bob saw it. The garage had burned down.

Like good parents, their first question was, "Is anyone hurt?"

"No," Bobby answered.

"Bobby did it!" chimed in younger brother David.

It had become sort of a family joke that whenever anything bad happened, it was Bobby's fault. This was no laughing matter, however, as the family's two-car garage/workshop was a charred mess. Bobby was too big to spank, but that wasn't his dad's style, anyway. Bob did blurt out a "What happened?!"

Bobby's infraction wasn't that he had been welding something in the garage (he had become an accomplished welder, building mini-bike frames and all), it was that he was welding something in the garage *by himself*, which was a big no-no.

"I can't remember what I was welding," Robert, now fifty-eight years old, says. "But there was this pair of overalls hanging over the workbench I was welding on, and when I was all done, I kind of wrapped things up and went into the house. I remember I was sitting there playing the piano when one of my friends started banging on the back sliding door, yelling, 'Your garage is on fire!' I ran out there and saw the overalls on fire. I ran over to a hose that was hanging on one of those hose reels, but I couldn't get it untangled. I kind of panicked. I jerked on the hose and busted it off right where it connects to the faucet."

Standing there between the faucet and the broken hose, with no way to get water to the fire, Bobby did the valiant thing. He ran into the burning garage and rolled out his mini-bike. Then, he returned a second time, this time saving his little brother's mini-bike. By the third trip – he can't remember what valuable item he was trying to retrieve – the fire was too intense. Besides, the wall of spray paint cans was starting to explode, and multi-colored missiles were shooting out through the flames.

"Dad took it pretty well," Robert recalls. There wasn't any yelling or screaming. No punishment at all, really, unless you consider a seventeen-year-old spending the rest of his summer tearing down what was left of the family's garage and rebuilding it with his dad and brothers as something bad. In fact, because they did all the work themselves and didn't hire a contractor, which the insurance estimate provided for, the ordeal turned out quite favorably for everyone. The escrow account their Allstate insurance agent had set up for the construction project had a balance of more than three thousand dollars when Bob and the boys finished the building.

So, they splurged, and put a built-in pool in the backyard. But what the entire family had been pining for was a boat. Bob Dietz, their neighbor across the street, had a ski boat, and every Fourth of July he would invite the Moores to go skiing with his family on Whiskeytown Lake. The boys loved it. Only problem was the Dietzes would bring a dozen or so family members, and it seemed like just when Ken or Bobby or David was getting the hang of getting up on two skis, Mr. Dietz would turn the boat back to shore and load up a different group. Bob would see the disappointment on his sons' faces, and it bothered him enough that he committed himself to buying them a boat.

For the rest of that summer, he religiously scanned the classified section in the local newspaper for used boats. He stopped at every boat shop in the area to inquire if anyone knew where he could find a ski boat for under a thousand dollars.

"They kind of laughed at me, because even these junky boats were going for two and three thousand dollars," Bob reveals. "But I only had one thousand dollars left from the insurance and that was my limit."

Months went by, and no luck. But Bob didn't give up. One day at work he happened to mention his fruitless search to a customer. Matt Mattlock, a retired fellow, said, "Oh, you're looking for a boat?"

"I said, 'Yeah, but I can't seem to find anything I can afford.' So, he says 'How much money have you got?' I said, 'Well, we're trying to find a boat for about a thousand dollars.' He said, 'I have a boat and I don't use it.' I asked him what kind it was, and when he told me it was an eighteen-foot such-and-such, I knew I couldn't afford it, and I let him know that. He said, 'Hold on there, that's up to me to say.'"

So, Bob and Charlee went to see Matt's boat.

"He lived a little ways out of Redding, in a nice area. He invites us in the house, a very nice house. We go in the kitchen. His wife has tea ready for us. We sit at the kitchen table and talk. I knew Matt pretty well because I had taken care of his car, but I didn't know his wife. She is very excited. She says, 'So, you're the ones who are going to take the boat!' They asked about our family and we told them we had three boys. I think I had pictures of them in my wallet. She says, 'Well, isn't this going to be nice!' And I'm thinking, 'I haven't bought this boat.' Besides, the way he described it, it's going to be four times the money I've got. But she keeps talking about how glad she is going to be to get rid of that boat. Finally, we go out to the garage to look at it. Apparently, every time she goes to the trash can, over on the other side of the garage, she has to walk around the boat. She is not a boater and she doesn't like the boat. She says her husband never uses the boat, and she can't understand why she has to walk around it all the time. She says she is going to be so glad when it is gone. Matt says, 'Well, you see what I'm up against.' I laughed. And then I saw this boat. It's beautiful. It's brand new. And every single accessory is on it!"

Apparently, Matt had taken the boat out only about three times, and

then he had simply parked it in the garage. He had bought all the gear –
skis, ropes, and vests – for skiing, and they had never been used. As Matt
continued to point out all the extras, like side curtains, he had purchased
for the boat, Bob kept glancing over at Charlee with that "we need to get
out of here; we can't afford this" look in his eye.

"I mean, this was getting ridiculous! That boat had everything you
could possibly dream of on it, but we were not going to go in debt to buy
it. That's all there was to it. So, finally I said, 'Well, this is just a wonderful
boat, but I only have one thousand dollars, and obviously this is worth
many times that. I'm sorry, we should go.' That's when Matt's wife gave
him a look like, 'Come on, Matt, speak up!' I guess they had already talked
it over. So he says, 'Well, I'll take a thousand dollars for it.' She's all smiley,
and takes my hand, 'You're going to have so much fun with the boys and
all.' I couldn't believe it! It was as if these two people had come down from
heaven, and they were sitting here, and after this thing was over with,
they were going to be gone. If anyone were to drive out there, the house
wouldn't even be there. It was kind of like that. It was marvelous."

Bob was speechless. Charlee started crying.

"I said, 'You could sell that boat for a great deal more.' Matt answered,
'You can have it for one thousand dollars…but there's one condition.'
Uh-oh, I thought, I knew this was too good to be true. 'You have to try
it out first,' he said."

After tooling around Whiskeytown Lake, where Bob confirmed it
had hardly any miles or time on it, they wrote a check for one thousand
dollars, hitched it up to the Buick, loaded in all the skis and accessories,
and drove off with a brand new boat.

"I can still remember taking that home, and driving down our street
where everyone knew us, with that ski boat on the back. It was so beautiful, so perfect, so new. Seeing my neighbor, Larry Banks, go, 'Nooo!'"

The Moores had many years of fun with that boat. Bob guessed they
covered just about every one of Shasta Lake's 365 miles of shoreline.
And when it was finally time to sell it, Bob did the same thing that Matt
had done. He got it in perfect running condition. Updated everything.

Waxed it from top to bottom. Bought new skis. Put a low price tag on it. And sold it to the first guy who came by.

"That was fun, too. He had a couple of daughters, and I told him, 'This boat is just right for you.'"

Even today, when Bob sees a boat like the one for which he paid the favor forward, he wonders if maybe those people were blessed, too, somewhere along the line by two angels from heaven. Plus, it's not lost on Bob that something good came out of the fire that burned down their family's garage.

"In a way, I'm where I am today running a very successful company because my mill burned down. Something good came out of it. Just like getting a swimming pool and a ski boat. I didn't know at the time how either of those fire-related events would turn out, but I believe there is a Providential energy beyond regular human activities that seems to drive certain aspects of life and make it work."

It had to be Providence which met Bob Moore at the Redding Public Library that day in 1968. It showed up in the form of a book called *John Goffe's Mill*. And it changed his life. Not that he wasn't happy with his life.

"The whole time I was with JC Penney, I liked my job. It was a good job. And I could see myself still doing it. I just felt I had a different calling."

His favorite part of the job was providing excellent service to his customers. And they loved him for it. To the point they would write letters of appreciation to the head honcho, Marvin House:

Dear Mr. House,

Your service manager, Bob Moore, and his crew have been very thorough and conscientious in their work. They have always been extremely helpful and very interested in having the customer satisfied. It is a pleasure to do business with your fine organization.

Sincerely,
Martin G. Nelson

And this note from Mr. and Mrs. D.D. Hoffman:

> Dear Mr. House,
>
> Just a note to express our appreciation for the excellent service we have received. The "Pit Boss" Bob (last name unknown) is consistently knowledgeable, courteous, and extremely efficient. These traits are also evident among the rest of his crew.

"You only meet a handful of people like Bob Moore in your lifetime," says Sue Martin, who with her husband Dick entrusted their 1965 Ford Country Squire station wagon to the man she knew as the Pit Boss. "He was a unique man, a mechanic with an exuberant personality. We were in our mid-twenties and knew there was something different about him. He was cordial, pleasant. And we knew we could believe him when he told us what was wrong with our car."

"It was nice to deal with someone in the service business who was real," adds Dick. "A very trustworthy guy."

And Bob had a happy home life. Charlee was working part-time and liked her job at Sears. By now, she had her entire family eating unprocessed nutritious foods. Even her husband, who had always been a voracious reader, was reading every book he could find on the subject of healthy eating.

"We were raised eating pretty healthy food, consciously so, back as early as when we lived in the farmhouse," Robert remembers. "And then by the time we moved to Redding, I clearly remember Dad did a lot of reading on different health things and what not. I think he kind of got a little carried away with some of it, just god-awful stuff they were mixing into all kinds of things, trying to get it so it was palatable for us kids."

The teen years, basically the late '60s, were fun times for the boys. With a dad, who, according to Robert, "went out of his way to participate in our lives and to provide us with the means to have things to share," it was sometimes like having four boys living under one roof.

Like the time they tried to blow up their old 1954 Pontiac. The car was on its last legs, ready for the junkyard. But the kid in Bob had a crazy idea. Since they were going to get rid of it anyway, why not drive it into the ground until the engine blew up. Literally. There was a dump area on the other side of the Redding airport where people would drop off old refrigerators, broken furniture, crashed cars, and other kinds of junk. With lots of hills and dirt roads surrounding the huge open pit, it was also a popular track for motorcycles, dune buggies, and go-karts. Neither Bobby nor David was old enough to drive, but their dad let each of them get behind the wheel that day. Bobby would peel out, slam on the brakes, skid, step on the gas again, do figure eights, doughnuts, the whole nine yards. David, who was probably twelve, could barely reach the gas pedal and still be able to see over the steering wheel. But that didn't stop him from flooring it. By this time, the oil gauge was reading empty, the rods were knocking, and smoke was pouring out of the straight-eight engine. It was time for the grand finale.

"We took it over to where there were a bunch of other cars, put it in park, and took turns sitting in the driver's seat with our foot all the way down on the gas pedal and the engine screaming, just screaming," the elder Bobby says. "Finally, I thought we ought to get out because it might start throwing pistons out the side of the block. So, we wedged a brick on the gas pedal and stood back, waiting for the engine to explode. You know what…after half an hour or so we got bored and walked away from that car, the engine still racing. The boys and I still laugh about that. They wouldn't think their dad would be a part of some crazy stunt like that, it sounds like such a kid thing. But I probably had more fun than they did."

He was happy at home and satisfied with work, but something was missing in his life. And he was ever conscious of it. It was what he dreamed of as a kid; what his dad and he talked about late into the night. What he had always wanted. What he probably *needed* to feel fully fulfilled. The desire deep down in his DNA was to be in business for himself. He wanted to be an entrepreneur in the truest sense of the word.

"I felt like an entrepreneur when I was in management at Firestone and JC Penney, in the sense that I had contact with the whole company, contact with the customers, and contact with the product. But I didn't make the master decisions. Somebody above me did. And I wanted that responsibility. My plan from the beginning was to eventually become that true entrepreneur. I am an entrepreneur. It comes out the ends of my fingers."

With that burning desire came an equally strong commitment. Not to be just a business owner. An entrepreneur anywhere. In any type of endeavor or industry. No, it had to be one he believed in. To the core of his being. Totally, one hundred percent.

Bob knew what he believed in, and the picture of his future started to become clearer to him. He had actually begun to write a plan down, sketch some things out. He was a prolific list maker. Always wrote his priorities and goals down on a piece of paper.

He believed in God.

"Of anything that I am confident in, it is the eternalness of my life; and my love and respect for the truthfulness, the veracity, of the existence of God, of His word, of everything we look at, His creation. It is just a part of me. There is no doubt in any way, shape, or form. Not a bit."

He believed, thanks to Charlee, in living a healthy lifestyle that involved eating whole unprocessed food – fruits, grains, and seeds. He even points to the Bible for inspiration. The first book of Genesis, verse twenty-nine:

> And God said, Behold, I have given you every herb bearing
> seed, which is upon the face of all the earth, and every tree,
> in the which is the fruit of a tree yielding seed; to you it shall
> be for meat.

And he believed in his God-given abilities to work on motors and machinery. He was good at working with his hands. He could fix things. Build stuff.

As he contemplated these things, Bob began to draw. He made a drawing of a building, with a waterwheel on the side, living quarters upstairs, and a store downstairs. With an old-fashioned stone mill in the back. Then, he stepped back and looked at it.

"Now you tell me," he told himself, "if you put a building anywhere where people congregated, anywhere, put in a building, quaintly constructed with a store downstairs, a waterwheel on the side, and a mill in the back grinding grain, you think people wouldn't want to go in there? I promise you they will,"

Nearly forty years later, sitting in his office above his milling operation, he answers his own question: "I tried it and it worked."

CHAPTER 17

JOHN GOFFE'S MILL

W HEN BOB FINISHED READING THE BOOK, HE THOUGHT TO HIM-
self, "You know what, if that guy can do it, and he didn't know
beans about any of it, I can do it, too."

"That guy" was George Woodbury, and Bob learned his true-life
story reading *John Goffe's Mill*. Woodbury, a seventh-generation descen-
dant of John Goffe (1701–1786), inherited the family's derelict Bedford,
New Hampshire, mill in 1938, and left his research position at Harvard's
Peabody Museum to resurrect the old mill. As an accomplished archae-
ologist and anthropologist with a PhD, Woodbury knew nothing about
milling. But, at thirty-eight years old, he taught himself how to restore
a run-down mill and grind wheat into flour using ancient stone mills. A
coincidence or not, Bob was thirty-eight when he was inspired by Woodbury to pursue the same lost art.

Bob had gone to the Redding Public Library that day to do some
research on flour mills, to compare designs to an image he had in his mind.
At a deeper level, he was formulating a plan that was driven by a vision.
The vision he couldn't seem to shake was him operating his own flour mill.

Of him in business for himself. Running his own company. One that provided healthy, nutritious food for moms to feed their families.

"I envisioned the mill as a change in my life to be able to do what I wanted to do, what I believed in, which was whole grains. And I could make a living out of it, by grinding grains the ancient way, and exposing 150-year-old machinery to the public so they could appreciate what I was doing. It was unique, it was healthy, and it fit all my aspirations for helping people. That was kind of the key to the whole thing. Working with whole grains was what I wanted to do, and how I would get the public to buy into it would be to do something no one else was doing. Nothing about that doesn't appeal to me. Even right now."

So, Bob began accumulating books on milling. He researched how historic mills were powered – primarily by windmills, waterwheels, and, in the past century, by steam engine and electric motor. Then he started contacting companies that had anything to do with millstones and flour-making equipment. In his letters, he referenced it was a dream of his to go into the milling business with his sons. What he discovered was there were lots of mills in existence, but most were in museums. Some even ran on weekends, but almost all were for display only.

Bob didn't want a museum piece. If he was going to follow his dream, it would have to be with the same equipment that afforded a miller a good living back in 1850.

One of the companies that received Bob's letter referred him to Dewey Sheets of Muncie, Indiana. Dewey was a postal worker who after retiring had run a mill with his brother.[5] Turns out he was just the man Bob needed to know.

In a letter, he gushed to Dewey about his love of old mills, his dream to start a business with his sons, and his quest to find working flour-milling equipment.

---

5 The Wildcat Mill in Cutler, Indiana, still stands today. Under the "Old Water Mill" brand, Dewey and his brother sold Good Luck Flour and Bob White Corn Meal. Today, you can buy antiques at the Wildcat Mill.

"Dewey was this real cute old guy – he lived to be one hundred. He was skinny, kind of wiry, and he had this real squeaky voice. He was so enamored with my letter."

Dewey wrote back that he would be going on a scouting trip along the Eastern Seaboard to source authentic milling equipment – stone mills, dust collectors, grain cleaners, bucket elevators – for restoration of the Metamora Grist Mill, which was a State of Indiana park attraction, and he would keep his eyes open for anything he thought Bob might want.

Bob was so excited when he got a letter from Dewey informing him he could get some equipment for him from a farmer in Fayetteville, North Carolina, who had an old mill building on his property. And it would only cost $350! Bob sent a check and then anxiously awaited the shipment as he and the boys cleared some space in the garage to store the stuff. It arrived cash-on-delivery, and about broke the bank. The cost to ship the heavy boxes from Fayetteville to Redding was a whopping $1,400, almost everything Bob and Charlee had in their savings account. And the equipment sat there…for years.

"I was struggling with how to make a viable business with all this old wooden equipment and these weird-looking stones. I knew that's what I wanted to do – and two of my sons were interested, as well – but I couldn't even get the electric power to run the mill in my garage because it needed at least a twenty-horsepower motor with three-phase power. And the county told me the only place I could get three-phase power was the industrial section of downtown Redding."

So, Bob started driving around downtown with his neck craned outside the driver's window, following transmission lines to see where three-phase power was available. He finally found what he was looking for in an old Quonset hut that had once been an auto body shop. The owner, a Mrs. Thompson whose family operated the local men's clothing store, was a customer of Bob's at the auto center. She said she would rent the building to him for $125 a month. But when she found out Bob planned to grind flour in there, her insurance agent told her she should charge more because of the explosive nature of the process. It could blow up your building, he told her. So, she charged an extra twenty-five dollars a month for "explosion insurance."

Now he had a building to house his milling equipment. He had three-phase power to rotate the milling stones. And he had a bunch of "how-to" books to teach him how to turn wheat and other grains into flour. He continued to read up on the subject, and got his two oldest boys interested in the project as well. Ken, who recently got out of the Navy, was working the night shift at Albertson's and could help out during the day. Robert was studying music at Shasta College and was able to pitch in between classes. David was still in high school and eventually went into the Army, never really getting involved in what ultimately became a family business.

"My dream was to get that mill operating, and go into business with my sons, a vision similar to the dream my dad and I shared."

The challenge was he couldn't quit JC Penney, because it was going to take a couple of years to get the milling operation up and running. And nobody knew how long it would be before the Moores would make a profit bagging and selling their flour to the public. One thing Bob knew, for sure, was he wouldn't make the same mistake twice, or actually, for a third time. He wouldn't leave a sure thing (a steady paycheck) until he knew for a fact he was stepping into a profitable business situation. Leaving U.S. Electrical Motors before the Mobil station was open was mistake number one. Mistake number two was leaving a very stable Mobil station in Los Angeles for a pipe dream of a gas station in the volatile environs of Mammoth Lakes. He would not, could not, screw it up again – and put his career and family in jeopardy – without a guarantee. He decided the only way he would ever leave the security of JC Penney was if the mill was already up and running, *and making a profit*. The only way that could happen, he knew, was if he set the boys up in the business and helped them run it behind the scenes. He could underwrite the funding, he could work there nights and on his days off, he could advise the boys on the mill's daily operation, and he could oversee the entire business. The only thing he couldn't do was let his superiors know what he was doing before eight and after five.

"I was so concerned about what JC Penney might say: 'Bob, what's going on down the street? What's that all about? Why does it have your name on it? How long are you going to stay here?' I had an important job and I was being paid quite well for it. The circumstances just didn't allow me to talk about my plans, so I had to keep everything kind of under the table."

Besides, it was a small town, and people would talk. So, the first precaution he took was registering the business permit at the county office in Robert's and Ken's names. Bob Moore's name was not officially associated with the family business they all agreed to call Moores' Flour Mill (there were arguments about where the apostrophe should go, but a local English teacher told them if the company was owned by three Moores, then the name was plural, and the apostrophe went after the 's'). If anyone asked, it was Robert's and Ken's business. As difficult as it was, Bob had to restrain himself from telling folks Moores' Flour Mill was actually a three-way equal partnership. It had been his lifelong dream to own a family business, and now that he did, he couldn't even admit it. He eventually would confide in a couple of his crew members that, yes, it really was his business, but otherwise, he essentially ran the operation clandestinely. For nearly two years.

It was slow going – transforming the Quonset hut into a working flour mill on a part-time basis took the better part of 1973. Robert had quit community college by then and was working as a logger. Ken was still stocking grocery shelves on the graveyard shift. Both sons chipped in hours where they could – they were usually exhausted from logging and working nights. When he wasn't at JC Penney or home sleeping, Bob was working on the family project.

They were basically building a small two-story building within a forty-foot-wide by sixty-foot-long convex building made out of corrugated galvanized steel. Building out that 2,400-square-foot space would require a lot of timber. Fortunately, the timing of the conversion process coincided with a major renovation of the downtown area, and there was lots of scrap wood available just a few blocks away. Dilapidated brick buildings were being torn down to make room for the new Redding Downtown Mall, and this demolition project provided ideal scavenging opportunities for the Moores. They salvaged fourteen-by-four-foot rough-hewn timbers that had been used as floor joists in the turn-of-the-century buildings and used them to build a heavy load-bearing room. They reclaimed boards to construct a packaging area; even an upstairs office and a main floor storefront.

As the setting up of the mill operation progressed in 1973 and '74, the inner transformation of the empty old Quonset hut was amazing. Insulation, wall paneling, and wallpaper covered the bare metal walls of the curved building. Stairs led up to the second floor where bags filled with wheat and corn would be stored. The mill room, with its heavy sets of millstones, had been carefully set up on the main floor. Next door was the packaging room where storage bins, tables, scoops, and scales would be used to fill the one- and five-pound flour sacks. Shelves were arrayed in a couple of aisles that made up the little retail area, with a cash register on a counter in the front. They added a large plate glass window between the store and mill room so shoppers could view the milling process.

"With all that wood we scavenged, we just about got the remodeling done at no cost," Bob reports, obviously proud of the accomplishment.

Robert, too, remembers the construction process, albeit from a different perspective. "We Mickey-Moused everything. If you needed something, you would never dream of buying it new. You went to a scrap yard and picked out something you could get for nothing. Everything was made of duct tape and baling wire. Now, if you go up to my dad's operation today, and you see how professional and down to every detail everything is, well, that's not the way we did it when I was a kid."

Now that they had the skeleton of the mill built out, they still had to figure out where to get the equipment (the mixers, hoppers, bucket elevators, forklift, and a truck, for example), and how they were going to pay for it all. Bob figured he would need to secure $10,000 to $15,000 to pay for start-up costs. He found a good-sized chunk of it in the town of Sutter, just north of Sacramento.

Bob was tracking down a grain cleaner for sale at a rice processing plant called WestLAM. While there, he asked if they had any other surplus milling equipment, and learned they wanted to get rid of their grain silos. There were fourteen of them, each eighteen feet high and eighteen feet in diameter. Bob knew he could use one or two to store wheat and corn behind the Quonset hut, but balked at the price of $500 each. Then the WestLAM guy offered, "Well, if you want them all, I'll sell them to you for $350 apiece. Only thing is, you'll have to take them apart yourself."

Bob secured a few days to think about the deal, and on the drive back to Redding he formulated a plan. He paid a visit to the newspaper office and placed a classified ad, offering twelve grain storage tanks he would deliver anywhere in the Sacramento area. Eight hundred dollars each. The first respondent, someone from a local dog food company, said he would take them. They agreed on $9,600 upon delivery, which Bob pushed out a couple of weeks because he knew it would be a herculean task to dismantle the metal tanks.

The silos had been out in the elements for ten years, which was evident by the rust and wear and tear. But the dog food guy saw a picture of them and agreed to take every panel and every screw. Now all Bob had to do to pocket upwards of eight thousand dollars was to take impact wrenches to every one of those thousands upon thousands of rusty screws.

"There were square head nuts on the inside, with round head screws on the outside, and every one of them was about this far apart," Bob explains, holding thumb and forefinger three inches apart. "We borrowed some scaffolding from Bill Mettlebaugh, one of my customers who was a house painter, and a flatbed trailer and pickup from my good friend, Phil Black. I took two weeks' vacation, and Robert went down there with me. We slept in the back of the station wagon in a couple of sleeping bags. We got in there with our impact guns, one of us on the inside with the scaffolding and the other on the outside with a ladder, and we got a rhythm going of taking those things down; every single screw and nut had to be taken out. After a while, we would go get something to eat, and then we would come back and work, and we'd work until dark. I mean, we really poured the coal to it."

Bob says, and his son would no doubt agree, "It was the most miserable job I ever did in my life! It was always hot in that darn valley down there, and the rice hulls they had been storing in those tanks were just like little needles. They were awful! You'd get sweaty and those little nasty hulls would stick you in your armpits."

Overall, the dirty job took about a month, and from time to time the entire family got involved in the project. Charlee would come down to give encouragement. Robert's girlfriend (later, his wife), Barb, and a friend of hers helped out. They would all go out for pizza at night and celebrate their progress. After the last panel and screw were delivered, Bob deposited eight thousand dollars in his Wells Fargo bank account. He had half of what he figured his start-up costs would be. Now he had to get the other half.

"By now, a lot of people were following what we were doing, and everybody got a kick out of it. I went to my banker, Bob Baker of Wells Fargo Bank, and asked for an eight-thousand-dollar line of credit. I told him, 'I won't use my eight I just deposited; I'll use your eight. That should be enough to get us started. And when I get ready to use *my* money, I'll come in and we will see how business is. If it warrants it, then I will start using my money. That would give me sixteen thousand, and we will go from there. You can't lose any money!' He thought that was pretty funny."

Now that he had the bankroll, he got serious about spending the money it would take to get the boys up and running. He bought a 1959 fourteen-foot GMC flatbed truck and a used forklift. He went to Montgomery Ward and picked out a brand new cement mixer, and after sandblasting all the paint off it, used it to mix ingredients, one hundred pounds at a time. He had acquired a second mill, a smaller one, and used it to grind cornmeal, pancake mix, muffin mix, and ten-grain cereal. The larger mill ground wheat into whole wheat flour. He had purchased a packaging machine to put the finished products into one-pound bags. They completed construction of an office on the second floor, next to a storage area where he was building up his inventory of raw materials. In the back, he re-erected the two grain tanks he had gotten in the WestLAM deal.

Their goal was to open before Thanksgiving and the upcoming baking season. Everyone had been working hard, making sacrifices, living on shoestring budgets, with hopes this crazy idea of running an old-fashioned flour mill would actually create cash flow they could all live on. It was a long shot. Nobody knew anyone who had ever tried something like this before. Yeah, some guy in a book apparently pulled it off at John Goffe's mill in 1938. But, there were no case studies, no business plans to follow, no how-to manual providing a step-by-step approach to milling flour with a century-old mill and selling it to the citizens of Redding, California. It took a huge leap of faith. Personally, Bob was ready to take that step, but he knew he had to wait until the business venture proved itself. When it was real, it would mean the realization of the dream he had shared with his father. He was a partner with his two sons, but, so far, he was a silent partner. Publicly, it was Robert's and Ken's business.

CHAPTER 18

MOORES' FLOUR MILL

IT REALLY WASN'T A VERY PROFESSIONAL OPERATION, BOB ADMITS. AND from the day Moores' Flour Mill opened on November 17, 1974, they had a big problem.

"We didn't expect to do much business, and that was the problem. We did better than anyone anticipated. It became more successful than we could have ever imagined. It was a force we had to deal with from the moment we opened the doors."

They had put a small newspaper ad in the *Redding Record Searchlight*, mirroring what it said above their front door entrance: Moores' Flour Mill; Stone Ground Flour & Meals; Grains, Beans, Nuts. They included the phone number and their address on South Market Street, along with this statement heralding their opening: The Millstones are Turning.

Apparently, a lot of people wanted stone ground flour, meals, grains, beans, and nuts, because Moores' Flour Mill was busy from day one. There were only three parking spaces and they were always full. The store, which was probably less than three hundred square feet, was so crowded people could hardly move around. It was a great problem to have, the Moores realized. But, it was a problem, nevertheless, and it had to be dealt with. Almost from the beginning, Bob began looking for bigger space.

While the Moores never expected their little natural foods business to take off so fast, there were external pressures at the time that contributed to their success. The counterculture movement of the 1960s had peaked, and mainstream America seemed to be hungry for alternatives to the "sex, drugs, and rock 'n roll" lifestyle and the troubles those excesses caused. Hippies were still around, but their "back-to-nature" subculture actually helped increase business for stores that sold healthy food. Young adults who had marched against the Vietnam War and for Civil Rights, but still wanted to demonstrate their rejection of conventional social norms, avoided traditional grocery store chains and supported the local mom and pop operations. All this was good news for Bob, Charlee, Robert, and Ken, as well as Robert's wife, Barbara, and Ken's wife, Dora, both of whom had started working at the busy mill and store.

But the biggest single contributing factor to their remarkable start had to be the timing of the release of a certain book. One that had been written by the author of a very popular title in 1969 called *Everything You Always Wanted to Know About Sex (But Were Afraid to Ask)*, and in 1972 was adapted into a movie by the same name starring Woody Allen. Dr. David Reuben followed up his book on sex with a book about health. It came out in early 1975, just about the time Bob needed that final push to get him to feel comfortable about leaving JC Penney. The book, which extolled the health benefits of eating fiber, was called *The Save Your Life Diet*.

Reuben wrote the book after five years of watching his father die slowly from colon cancer. He read every scientific report he could find about how fiber affects the human body, concluding, "I am now convinced that not only could my father's life have been saved, but millions of other cancer victims would be alive today if they had simply been able to add a few cents' worth of vegetable fiber to their daily diet."

He goes on to say the key to survival – protection from colon cancer, heart attacks, appendicitis, and overcoming obesity – is ensuring that dietary fiber is an essential part of the human diet. He specifically adds in his "ideal" diet plan for mankind, we should avoid refined flour, substituting for it whole grain flour products such as whole wheat bread, whole wheat crackers, whole wheat pastries, pies and cakes; and avoid all refined cereal products, substituting instead whole grain cereal products such as whole wheat, brown rice, and whole grain corn meal.

Internationally respected publications like the *Journal of the American Medical Association* and *Medical World News* had jumped on the fiber bandwagon with articles published respectively in August and September of 1974. Even mainstream magazines, like *Reader's Digest,* the largest paid-circulation magazine in the world, (which at its peak in 1974 when the article hit sold seventeen million copies) wrote that the lack of fiber in the American diet may be a contributing factor in a number of diseases, including cancer and heart disease. The headline and subhead from that December, 1974, issue did more promotion for whole grains than any ad could do:

> Is a Vital Ingredient Missing From Your Diet? *A startling new theory suggests that the addition of fiber to the daily diet may prove to be an important defense against colo-rectal cancer and other diseases.*

"The timing was perfect, and it hit our business like a ton of bricks!" Bob remembers. He ordered 10,000 copies of that *Reader's Digest* article, and the family handed them out to everyone who came to the store.

It was like a commercial for Moores' Flour Mill. All the products these esteemed sources were citing were available in their little store. Business was booming, and still, Bob sat on the sidelines. He would see his exhausted family members after work hours and join them on Wednesdays (they were closed on Sundays, his other day off). It seemed like every week sales were outdoing the week before. And every month was getting better and better. A January 15, 1975, article in the *Record Searchlight* provided an additional boost in sales, and there was no doubt the business would soon be turning a profit. The story didn't even mention Bob.

"The business was one hundred percent my dream, and sometimes I've wondered whether I should have done it different in the sense that I should have been a part of that. I remember feeling a little pang of being left out or something, but was I jealous? No, I don't have time for that foolishness. I've made a lot of mistakes in my life, but jealousy is not one of them. I enlisted the boys in this and they obviously picked up on it. For whatever it's worth, that's how it worked out. And, today, both of the boys are still working together, and they are still in the business."

It wasn't until September, 1975, almost ten years to the day since he became the Pit Boss of the Redding auto center, and more than six years after reading *John Goffe's Mill*, that Bob quit JC Penney and went all-in at Moores' Flour Mill. At age forty-six, he would – publicly – finally have his family business.

Technically, his "all-in" was a lot less than he had expected. He had been counting on cashing out his JC Penney retirement fund to support the expansion of the business – he already had his eye on an 8,000-square-foot space that was soon to become available. But, when he received his final paperwork, he was shocked to learn JC Penney stock had taken a nose dive in the past several months. He had been expecting a check in the neighborhood of $20,000. He almost fainted when he saw the amount – $3,500.

"It was an incredible disappointment," he understates. "That was my first experience with the big world of investments, and I can honestly say I have never not been disappointed with the stock market function of this country since that day."

Where he worked, everyone opted to direct all their retirement funds into JC Penney stock. The company even matched their contributions. For years, Bob had been accumulating shares at a cost of $115 each. When he cashed out, a share was worth about twenty-two dollars.

It was a major setback, but it didn't slow Bob down from pouring his heart and soul (and finances) into Moores' Flour Mill. He was finally free to spend one hundred percent of his workday at the mill. His mind and spirit had been with the boys since the three of them started the project twenty-two months earlier, but physically, it had been Robert's and Ken's show for the ten months they had been open to the public. Now, Dad was on the scene full-time, and working side-by-side with his two partners. And as busy as they all were, sometimes that "full-time" schedule meant working around the clock, especially when the millstones needed sharpening.

Bob was the only one who knew how to "dress" the stones when they became dull from wear, usually about every two to three weeks. He learned the ancient art by reading a book on the subject. Using firm strokes on a "bill," a cutting tool resembling a double-edged wedge forged from high carbon steel, and a pointed "pick," he would chip away at the surface of the stones, chiseling out peaks and valleys called "lands" and "furrows." It was a precise undertaking, also involving cutting fine parallel grooves along the surface of each "land." Experienced millwrights could cut as many as sixteen of these "stitches" or "cracks" to the inch.

Adding to the degree of difficulty were the unwieldy stones, some weighing as much as a ton. They were usually about four feet in diameter, arranged in pairs with the upper "running stone" rotating most efficiently at a speed of 125–150 rotations per minute above the lower fixed "bed stone." The face-to-face stones never touched, but when perfectly dressed, the "furrows" would cross at each revolution, cutting the grain with the action of scissor blades. The actual clearance between the grinding surfaces of the 2,000-pound stones required very fine adjustment in order to produce meal or flour of the desired texture. "French buhrs" made from blocks of quartz quarried near Paris were the most highly prized millstones. Matching shapes of quartz were skillfully pieced together, jointed in cement, bound with iron hoops, and backed with plaster of Paris.

Once the millstones were sharpened and perfectly balanced – akin to today's automotive wheel alignment and balance – they were housed in a wooden structure called a "vat." Across the top of the vat lay a framework called the "horse," which supported a wooden hopper and a tapering spout, or "shoe," which fed grain into the eye of the runner stone. This arduous task could take all night – or longer – and if not done correctly, friction from the stones touching could produce more wear in minutes than weeks of grinding. There was also the very real danger two stones rubbing together at high speed could throw off flying sparks, igniting an explosive fire in the dust-laden air.

Hundreds of years ago, the craft of milling was usually handed down from father to son, and that heir had to have the physical strength to man-handle heavy loads in confined spaces, as well as possess the ingenuity to operate waterwheels and, eventually, machinery to power the grinding process. That blessing (or curse, depending on how you look at it) fell to the middle son in the Moore family. Robert took a bigger interest in run-ning the milling operation, while Ken's attention veered more toward con-struction, and he ultimately went into the home-building business. It was Robert, who, like his dad, would earn the "thumb of gold." That's the term Chaucer reportedly used to describe what expert millers got from a lifetime of gauging by touch the fineness of meal and the quality of grain. Others called it "miller's thumb," a curious flattening of the thumb that occurred from years of testing meal by rubbing it between the thumb and fingers.

As Robert stepped up to take on more responsibility, one of the areas he focused on was building relationships with suppliers. They sourced from several companies in San Francisco the raw materials such as spe-cialty flours, baking ingredients, nuts, seeds, beans, and other ancient grains Moores' Flour Mill needed for blending into their pancake mixes, bread mixes, meals, and cereals. One of their major suppliers was Giusto's Vita-Grain, a family-run business started in 1940 with a bakery and small health food store. By the mid-1970s, Giusto's was a major processor and wholesaler of every kind of grain and baking ingredient home cooks or professional chefs needed, and Robert would make a couple of trips a week to buy from them.

Both Robert and Bob credit Fred and Al Giusto, the two brothers who were running the company, with providing them insights about the grain business, which accelerated their respective learning curves. As the business continued to grow, fueled by the medical community's endorse-ment of including whole grains and other forms of vegetable fiber in a healthy diet, new opportunities surfaced. Should the company expand from retail only to wholesale? With limited manufacturing capabilities, how were they going to keep up with demand? They definitely needed more than 2,400 square feet. Where should they relocate? Should they lease or buy a new manufacturing facility? They had recently purchased a refrigerator in the store and were selling gourmet cheeses on the side; should other specialty gourmet products be added?

With three equal partners struggling to make the right decisions, there were oftentimes three different answers to the questions. Limit risk or take a chance? Spend or save? Grow or stay small? Expand with new products or sell more of what you have? These were business dilemmas most healthy companies face on a regular basis. But, add the dynamics of a family business – with a dad and two brothers each owning a third of the company – and you add another layer of challenges.

"Well, it was one of the things I got kind of used to: Dad and Ken always disagreed on everything; so, because it was an equal partnership, I would let them pick their two sides, and then I would get to be the tie-breaker. So, when it came to voting, basically, I got my way," Robert recalls.

Bob remembers those start-up years with their growing pains as "fun for a while, even butting heads with these kids. They were both in their twenties, and, sometimes with the three of us, it was like having an adjustable wrench that just would not adjust."

It was those times – when Bob was in his mid-forties – that he wanted to start enjoying life a little more. He worked hard. The boys worked hard. And he liked nothing better than taking a break and escaping with Charlee.

"The boys could run the mill, so finally Charlee and I were able to take off. We had a lot of fun, some nice moments. We went over to Napa Valley for about a week, to the wine country. I can remember eating at this pizza restaurant, up on the patio, up high, on the top of the building. We were sitting there in the middle of the day. They had umbrellas, and looking out over the vineyard and down the street and whatnot, I told Charlee, 'I have never been happier or felt any better in my entire life than I do right this minute.' I remember telling her that."

But, back in Redding, working side-by-side with two guys who had different ideas than their dad did about how to run the business became a grind. It just wasn't the satisfying experience Bob had hoped it would be.

"I had such an energy for that business. And each of us had strong feelings, determination, and stuff like that. But we didn't have a shared vision. I finally came to the realization that the long-term viability of it just wasn't meant to be. That's all. Plain and simple."

Robert agrees. "There were definitely dynamics at work that would have precluded us from working together much longer on an equal footing, which is the way we had set it up. In any combination of people, I think it probably works best when you have one dominant person, and everybody else tends to be a little bit more submissive. But, I was certainly not that. I think Dad tried to give me free rein a little bit, but I was twenty-one, twenty-two years old, and I wasn't interested in knuckling under and always doing things the way he wanted them done. Of course, you think you know everything at that age."

In spite of the tension, the business was going gangbusters. Within two years of opening, it was time to move to larger space. Bob had begun negotiations with the E.W. Scripps Company, owners of the *Record Searchlight* newspaper, to rent space in the 18,000-square-foot building they were leaving to move into a brand new building. Scripps wanted to keep 10,000 square feet in the back for storage, so Robert signed an agreement to rent the front 8,000 (by this time in 1976 it was pretty clear Dad wasn't going to be a long-term partner in the business, so there was no need to put his name on the document; Ken opted out about this time, as well, and started spending more time building and selling houses than working at the mill).

For the second time in less than three years, the Moores took on the after-hours job of converting a building into a flour mill. It was similar to what they had done with the Quonset hut, only with about 5,000 more square feet in which to operate: store in the front, office above on the second floor, mill room, packaging room, storage area, grain tanks in the back. Bob kept the mills running at the old location until it was time to haul them over to 1601 Shasta Street.

When they were fully functional at the new place, it effectively tripled their capacity. Of course, it increased their overhead as well. In addition to the family members who were working in the business, they had hired three or four people to work in the expanded mill and store. And the rent had skyrocketed from the steal-of-a-deal $150 a month they had paid for the Quonset hut.

"Redding was still a small town, and the business as it was really wasn't big enough to support all of us," Bob reasoned. So, he began to consider his options. He ruled out staying on as a partner, because he loved his sons

Charlee stocking shelves at the retail store (1976)

too much to fight with them. He entertained the idea of buying a nearby gas station that had closed because I-5 had changed local traffic patterns, but he realized that would be a struggle, and probably too big a risk. One day, he mentioned to Charlee that instead of a career change, now might be the perfect time for him to do something he had always wanted to do, but never thought he would get the chance. Maybe he should go back to school. But not just any school. It had been a goal of his to read and study the Bible in its original Greek and Hebrew languages. In order to accomplish that, he would need to go to a theological college.

"I loved the business, but the more I thought about it and prayed about it, I became totally enamored with the idea of going to seminary school."

While Charlee knew that would mean leaving Redding, their children and grandchildren (Barb had two children, Chad and Monica, before she married Robert, and by this time they had Sarah together), she supported her husband's dream. It would take some planning, but she was willing to go on this journey with him. The first step would be to approach Robert with the concept.

"I said, 'Son, you can handle this business on your own, but I don't want to put any type of burden on you. I'll stay on for a year. I'll work for you – sack flour, run the mills, drive the truck, build machinery, whatever you need. You pay me one thousand dollars a month, and at the end of twelve months, I'll consider myself bought out, and the business will be all yours.'"

Robert agreed. It was the summer of 1977, and the transition plan was in place.

CHAPTER 12

HERE WE GO AGAIN

WESTERN EVANGELICAL SEMINARY (NOW GEORGE FOX EVANGEL-
ical Seminary) is nestled alongside the Willamette River in the
Jennings Lodge area east of Portland, Oregon. Bob and Charlee Moore
began auditing classes there Fall term of 1978. They had applied to four
seminary schools, but getting accepted at a college not far from where
Bob was born made them feel WES was the best choice. That June, Bob
had fulfilled his commitment to his son for a one-year transition out of
the Moores' Flour Mill business, and their house had sold in short order
for $59,000, almost five times what they paid for it ten years earlier.
When they said their goodbyes that Fourth of July weekend, they alluded
to "retiring for a while" in the Pacific Northwest. Bob told Charlee he
estimated they could live for about four years on savings and the profit
from the sale of the house before they had to look for work again (they
had about $89,000 in the bank).

"I love my boys with all my heart and all my soul, and we were so
joyous that we could let Robert have the business, and Ken and David
could work there if they wanted. Charlee and I were so happy to be
going to school, learning more about the Bible, becoming part of a local

church, and actually feeling retired. Plus, I knew way off somewhere that with my fascination with gas stations, repairs, and stuff, I felt young enough that I could get a job in Portland with Les Schwab or some other tire outfit."

At least once or twice a month that summer and early fall, Bob and Charlee made the seven-hour drive south in their 1966 Ford station wagon to visit their kids and grandkids. Robert and Barb were managing the business quite handily, and they appreciated the frequent visits because they could get Bob's help tweaking a mill or two. Charlee was quite homesick, and relished the time she could spend with her new granddaughter, Sarah. Ken had struck out on his own and was building a Moores' Flour Mill in Ukiah, about 100 miles southwest of Redding. It was a small operation with a waterwheel, store, and living quarters upstairs, loosely based, Bob says, on his original plan and sketches. "I thought it was kind of neat that both boys had a Moores' Flour Mill."

As September rolled around, Bob and Charlee readied themselves for the school semester. They were renting a very comfortable two-bedroom townhouse for $250 a month about a half mile from Western Evangelical Seminary. Here they were, almost in their fifties, buying books and school clothes like a couple of college kids.

"We were having a wonderful time! We were semi-retired, spending a beautiful summer in Oregon, going to Redding about every other week, and studying the Bible. Sometimes you might wonder if you are in the right business or if you are doing the right thing, but I can promise you when you sit down with the Bible in front of you, you are doing the right thing."

The coursework was difficult – learning to read the Scriptures in their original languages – but Bob approached his studies with an intense passion and commitment. He would stay up late reading Greek and Hebrew interpretations of the Bible. During the day, he would attend classes and focus on his homework. Learning languages required a lot of memorization, and one of his favorite study methods was to walk the neighborhoods of Jennings Lodge and adjoining Milwaukie with Charlee, reciting passages as they went along. It was on one of these long walks with his

**Robert Moore's mill in Redding, California;
Ken Moore's mill in Ukiah, California**

wife and study partner that he happened upon an old feed mill. The run-down building was on the fringe of a neighborhood on Roethe Road that transitioned to an industrial area leading to busy McLoughlin Boulevard a block away.

"Well, there was no way I wasn't going to go investigate it," he justi-fies, referencing his passion for old mills. While Charlee hung back, grip-ping the study manuals a little tighter than she had before they stumbled upon the old building, her husband slowly walked up to the side of the weathered structure, stood on his tippy toes to peer into a dirty window, and, as Charlee explains later, "he seemed lost in his thoughts." Mesmer-ized, as if gazing at a thing of beauty instead of a dusty, sun-bleached hunk of tinderbox blight on the neighborhood, the miller inside him – the one that never really left his DNA – started wondering, "What if… what if I could…if we were just able to move that wall, and…" Almost hesitatingly, he continued his exploration; stooping to touch a piece of siding, stretching to see if a loose board could be put back in its place. When he disappeared around the back of the building on his circuitous route, Charlee's heart started beating a little faster.

"What if…" she started. She knew her husband. "But, what if it doesn't work out," she declared to no one within hearing distance.

He came back into sight. This time with a little quicker gait. He wasn't looking at the old mill as much as he was taking side glances at the woman who was waiting for him. He was beaming, actually, but trying to furrow his brow at the same time. It wasn't working. She could see right through him.

"Whatdya think, hon?" he asked almost rhetorically, not really expecting an answer or wanting one either. She smiled, maybe a little tighter than she wanted.

"Looks nice." Could have been a used car he was pointing out or an ugly painting. She loved her husband, and could see there was something already smoldering inside him neither of them wanted to extinguish.

"I found a phone number; it was on a 'For Sale' sign over there," he said as he pointed to the far side of the tired-looking building. "I guess it won't hurt to at least call the number."

Charlee took her husband's hand and squeezed it as they turned and walked away from the old mill. Bob couldn't help but turn back for another look – twice, actually – as they headed back to school. They both looked down at the phone number he had written on a scrap of paper. Neither could have ever guessed where that chance encounter would lead them.

When Bob got home that night, he called the number and learned a local car dealer owned the land. He said he was planning to raze the building and use the two-acre lot to store some vehicles on it if he couldn't sell it. The asking price was $95,000. "Well," Bob told him, "I may be interested."

He also learned the building had originally been constructed in Montana, was dismantled, transported to Oregon, and rebuilt on its present two-acre location. The Martin brothers, who owned it, had run a chicken ranch nearby and used the building as a feed mill. When the nearby Milwaukie Railway, one of the Pacific Northwest's first electric interurban lines, closed in 1958, the Martins were no longer able to ship grain to the mill, and shut down the operation.

Bob was only several months removed from the flour milling business, and there was a lingering feeling of disappointment about the way it had ended. His dream of having a family business, at the least, had been put on hold. For the near term, he had resolved to take a break, to sort of retire, and then pick it up again after Bible college. But Moores' Flour Mill in Northern California was a different situation than the one that was starting to creep from the back of his mind to the forefront. He was not a majority owner there. He was one of three equal partners. He didn't have the final say-so in the Redding operation. One thing he did know, for sure, coming out of that experience, was if he ever went into business with anyone again, he would have to be at least a fifty-one percent owner. He had had time to think about it, and he had come to the realization that as an owner, he was wired to be in charge, or else it wouldn't work for him.

Overnight, and for the next several days, he couldn't get the thought out of his mind of what it would be like to resurrect that old mill into a functioning flour mill. He was completely out of the business – didn't have any millstones or equipment. The building looked like it was about to fall down; what would it take to reinforce the structure and refurbish the mill room, second-floor storage area, and grain-cleaning room. Plus, they would have to build a packaging room, a store, and an office. He had done it all before, twice, actually. But, now he was nearly fifty years old. Did he want to start over again? Could he afford to do it? Most of all, what would Charlee think?

Turns out, she had already thought it through, and probably knew before her husband what was going to happen. "At first, it was like, 'Oh, no!' But I could see the writing on the wall. Here we go again; we were going back into the business."

Of course, they prayed about it. And Bob said he felt an incredible spiritual energy to move forward. "After leaving Redding, I had no thoughts about ever going into the milling business again. Not a thought...until we walked around the corner and there was that crazy mill, right there. It certainly was not my intent when I moved up here. It just seemed obvious to me now, though, that the Lord was saying, 'It's okay to learn about Me in the Bible, but I want you to do something else.' And getting that mill was what I was supposed to do."

Bob did his due diligence. As he always did first, he went to his banker and asked what kind of credit he could get. He went to the Clackamas County office of development to share some preliminary sketches, some initial plans. They told him he would not need a permit to transform the old feed mill into a working flour mill. He contacted his mentor, Dewey Sheets, to put him on alert he might be needing some millstones and equipment. He got recommendations from his church, Oregon City Bible Chapel, about which members did construction work.

When he had everything lined up, he called the car guy who owned the property and proposed a rental agreement with an option to buy. The owner, curious to know what his plans were for the property, laughed at him when Bob said he would get the mill going again.

"He was a real smart aleck, and I could tell he had a bunch of hotshot used car salesmen in his office, because they were all kind of cackling in the background when he repeated what I had just told him: 'Really? I was going to tear that old building down, and you're telling me you're going to get it going again?' Anyway, I guess it was kind of funny, but I knew what I had done in almost five years with the boys, and I didn't have a building that even looked like a mill! This one did. I thought, 'My gosh, we did pretty good down there, what could we do with this!' It was just a piece of cake."

With the deal done, Bob gave himself three months to get the mill up and running. That was awfully aggressive, but it wasn't like transforming a metal Quonset hut or a newspaper office into a mill – he already had a mill with some usable guts and salvageable equipment. Plus, Dewey, now nearly ninety, told Bob he could have all the milling equipment he had been collecting over the years, and he wouldn't accept any money for it.

Bob said he grew to expect things would fall in place. "It just never occurred to me I couldn't do it," is how he put it. But he knew he couldn't do it alone. He successfully negotiated with U.S. Bank Manager Bruce Cullison to match the $50,000 he and Charlee had on deposit there with a $50,000 line of credit, giving him $100,000 to bankroll the new venture. Because he was renting the mill and the property, he only had to make very reasonable monthly payments, which protected his cash savings for operational purposes.

He opened up a checking account and promptly went out and made his first major purchase – a $22 coffee pot. Then he paid $3,200 for a 1969 Ford C-600 cab over truck. The next several days and weeks he was consumed with retrofitting the feed mill. Set back on its two-acre lot, the forty-by-three-hundred foot wood building was an imposing sight in the daylight. It had been his lifelong desire to someday own a classic American flour mill, so Bob had it painted bright red with white trim. A large bay at the front provided access for delivery of raw products, and the doors opened into a sixty-foot-tall milling room where overhead belts on steel shafts that ran the length of the building would turn the massive quartz wheels. Two guys from church, John Bierwagen and Jack Sherman, did the construction work, including the mill retail store, which was actually a rebuilt milk barn Bob had purchased from the Skoko Farm on Highway 212 in nearby Clackamas. The Skokos, who had operated their family milking business on that site since 1900, sold the actual wooden barn to Bob, and the construction crew carefully rebuilt it inside the mill warehouse to serve as their store.

But there was still one key component missing. Bob needed a right-hand man, someone who knew how to operate a mill.

In his travels (he loved to visit old mills), he had discovered Butte Creek Mill in Eagle Point, which is located in Southern Oregon approximately halfway between Redding and Portland. Billed as "the last water-powered grist mill, still commercially operating, this side of the Mississippi," the 140-year-old, water-powered flour mill is listed on the National Register of Historic Places. Bob got to know its owner, Peter Crandall, sort of a modern "John Goffe's Mill" story himself (a graduate of Cornell University, he became a research engineer in the space industry who examined moon rocks). He left his job at North American Rockwell Science Center in 1970 to begin a thirty-year career as a flour miller and proprietor of the Butte Creek Mill country store.

It was Crandall who introduced Bob to Craig Ratzat. Craig, from the nearby Grants Pass area, grew up around the grain business. His dad, Carl, worked in a feed store. Craig worked there part time during high school, and after he graduated, he spent three years working at the Butte Creek Mill. When it was slow in the wintertime, he would work construction, and it was during one of those lulls that Bob called Craig and offered him a job. He was the first employee of what became Moores' Flour Mill in Milwaukie, Oregon.

"It was interesting how it turned out," Bob remarked. "All three of us got mills, and we each called it 'Moores.' We were the milling family."

With Craig's help, Bob got two stone mills operational and the remodeling finished exactly three months to the date set out in his plan. Moores' Flour Mill in Milwaukie, Oregon, opened in early May of 1979 (a picture of Charlee accepting the first dollar on May 2 hangs on a wall at company headquarters). And, just like the opening-day experience in Redding four-and-a-half years prior, they were busy from the get-go. Bob had timed it just right, with a print ad in the daily *Oregonian* newspaper announcing Moores' Flour Mill was now open for business. In addition to being a big believer in advertising, Bob understood the value of good PR. Just two weeks after he opened the door, TV news reporter Kathy Smith from the local ABC affiliate KATU came out to do a story. The media has been enamored with Bob and his authentic old-fashioned milling operation ever since. Over the ensuing months, the NBC affiliate, KGW, sent "Faces & Places" anchor Cheryl Hansen over to broadcast live. Hansen's field reporter Kev Reilly did a five-minute profile on Bob and his mill – basically a commercial – describing him as "a man who's forsaken the rat race for the simple satisfaction of grinding his own flour and sharing it with his customers." He concluded his story with, "You're one of the rare guys who actually can say he likes to get up and go to work in the morning," to which Bob responded, "I work long hours because I want to, because I enjoy what I'm doing. Here's the thing – I get a business going that I absolutely love, one that I have worked my entire life to get, and I find myself saying, 'This is who I am. I'm never going to do anything different. This is always what I'm going to do.' Almost immediately I had enough money to make it all go; I didn't have any problems paying the bills. Now, I know what it feels like to lose money; I know what it feels like to go broke. But when I opened my own mill, I didn't have those feelings about not making it. What I did feel was, 'I've learned my lessons; now I need to start living my life. I'm ready now.' When I opened that mill, I said, 'I am my own person. Truly, truly, I am my own person. I am unique to anybody else.'"

To keep up with the demand in the early going, Bob ordered truck-loads of raw grains and products from Robert's Moores' Flour Mill in Redding. Nobody thought twice about any competition, because at the time, all three Moores' Flour Mills were only selling to their local customers out of their own retail stores. Nobody was selling wholesale. None of the three was even thinking about it.

As Bob's business continued to grow, he approached Craig about the prospect of partnership. Craig had been in the grain business his entire working life, and Bob needed what he had. Craig knew construction, he did the milling, he ordered all the grains, he drove the truck, he was good with customers, and he had tons of energy. Craig's wife, Gail, worked in packaging and retail alongside Charlee, and the two couples got along splendidly.

"There was a lot of joking and laughing together, just a very nice relationship," Bob remembers fondly. "They didn't have a babysitter, so Gail would bring their two little kids to work, and they were running around the mill laughing and playing, which I thought was kind of homey. And Craig, he is absolutely honest; I would trust him with anything."

Craig held Bob in high regard, as well, describing him as "a father figure," and someone who was "always more than generous to me."

"We got along very well," he says. "We never fought, but we certainly didn't agree on every tactic. I just remember we would always get over our disagreements. And in the big picture, Bob was a big inspiration to me, especially about what it takes to be successful in business."

The two millers were building something very unique together, but as Bob describes it, "Craig was doing a really good job, but he was just working for me. One day, I told him, 'Craig, you need to be a partner in this thing. We need to be partners together.' I told him I was willing to put thirty-percent ownership on the table."

Craig favored the partnership idea, but told Bob he didn't have enough money to buy his way in.

"Well, how much do you have?" Bob asked.

"Fourteen hundred dollars," was the response, profit from a house sold in Eagle Point.

"I said, 'Okay, you give me fourteen hundred dollars, and I'll give you a thirty-percent ownership in the company. We'll both take home the same salary, and we'll split all the profits down the middle.'"

At first, it didn't make any sense to Craig. "I pay you fourteen hundred dollars, you give me thirty percent of your company, we make the same salary, and we share the profits fifty-fifty," he parroted. To most, it would seem to be one of those stories too good to be true, but as Craig thought it through, he realized that Bob's offer, while kind of strange, was consistent with the man's philosophy he had come to appreciate. It was never about the money.

"I didn't need his money," Bob explains. "I needed *him*, and the deal worked for me. It was fine. Craig was my partner. I don't think it made any sense to him, didn't make any sense to the accountant, wouldn't have made any sense to the government, wouldn't have made any sense to anybody – but that's what I did. You read stories in the Scriptures, where the rich man gives only a little and the widow gives all she had, and who was blessed? The widow. That's exactly how life is. That's the real world – the world God made and watches over. It's just that the rest of us have our own goofy ideas sometimes."

Some thirty years later, two hundred of Bob's employees would be shaking their heads in another "this-doesn't-make-sense-to-me moment" when they would learn they had become owners of the company through an Employee Stock Ownership Plan (ESOP), and they wouldn't have to pay a dime for their share of ownership.

CHAPTER 20

BOB'S RED MILL

W HEN MOORES' FLOUR MILL CELEBRATED ITS ONE-YEAR ANNIVER-
sary in May, 1980, Bob, who carefully wrote on a calendar every
day's revenue figures, noted the company was averaging $951 a day in
sales. They ended that calendar year with $266,552 in total sales, with
nearly twenty percent of that in wholesale sales to local grocers like
Zupan's, Corno's, Spicer's, and Sheridan Fruit.

The potential for wholesale to grow was evident, and Bob recognized
he would have to add capacity to keep up with increased demand. He
needed another set of millstones. Maybe two. At the time, most centu-
ries-old millstones in America were part of historic museum exhibits or
buried in decaying flour mills long ago abandoned. That didn't deter
the determined miller in his quest to find and own one or two of these
ancient relics. In his research, he had discovered that as late as the 1890s,
there were 187 operating flour mills in Oregon. So, he did what he loved
to do – grab Charlee and go on a road trip to visit old mills. It was on one
of those driving excursions that the couple stumbled upon a rundown
mill near Dufur, Oregon.

"We had stopped at this old store for an ice cream, and on one of the pillars was a newspaper article about this mill. I read it and asked the storekeeper where it was. They told me right up the road on 15-Mile Creek. We drove over there, and I didn't see it right away because the mill was down in a draw where the water was. I trotted over, jumped up on this little porch thing, looked through the windows back in there, and saw that mill. I had never seen a derelict building with a completely intact stone mill. I could not believe it. In fact, to me, the whole thing was kind of mystical. It's right there — completely intact! Covers on it, hopper on it; sitting there, absolutely complete. My heart just went pitty-pat. I just couldn't hardly believe it."

It was the Boyd Flour Mill, Bob learned from owner Ted Marvel. The mill had operated there since the millstones came around the Horn in 1870. The operation shut down in 1933.

"Ted said he remembered me from one of the TV stories. He got a key and opened the door to that old mill. Never in my life was I any more

PHOTO CREDIT: MARVEL FAMILY, DUFUR, OR

Boyd Flour Mill near Dufur, Oregon

thrilled at seeing what I saw – a full-fledged flour mill, shut down, sitting there. I said, 'Ted, I just really need to get this mill.'"

Ted was having a hard time parting with the stones, but he agreed to lease them to Bob for $200 a year…for ten years. He had no intention of getting them back; he just couldn't in good conscience sell them.

"I told him it's kind of a crazy way to do it. But the mill was priceless. Plus, I was probably the only person in the entire world that had any use for it."

Bob returned later with Craig and John Bierwagen to haul the equipment back to Milwaukie. It was quite the feat to load the intact two-thousand-pound mill onto their truck. John remembers their relief, almost a giddiness, as on the return trip they couldn't stop laughing about the phrase he had coined: *"Ask not what Dufur can do fer you, but what you can do fer Dufur."*

The large forty-eight-inch stones and the smaller set allowed Bob and Craig to more than double their production. They needed the extra capacity, because heading into 1981, they never again averaged below a thousand dollars in daily sales. Although they were busy, Craig remembers they kept it fun. Years later, he still remembers the little ditty Bob would sing out to lighten any moment:

> Today is the day they give babies away,
> with every pound of tea;
> If you know any ladies who want any babies,
> just send 'em on over to me.

And Craig got a kick out of his partner, who he remembers one day telling him he wanted two things – to be known as the Colonel Sanders of the milling industry, and, to eat all his meals at a restaurant. "I always got a kick out of seeing him come back to the mill after every breakfast, with a cup of coffee – he lived with a coffee cup in his hand – and a little bit of soft egg yolk in his beard."

For those first two years at Moores' Flour Mill in Milwaukie, it was pretty much Bob and Craig who did all the back-end work – anything to do with the mills, equipment, purchasing, cleaning, repairs, etc. Charlee and Gail did the books, handled the packaging, and managed the store up front. They cycled in a half dozen or so part-timers to clean the grain, sweep up, stock shelves, and man the cash register.

But being open six days a week and trying to keep the old mills turning and the antiquated machinery running took its toll. Craig remembers, "I often worked sixteen and twenty hours a day." Bob, then fifty-two, was tired of wearing all the hats of a manufacturing, sales, and retail operation, plus sweeping floors and sacking flour. The two partners decided it was time to hire their first full-time employee.

Bob remembers that day in May, 1981, when he grabbed a manila folder and with a felt pen wrote "Help Wanted" on it. As he was about to hang the sign in the window, the mailman, Paul Geiter, walked in and asked how he was doing. "Well, I'm staying busy running the mills, sacking flour, giving tours, and sweeping floors," he answered. "And it's about time I hired a young man to help out around here."

The mailman thought for a second, and then told Bob he had a nine-teen-year-old son who was looking for work. "Okay, send him down," Bob replied. The "Help Wanted" sign never went up.

Dave Geiter got the job. He was a local kid, born and raised in Mil-waukie, graduated from Milwaukie High School, and attended Multnomah School of the Bible in Northeast Portland for one year before hooking up with a landscaper who couldn't provide steady work. Then, "out of the blue," his dad told him about the opening at Moores' Flour Mill.

The timing, according to Bob, was Providential. "David turned out to be a wonderful lad, hard-working, a charmer. As time went on, I remember looking at him and wondering what he thought about this business. How long was he going to stay with me? I kept waiting for him to quit working for me, and go to work for the U.S. Postal Service like his dad, or get a job at a "real" business. But David just kept working, and I began to believe he was looking to Moores' Flour Mill as a permanent place of employment. Up until that time, I felt my company would be no responsibility to anyone but me and Charlee. I felt I had a good business, an interesting one. But I didn't consider it something I would do for the rest of my life. David changed that."

It could have been the lucky PR that resulted in numerous TV stories and newspaper articles. Or it could have been the print ad they ran every week in *The Oregonian*'s FOODday section. Either way, Moores' Flour Mill was getting noticed. And not just by customers who bought their whole wheat flour, cornmeal, bread mixes, and 10-grain cereal (which were among the forty or so whole grain products the little store carried). Other retailers were starting to pay attention as well.

It was a representative from Fred Meyer, the Oregon homegrown grocery retailer, who came calling first. They wanted to buy Moores' Flour Mill products and sell them under the Fred Meyer Nutrition Center label. Bob told them he wasn't interested. He had a nice little business, and had no intention of expanding into grocery stores. A few months later, Fred Meyer showed up again, a little more desperate. They told Bob the company, Manna Milling of Mountlake Terrace, Washington, from whom they were buying their whole grain products, couldn't fulfill orders in a timely fashion. They wanted to know if Bob thought he could do a better job.

"That was kind of like waving a red flag in front of a bull," Bob remembers feeling about the challenge. "I felt I could always do better."

So, he made a little reconnaissance trip north of Seattle and asked the nice people at Manna Milling for a tour. When he saw they were using a "Meadows" mill, which uses softer stones designed for grinding cornmeal and not whole wheat flour, he knew the operation was in way over its head. No way did they have the capacity to supply all of Fred Meyer's nutrition centers. On the drive back down I-5, Bob's entrepreneurial spirit was tingling. He was basically being invited to double or triple his business. As the mileposts ticked by, he started running the numbers in his head. He'd have to hire some more people. Probably go to a second shift. He needed to find out exactly how many products Manna Milling had been providing and work out his pricing. By the time he crossed the

Columbia River into Oregon, he had made the decision. He would take advantage of the opportunity to supply products to Fred Meyer.

When he got back to Milwaukie, he asked his rep at Fred Meyer if he could see a copy of Manna Milling's order sheet. The March 23, 1982, report listed each of the thirty products Fred Meyer was willing to now buy from Moores' Flour Mill. There were sixteen kinds of flour, including barley flour, buckwheat flour, corn flour, graham flour, oat flour, and wheat flour. There was four grain cereal, seven-grain cereal, soy grits, cornmeal, and raw soy beans. The only items on the list Moores' Flour Mill wasn't interested in supplying were carob chip oatmeal cookie mix and carob brownie mix. Before the deal was done, Bob had added eight more products, including pancake mixes, soup mixes, and oat groats.

With the expansion into private label, Moores' Flour Mill sales soared. Not even a full year into the relationship with Fred Meyer, 1982's year-end sales were up fifty-seven percent over the previous year. And the company nearly hit the one million mark by the end of 1983, along the way earning the "Supplier of the Year" award from Fred Meyer. The only problem Bob had with supplying several dozens of his products to Fred Meyer was there was no mention of Moores' Flour Mill on the packaging. Eventually, he approached Nancy Moon-Eilers, vice president of natural foods merchandising and procurement for Fred Meyer, and proposed putting a Moores' Flour Mill label on his products. She thought it was a good idea. Bob was so excited by the prospect of some brand awareness for his company, he immediately printed a bunch of new Moores' Flour Mill labels. He loaded up the station wagon with boxes of them, and he and Charlee spent the next two weeks driving to every Fred Meyer Nutrition Center in the Northwest. They opened every box of product at every store, took out each bag and applied the new label, and then taped the box shut again.

As tiring as it was, Bob and Charlee had a ball. They loved taking trips by car. They ate in different restaurants, stayed in funky hotels, and just enjoyed being together. They were loving life. They were in their early fifties, some might say the prime of their lives. The kids were all grown, and they were proud grandparents. Frequent trips to Redding to visit family were always happy times. The business was doing great, generating well over a million dollars a year. By this time, Bob and Charlee had been able to exercise their option to buy the property they had been renting. Apparently, the owner was in desperate need of a lump sum of money due to a divorce settlement, so they pulled together twenty-five thousand in cash, and financed the rest with a bank loan. They were less than four years into their new business, and they held the title to the mill property.

It was a heady time. In addition to Fred Meyer, Safeway in Oregon was now purchasing its stone ground flour from Moores' Flour Mill. Franz Bakery, the largest bakery in Oregon, bought flour from them. By 1984, less than two years after hitting area grocery shelves, Moores' Flour Mill products were readily available in stores throughout the Northwest. And beyond.

It was the "and beyond" that tripped him up. Unbeknownst to Bob, some of his products were being shipped to stores in Northern California. Normally, that type of expansion would be welcomed, but with two other Moores' Flour Mills in California – one of which was just trying to get into the grocery channel – it could cause confusion and consternation.

It was one of those perfect storm situations that seemed to hit everyone overnight. Moores' Flour Mill in Milwaukie, Oregon, had just signed on with Oroweat to supply whole grain flour for its bakeries. Oroweat had a thrift store outlet in Chico, not far from Redding. Moores' Flour Mill in Milwaukie, Oregon, had just inked a deal with United Grocers to distribute its line of products. United Grocers delivered to a store in Redding. Fred Meyer, with its dozens of stores in the Northwest, was just opening one of its first stores in California. In Chico.

The timing for both Bob and his son, Robert, was unbelievable. Robert's Moores' Flour Mill in Redding was just in the process of trying to get his product into area stores (Ken's Moores' Flour Mill in Ukiah wasn't selling any product outside its own store). Bob's Moores' Flour Mill in Milwaukie was expanding into retail so rapidly no one knew exactly which stores in which cities were carrying his products.

"I was trying to get into Raley's, and one day I was on the phone with the buyer," relates Robert of Moores' Flour Mill in Redding. "When she came back on the line, she says, 'Oh, we're already carrying Moores' Flour Mill products.'"

Indeed, they were. United Grocers had just delivered a shipment of Moores' Flour Mill products from Milwaukie, Oregon. When Bob learned about the mix-up, he was aghast. That incident became the impetus for a name change. He toyed with Moores Natural Foods, but settled on Bob's Red Mill Natural Foods.

"When my dad started his business up in Oregon, he asked if I minded that he use the Moores' Flour Mill name," Robert says. "You know, there were some advantages to it because we could go in together and buy things like printed bags, which were sold in large minimum quantities; and so, for a while, we were both Moores' Flour Mill. And it was fine, as long as he was up there and I was down here. But we both were growing, and suddenly we had this conflict down here."

Bob was so troubled that the foray into his son's territory could have been perceived as purposeful that he immediately drove down to Northern California to remove his Moores' Flour Mill products from store shelves. "I wanted to dig a hole and crawl in it," he says. "It was awful; a terrible situation."

"Once Dad came up with the Bob's Red Mill name, we didn't have that kind of conflict," Robert explains. "I totally pulled out of retail and am now in a compatible business with him. It's worked out as a better opportunity for me to supply him with some things, like our granola, which he has been good enough to include in his product line. We make it, and he markets it. It's a good deal for us." Robert estimates Bob's Red Mill makes up at least ten percent of his business today.

Now that the name change was completed, and the conflict of interest averted, Bob set about creating awareness for the new brand, "Bob's Red Mill," and taking the business to the next level. He hired a broker, a pretty common practice for growing companies, named Phil Bayha, and it was Phil who convinced Bob that calling the company "Bob's Red

Mill" was a smart idea. "I thought it was awful," Bob admitted. "I mean, what about the public's perception of using the most common name in America?"

Apparently, they liked it. Sales in 1985 were up sixteen percent over 1984. They hit $1.4 million by end of 1986. And Bob's name was becoming well known nationally in the milling industry, thanks in no small part to his mentor, Dewey Sheets.

CHAPTER 21

MONEY MATTERS

I T WAS DEWEY WHO RECOMMENDED BOB MOORE TO BOB EVANS.
Bob Evans Restaurants was a chain of hundreds of restaurants, primarily on the eastern side of the United States, owned and operated by Bob Evans. After he suffered a heart attack in his late sixties, his doctors told him he needed to change his diet and lifestyle. They specifically told him to eat more whole grains. Not known as a man to do anything halfway, Bob decided he would not only eat more whole grains, he would build his own mill on his property in Rio Grande, Ohio, to grind his own flour. When he researched who in the United States was *the* expert who could help him build a mill, the name Dewey Sheets kept coming up. Bob contracted with Dewey to scour the country to source the best millstones and equipment, and make provisions to have everything shipped to his farm. Sparing no expense, Bob assembled a crew of Amish carpenters to build him a grand oak mill building and some of his farm mechanics to set the stones. When it was all done, there was only one problem – the millstones didn't work right. Bob tried to convince Dewey to come out and fix it, but Dewey, now in his late eighties, declined. Bob, not being one to settle for less than the best, asked Dewey if there was

anyone else in the country as good as he was, someone who could come to Ohio and get his mills working. Dewey told him there was only one guy – Bob Moore from Oregon. Bob Evans immediately made plans to fly out to Portland with Dewey to meet this so-called mill expert.

Bob and Charlee had a nice 4,500-square-foot home at the time, and offered to host their two guests. When they arrived, Bob ushered Dewey to the nicest guestroom with its own bathroom, and gave Bob Evans the small bedroom with the bathroom down the hall. Dewey was mortified. He was a humble man and obviously uncomfortable getting better treatment than the big shot with whom he was traveling. Dewey tried to explain to his host that Bob Evans was a very important person, a very rich man, and he deserved to have the biggest and best room. But Bob would have nothing of it. "You're my friend, this is your room," he told Dewey.

Bob Evans and Bob Moore would get along famously. "His ego barely fit through my front door, and he spent most of his time in Milwaukie trying to impress me," Bob remembers. "But after he showed me these catalogs and pictures of his thousand-acre farm, mansion, and horses and stuff, I started to get a grasp of just how wealthy this guy was, but it didn't change my mind about the sleeping arrangements."

A couple of weeks later, Bob got a call from Bob Evans, asking him to fly out and help get the mills working. Bob said he would, under one condition – that Charlee go with him. Bob Evans resisted paying for two airline tickets, but when Bob told him, "My wife goes everywhere with me, so…," Bob Evans relented.

When they arrived at the Homestead, as Bob Evans' home was called (the brick farmhouse is listed on the National Register of Historic Places), Bob thought it looked like a Louisiana plantation. "It was huge! Really, really something. With a big pool out back. And they had a maid, a butler, a cook. They gave us the guest quarter, which was literally a quarter of the entire house. Of course, I had put Bob up in this dinky little room with a single bed. We really laughed about that."

Bob and Charlee spent ten days at the Homestead. While Bob got two of the six mills operational, Charlee enjoyed Jewell Evans' company and hospitality. Bob had to dress and re-dress all the stones, and was at least able to show the mechanics the proper way to do it. He also had them replace several pieces of faulty equipment. One day, while they were waiting for some pulleys to be delivered, Bob Evans invited Bob to go horseback riding with him.

"Now, I didn't know the first thing about horses; I'm actually very uncomfortable around them, but I think he just wanted to show off. He introduces me to his horse keeper, a beautiful blonde; she looked like she might have won the Miss America pageant. She gets us three horses, and we ride over hills and across all of Bob's property; and even I could recognize this horse was magnificent. We were gone a couple of hours, and we had a lovely time. It was just delightful."

When they got back to the barn, Bob Evans asked the young lady to get back up on the horse Bob had been riding and "show him what the horse can do."

"So, she gets up on the horse – it's a cutting horse – and, of course, none of this stuff means much to me. Bob is just having a ball trying to impress me. She's riding back and forth, doing all this crazy stuff, jumping around and all. It was just astounding how responsive this horse was. When we got back to the house, and we're sitting in Bob's beautiful oak den, he reaches over, opens up this magazine to the center spread, and says, 'Here's the horse you were riding.' I think the magazine was called *Cutting Horses*. The headline read "Horse of the Century," winner of all these awards. It's the horse I was on. Bob got such a kick out of it. He had a lot of money and a big ego, and he liked people incredibly well. He liked me, too. We had a lot of fun together."

Before Bob and Charlee left, Bob Evans said he needed to go to Cincinnati and he wanted Bob to go along. When they got to the capital city, Bob Evans said he wanted to introduce Bob to a friend of his, the governor of Ohio.

"I said, 'Bob, *you're* going to meet the governor, and I'm going to wait for you right here in this bookstore.' There wasn't a reason in the world for me to meet the governor, except maybe for Bob Evans to show off. I just wasn't interested. So, I never did meet the governor of Ohio…but I could have."

Asked what princely sum Bob Evans must have paid the country's top milling expert to get the six sets of millstones operational, Bob gets somewhat indignant.

"I wouldn't let him pay me anything, except reimbursing me for the airfare. I told him I didn't want his money; I didn't need his money. If I had taken his money, it would have belittled me in his eyes. I could tell. I was an entrepreneur, he was an entrepreneur. In all ways we were equal, he just had more money than me. I wanted to be equal, and I was equal by not taking any money."

Moores' Flour Mill was generating more than a million dollars a year in revenue. Bob and Charlee had a nice five-bedroom home. They had traveled to Europe and the United Kingdom on vacation. They had nice cars. Financially, they were doing fine. But not even a consulting fee for his expertise?

"My time was valuable, of course, but for what? Isn't the goal of life to do what you want to do? That time with Bob and Jewell Evans was fun. It gave me some new insights on life and some new experiences. It didn't have anything to do with money. To me, life isn't about the process of accumulating money, because you can't take it with you when you die."

It's not that Bob wasn't a capitalist. There's no doubt he was in business to make a profit. He loved making payroll each month to provide for his employees. But he stopped short when it came to loving money for money's sake.

"Sometimes, people misinterpret the Scriptures when they say, 'Money is the root of all evil.' That's not what the Bible says. It says '*the love* of money is the root of all kinds of evil.' (I Timothy 6:10, New Living Translation) I don't have a problem with making or having money, as long as it is managed well. But I've never been interested in accumulating wealth. I was totally happy coming back from being with Bob Evans in 1986 or '87 and being a little entrepreneur. But I was just as independent as anybody could be. I would rather have a little corner in the world that is mine than have the whole world."

Money really didn't matter to Bob, and it cost him dearly. For the first several years in the new business, he and Charlee paid all the company's bills out of their own pocket. In retrospect, that was a big mistake. Instead of running everything through the business, they used their own personal money for most transactions. And their accounting procedures were lax, at best. They had kept their same accountant from Redding, so at the end of every month, Bob would send him an envelope with his ledger of accounts receivable and accounts payable, his bank statements, and payroll information. Three or four months later he would get the reconciled packet back. In the meantime, all the financial knowledge he had to go on was in his checkbook. If he had a positive balance, he could go buy a load of wheat. If not, he figured he couldn't afford it.

"I made the mistake of treating the business like a baby. You don't expect anything out of a baby. You just nurse it, feed it, change its diapers, and put it to bed. But you don't expect anything from it, and that's the way I ran the company in the early going. I was paying all the bills with our own money, and trying everything in my power to make it look like the business was profitable, but that was really stupid. I was probably thinking about the bank, and maybe my own pride."

Later, he discovered if he had run all the income and expenses through the business, and showed a loss when there truly was a loss, he and Charlee would have been in a much better tax situation.

Mary Bierwagen remembers those days when she didn't get a monthly check, but was paid "under the table." Granted, she was only twelve years old when she started working Saturday mornings at Moores' Flour Mill. Her dad, John, had helped renovate the mill (and gave Bob an early financial boost with a $5,000 loan), and her brothers Mike and Mark worked there as well.

"I did everything, everything the adult ladies could do," Mary remembers. "I did packaging and ran the cash register. Bob taught me how to count back change, and I have done that ever since. Not just,

'Here's your $7.24,' but counting back their change if they gave me a ten- or a twenty-dollar bill."

An independent youngster (Bob called her a fireball), Mary bought all her own clothes starting when she was twelve. She got twenty dollars cash from Bob every Saturday, earning more money in a year than probably any other twelve-year-old girl in her neighborhood. By the time she turned sixteen, she could afford to buy a car.

Turns out Bob was selling a car – a 1975 Mercury Comet, white on the outside, pea green on the inside – and Mary bought it for eight hundred dollars. She financed the purchase through the bank, agreeing to a ninety-one-dollar-a-month loan repayment plan. She was so proud of herself driving that car to work the next Saturday, knowing she had worked hard for four years to be able to pay for it on her own.

A week later, the transmission went out. The cost to repair it was almost as much as she had paid for the car. "Okay," she told herself, "this is my responsibility; I'll pay for a new transmission."

The next Saturday when she showed up for work, Bob looked out in the parking lot, and not seeing the white Comet, asked why she didn't drive it to work that day. She hemmed and hawed, knowing the inevitable if Bob were to find out what happened, and desperately not wanting that to happen. Finally, Bob badgered it out of her.

"Well, I didn't know I sold you a car with a bad transmission," he said. "I'll pay for the repairs."

"No!" Mary replied. "You won't. It's my responsibility."

The sixteen-year-old and the fifty-something-year-old argued. She wanted to be all grown up and pay her own way. He felt bad for her, wanted to make it right. Neither would relent. They finally agreed to disagree.

Mary, still defiant at the end of her shift, gathered up her things and headed out. Bob didn't say anything. When she got home, she looked in her purse, and there was eight hundred dollars cash.

"I didn't know what to do," the now forty-four-year-old mother of four would say. "My mom said I should just keep it, but I didn't want to. I didn't think it was Bob's problem. I wanted to do it by myself.

Ultimately, I did keep the money, but I still remember being troubled by that."

Mary's older brother, Mike, also had an encounter with Bob that involved a car transmission, albeit on a much lighter note. He worked there six years, and, like his sister, had earned enough money to buy a car – the sporty Datsun 280ZX. He loved racing around in it, and carefully parked it across the street where no other vehicles could put a ding in it. As he was leaving work one day, he put the car in reverse, stepped on the gas...and nothing happened. The engine revved, but the car didn't move.

"I freaked out, just panicked, because I didn't have the money to replace the transmission," he remembers. He ran back into the mill, and announced to Bob and Craig, "My transmission is stripped!"

Their howls of laughter brought him back from the edge of despair. As they followed him back out to his car, chuckling all the way, Mike could see his back tires spinning. A closer examination revealed the problem, more accurately, the practical joke. Bob had used a portable lift to raise the back end about a half inch off the ground.

"He was always doing stuff like that," Mike goes on to say. "Even though I was only about seventeen or eighteen at the time, when we were working with Bob, he was just one of the guys. He was just us, you know. He loved us. He and Charlee are just wonderful human beings."

Mike was the first employee Bob ever sent out on sales calls. "It was quite a rush when you're an eighteen-year-old or nineteen-year-old kid, and you walk into a store, trying to sell a product you believe in, but you don't know if anyone else does, and they do, and they want to buy it. You go back and tell Bob, and you get this grin, and he winks at Craig. I mean that was huge for me. That was a memorable moment for me."

The three Bierwagen kids, their friends the Shermans (Dave, Steve, and Carol), and a dozen or so full-time employees stayed very busy through the end of 1987 and into 1988. Money was rolling in in record-breaking fashion. Sales topped $1.6 million in 1987. With his first-ever $200,000 months (March and May), Bob was predicting going over the $2 million mark in 1988.

The crew that got the mill running on Roethe
Road in Milwaukie, Oregon

One of the reasons sales were booming was what has been coined "the oat bran craze" that swept the country in the late 1980s. Historically a feed for livestock, particularly horses, oats earned a health-food label for humans, primarily due to the discovery of its cholesterol-lowering properties. They are also recognized for containing more soluble fiber than any other grain, resulting in slower digestion and an extended feeling of fullness. Moores' Flour Mill was selling tons of oats packaged as rolled or steel cut for hot cereals, included as ingredients in cold cereals like granola and muesli; ground as oat flour; and used in a variety of baked goods such as oatmeal cookies and oatcakes.

And when reports came out that oat bran (the outer casing of the oat) was believed to lower LDL (the "bad") cholesterol and possibly reduce the risk of heart disease, manufacturers couldn't produce enough of the stuff to meet consumer demand. The food fad was short-lived and faded by the early 1990s, but it spiked a tremendous growth spurt for companies like Bob's Red Mill and Moores' Flour Mill in Redding. It didn't hurt that TV celebrities like Johnny Carson poked fun at the fad. In one of his Carnac jokes, Carson asked to name three things that tasted like oat bran. The answer? Sawdust, old socks, and oat bran.

The Moore family had been making and selling oat bran since they opened that first mill in 1974. In fact, Robert fancies he may have invented it. "I had never seen it anywhere else," he recalled. "It was just one of those little things we put out on our shelf in the store."

In Robert's opinion, it was the oat bran craze that woke the sleeping giants like Quaker Oats and General Mills, and forced them to start paying attention to health foods. "I think that was one of the first things that really lit a fire under these big companies. A lot of these whole grains and all of this organic stuff were just kind of under the radar, made by these little mom and pop outfits. And when oat bran caught fire, I believe it was actually Quaker Oats who instigated all of this research on cholesterol and what not. That made things just absolutely take off. It felt like we were on a merry-go-round. Suddenly, every company in the world that was making anything edible had to have oat bran in it. Oats got scarce, so we were bringing containers in from Australia, South America, and England. We went through hundreds of truck loads of oats from all over the world to meet the demand for oat bran. It seemed like it was all we were doing here for a couple of years."

In early 1988, Bob had so much oat bran in the mill he had to rent additional warehouse space across the street to store it all. It was on one of his oat bran delivery trips to his dad's operation that Robert made the comment, "one of these days the fire marshal is going to come in here and close up this old building." Bob took note, and decided to get a bid on a fire sprinkler system. In fact, the paperwork was on his desk on June 14.

CHAPTER 11

THE FIRE

J UNE 14, 1988, STARTED OUT AS A GREAT DAY FOR DAVE GEITER. HE
had taken time off from his mill room duties that morning so he and
his wife could sign a thirty-year mortgage on a house. He and Eileen had
been scrimping and saving for five years in anticipation of this monumental day. To them, signing those papers meant their dream to have
kids would be realized. It put into motion their plan to have Eileen quit
her job at U.S. Bank and be a stay-at-home mom. It represented their
secure future, because Dave had just celebrated his seventh anniversary
working for Bob; and as the company's number two man in seniority, he
envisioned a long and stable career as a miller of flour. Besides, with the
new bonus program Bob had announced two weeks earlier, the Geiters
were anticipating at least another thousand dollars a year in income.

Back at work after signing his life away, Dave was as happy as he had
ever been. A reserved and intense sort, he managed a wide grin when Bob
congratulated him with an enthusiastic handshake and a chummy slap
on the back. It was a great day all around. Bob's partner, Craig, was sun-
ning himself on some beach in Hawaii, on his honeymoon with his new
wife. His crew was hitting on all cylinders in his absence, basking in the

glow of the promising message freshly posted on the bulletin board that kicked off the new financial incentive program for the rest of the year.

Essentially a profit-sharing structure, the memo outlined how each employee would receive a penny-per-hour bonus for every $25,000 in gross sales over the previous year's total sales. At the rate current sales were going, he told his employees they could expect a five-hundred-dollar bonus for the second half of the year. Bob felt an "open book" management style was the best motivator, so he regularly posted the company's sales figures on the bulletin board. "That way," he wrote in a memo, "everyone will be aware of how we are doing, and you can watch our growth in a more personal way." He went on to report that "as of June 1, here's where we stand: Last year (1987) to date, sales were $630,549; this year to date, $898,349. This is a forty-two-percent increase over 1987, so the bonus figures would be somewhat higher than I have indicated if we keep up our present sales." He signed off with "Thanks, and good luck to us all!"

To the employees, bullet point number five of the memo was their favorite:

> This program will net a full-time employee a bonus of approx-
> imately one thousand dollars at the end of a year. As sales
> increase, this figure would naturally continue to rise.

They especially loved that last part, because every year (and almost every month), sales had gone up. They could almost count on it. Bob was pleased, too, as at the end of that Tuesday workday he checked the month's revenue to date – $92,433. Almost halfway through the month, and June was on track to be the third $200,000 month in the company's history, the third in the past four months.

While Tuesday, June 14, seemed to be such a great day, Wednesday, June 15, 1988, would be remembered as the worst day in company history. The fateful day kicked off shortly after midnight with a report of a fire at Moores' Flour Mill. David Noble, a security guard for U.S. Protective Services, was making his rounds at the nearby Bob Frink Nissan car dealership when he saw the smoke and called 911. Nancy Winston, an employee at Moores' Flour Mill, lived around the corner from the mill and was awakened by the first siren. She saw flames shooting out of the building's roof, and immediately called the Moores' home number. Nobody answered, so she left an urgent message. She later learned the Moores had recently remodeled their home and had yet to install a phone in their bedroom. Charlee heard the ringing and went upstairs to listen to the recorded message. Less than a minute later, the phone rang again. This time, Bob answered. It was a 911 dispatcher – she happened to be the sister of Dave Sherman, a worker at the mill. As she was monitoring the Clackamas County police and fire emergency calls, she picked up on the location and overheard the reference to "the old mill." She called immediately to deliver the devastating news to her brother's boss.

"Hello," Bob said.

"Oh Bob, I hate to tell you this, but we have a two-alarm fire at your mill. I'm so sorry."

The blood drained out of his face, as he replied, "I'll be right there."

Charlee wanted to come, but Bob was already in the truck and backing out the driveway. Their house was located a mile north of the mill in a nice section of Milwaukie. As he headed down the street, a gasp escaped him. At first he saw the smoke. Big billowing clouds of darkness tinged with an amber hue. And as his gaze focused on the site of his and Charlee's livelihood, he could see the orange flames reaching for the midnight sky.

A few minutes later, Charlee got in the car and experienced the same unfolding drama that her husband had seen. As if on automatic, the car followed the familiar route to the mill. Her thoughts were lost in the frantic fever of what would be revealed to her in just a few minutes.

When Bob arrived on the scene, several fire trucks with their red lights flashing were piled up on the narrow side street, blocking the road and his view of his building. All he could see were flames painted against a dark background beyond the red trucks. Other vehicles – must be police cars, he thought – were haphazardly arranged in front of him with their headlights pointing in all directions, casting eerie shadows as firefighters with long hoses were making their way to the burning structure.

When he maneuvered his way through to the front, he could see clearly what was left of the building. It was disappearing before him with a whoosh and a roar. As he watched, a portion of the roof and two walls collapsed in front of him. When Charlee caught up with him, they both tried to edge forward to get a closer look, but emergency personnel held them back.

"We were in shock, I think," Bob relates, reliving the awful moment. "You know, it's kind of like all your body juices are dried up. I think we were so numb that we weren't crying. I'm not so sure. Anyway, we cried though. Charlee and I, we definitely did have some, I guess, good moments. I don't know what kind of moments they were, but we were sure glad we had each other, I know that. Really glad we had each other."

As they stood there, hugging each other and witnessing their dream incinerating, two hands reached out to touch them. It was Dave and Eileen Geiter. Someone had called to tell them about the fire. At 2 a.m., they drove over from Clackamas and stood next to Bob and Charlee. As they tried to console the Moores, they couldn't help but think less than twenty-four hours earlier they had signed papers committing themselves to a thirty-year mortgage. Later, as they tarried a bit longer on the perimeter of the fire scene, they wondered if they should go back to the bank later that morning to see if they could cancel the deal. Not knowing if their dream of home ownership was morphing into a nightmare right before their eyes, they finally left and drove back to their little apartment.

As the Moores huddled together, alone now with their thoughts, and framed by the streams of water still trying to douse the flames, they were independently thinking the same thing, "How in the world did this happen?" Wracking their brains, they played out in their minds the final hours of that working day. It was only five or six hours earlier, but did anyone smell smoke? Could someone not have extinguished a cigarette out on the loading dock? Were any of our electrical cords frayed? Loose wires? What about spontaneous combustion? It had been an unseasonably hot June day, and flour mills have been known to explode when fine particles of grain or flour dust are suspended in air and ignite (a gigantic explosion of flour dust destroyed a mill in Minneapolis in 1878, killing eighteen workers at the Washburn 'A' mill). Was there a spark that had inadvertently ignited a fire? Yes, the Moores would later learn, there was a spark. But there wasn't anything inadvertent about it.

It was nearly four-thirty in the morning, and everything that could be done had been done. More than forty firefighters from Gladstone, Milwaukie, Portland, Clackamas, and Oregon City fire departments had responded to the alarm. It was one of the area's largest fires of the year, and it took them over two hours to suppress. Fire Marshal Hart encouraged Bob and Charlee to go home and get some rest. They could come back later to see if any of the three millstones had been saved. Pretty much everything else was lost, he told them.

Hand in hand, they turned away and walked to their vehicles. Bleary-eyed and smelling of smoke, they held each other close as they thought about their mill. It was reminiscent of a summer day almost ten years earlier. Back then, they had just discovered the old mill building and were dreaming about starting over in the flour milling business. A decade ago, as they walked hand in hand back to seminary school, they had wondered what the future might hold for them. Just like on that fateful day, as he squeezed his wife's hand, Bob looked back at the mill one more time. Shaking his head, he turned away, got into his truck, and Charlee followed him home. When they got there, he remembers the moment: "We spent some time praying and just holding each other; not knowing what tomorrow would bring."

Around 5 a.m., the fire marshal cut loose the Gladstone crew, so warehouseman and volunteer firefighter Dean Hauck drove the truck back to the station. Buoyed by the adrenaline rush of just having battled one of the biggest fires of his life, he immediately started cleaning up the truck, refilling air tanks, wiping off masks, and getting everything ready for the next call. When he got home, it was around 7 a.m., so he showered, got dressed, and did what he usually did on a weekday – he went to work. The warehouse was across the street from the burned-down mill, so maybe, he thought, Bob would pay him for a couple of hours to wrap things up. Then he could start looking for another job.

The rest of the team at Moores' Flour Mill wasn't so lucky, except for Bob's partner, Craig, who was honeymooning in Hawaii and was oblivious to the disaster. He didn't find out about the devastating fire until his new sister-in-law told him when she picked the newlyweds up at Portland International Airport three days later. The employees who had enjoyed a peaceful night of slumber were in for a rude awakening. When they arrived at the work place, they discovered the entire lot was cordoned off with yellow police tape. Poking around the blackened structure were investigators from Oak Lodge Fire Department and Oregon State Police. What surprised the handful of employees who were held back by a couple of Clackamas County sheriff's deputies was the presence of the U.S. Department of the Treasury's Bureau of Alcohol, Tobacco, and Firearms. The feds were on the scene? That seemed odd to the young millworkers. What they didn't learn until later was ATF and the local authorities were hot on the trail of a serial arsonist. Turns out the mill fire fit the model of several other deliberately set blazes in the area.

The days after the fire were surreal to Bob. Did this really happen? Am I finished? Odd thoughts shot through his mind from dawn to dusk. When he came back to the scene later on the day of the fire, he walked around in a daze. Dean described him as being very quiet. That definitely wasn't normal. Dean and Bob set up temporary quarters in the ten-thousand-square-foot warehouse across the street. There was an inventory of oat bran and finished product stored there, pallets of cellophane bags filled with whole wheat flour, oats, corn meal, and mixes ready for delivery to area grocery stores. Moores' Flour Mill had been manufacturing about 120 different whole grain products at the time, and a smattering of the final batch of production was housed in the safe environs of the concrete storage building. Bob could take some solace in knowing he wasn't completely wiped out. Oddly enough, one of the items that survived the fire was the company's ledger he had meticulously written sales figures in every day. Somebody had found the charred notebook in an area that used to be the office. The hardbound cover was black from smoke damage, except for a round circle of white in the middle of it. The ever-present coffee cup that Bob carried was gone, but at least now he knew where he had left it.

Carefully opening the thick notebook of singed paper calendar pages, he turned to June, 1988. He noted June 14's retail sales of $541, and wholesale sales of $153, for Tuesday's total sales of $694. Then, in capital letters he filled in the Wednesday, June 15 box with the letters F-I-R-E. No sales were logged on June 16. But, interestingly, two days after the fire, there was a nine-dollar sale.

A few of his employees showed up to help Bob sift through the charred ruins. The others drifted away to look for work elsewhere. With gloves and masks protecting them from the soot, workers used crowbars, sledge hammers, and shovels to tear down what was left of the building.

Bob's calendar somehow didn't get burned up in the June 15, 1988, fire

Bob was right there in the middle of the demolition crew, carting blackened pieces of wood and debris into piles that a tractor later loaded into a truck for disposal. There was nothing haphazard about his approach. Profusely sweating in the heat of the day, he worked like a man on a mission. Because he was. All he could think about was getting to his millstones.

Clawing through the wreckage with the same driving energy that had built the damn thing, Bob realized he was getting close to where the mill room once stood. He knew, because every small step he took, his shoes were starting to disappear deeper under a covering of wheat. As he shuffled forward, the mound of wheat was over his knees, black on the top, but surprisingly normal-colored underneath. Waist deep, he began sweeping the grain aside in wide swaths. Until he hit something. He didn't even flinch from the sharp pain on the back of his hand as it slammed against the rock-hard surface.

It was a "runner stone," the one-ton rock wheel stacked on top of the lower stationary "bed stone." The two round millstones stood waist high and were about four feet in diameter. As Bob and his crew continued to shovel their way through what was left of the mill room, he was amazed to find out the three mills were salvageable. By a stroke of Providence or sheer luck, thousands of pounds of wheat that had been stored above the mill room came cascading down on top of the giant wheels as the second-story wooden floor burned. The piles of grain were heavy enough to push the fine particles between the grinding surfaces, the iron hoops that surrounded the stones, and the tin covers on top. The fresh grain blanket provided an insulating effect that had protected Bob's cherished millstones from ruin.

Later that week, the 2,000-pound stones were hoisted from their blackened supports and moved across the street to the warehouse. Wood that could be salvaged had been chopped up and hauled away. Then Bob rented a bulldozer and hired an operator who demolished what was left of the fallen building. Because there was a basement – and thus the potential of someone falling in – the fire marshal required dirt be brought

PHOTO CREDIT: © *THE OREGONIAN*, BOB ELLIS

Only the millstones were saved after the June 15, 1988, fire

in to fill in the hole to alleviate any safety hazard. Soon, all that was left was the cement foundation.

Late one afternoon when the Cat, the trucks, and the demo crew were finally gone, Bob found himself alone on the barren lot. As he circled the bruised foundation, his thoughts took him back to that glorious July day almost ten years ago when he walked around the old feed mill for the first time. He remembered the trembling feelings of a decade ago, the pleasant ache in his gut that got him wondering about the possibilities. Tracing the outline of what was once there, his inner voice started up again with those pesky questions. He couldn't help it. It was engrained in him by his father to keep showing up, keep moving forward, no matter what. Yes, thoughts of quitting, of retiring, of doing something else, were swirling around in his head. But so was rebuilding. And starting over. The argument he was having with himself created a tension in his brain that was unbearable. He needed to go home. He needed to talk to Charlee. And to get the tangled mess of conflicting thoughts out of his head, he knew he had to write it all down. Just like he had always done when faced with uncertainty, he would create a list. One column for "pros," the other for "cons." But at the top of this very important list, he had already mentally written down a critical first step. Call Bruce Cullison.

Bruce Cullison was Bob's banker. He worked at the same U.S. Bank where Eileen Geiter was a teller. Since early on in his career, Bob had made it his highest priority to always have a good working relationship with the bank.

In his pocket was the insurance check. There were very few insurance companies around that would even consider offering coverage to a milling operation. Especially fire-prone flour mills housed in old wooden buildings. But Bob had found one – Mill Mutual. The company isn't around anymore, but at the time, they paid out the maximum the fire insurance policy was written for – $155,000. That was all the insurance he had on a business that was doing over one million dollars in annual sales. Even if he did decide to rebuild from the foundation up on the same spot, Bob figured it would cost at least $500,000 for the structure itself. He realized he was totally upside down on that deal.

And there was the matter of the business loan he had with U.S. bank for operations. The balance on his line of credit was $150,000. And that wasn't taking into account the check for $10,000 he had just written to clean up the aftermath of the fire. At best, walking into Bruce Cullison's office, Bob estimated he would still owe the bank $5,000 after handing over the insurance check. Where that repayment would come from he had no clue. Moores' Flour Mill was gone. He had no income. No job. Only the prospect of more debt.

The realization of his situation struck hard when he stepped through the door of U.S. Bank that morning. Entering into that financial institution – committed to paying off his loan – meant he would be walking out with nothing. He would be broke. Finished. At fifty-nine years old, there weren't too many prospects for employment. And there's no pension safety net for entrepreneurs who risk everything to be their own boss. Maybe I could get a job busting tires at Les Schwab, he remembers thinking.

Bob was a familiar face at the bank. Eileen greeted him from behind the counter. Bruce welcomed him and called him over. There was little need for chit-chat. As they sat down in his office, Bob took the check out of his pocket and handed it over. Bruce examined it, looked up, and handed it back.

"The check is made out to you personally, Bob. You need to endorse it."

Bob signed his name on the back of the check and slid it across the desk. Bruce also added his signature, as if to accept payment on the outstanding loan. He then said something so curious that even today Bob shakes his head when he thinks about it.

"So, Bob, would you like me to go ahead and just deposit this in your checking account?"

Maybe the banker didn't understand what he was doing. "No, this should just about pay off my line of credit. That's why I'm here."

"I know why you're here, Bob. But you're going to need this money. So, it'll be right here in your checking account."

Bob couldn't believe what he was hearing. As the gesture of generosity – no, the *risk* of what this man was assuming – began to settle in, he slowly stood and reached over to clasp Bruce's hand. There were no words as each of them shared a silent handshake.

More than twenty years later, Bob still marvels at what a banking relationship used to mean. "That just doesn't happen today. That check would have been cashed and deposited in the bank's account before the door hit me on the way out. Bruce knew I didn't have any collateral, but he had faith in me. As I walked out of there, I slowly began to realize what he must have seen. My collateral was in the Fred Meyer account. It was in the Safeway account and the other grocery stores I supplied."

On July 1, 1988, when Bob penciled in the daily wholesale sales tally of $10,324, he realized he hadn't yet added up the numbers from June. Finished goods stored in the warehouse were still being shipped, but the inventory was drastically shrinking. He had been so preoccupied with the clean-up, the arson investigation, the insurance paperwork, media interviews, and the outpouring of support from the community that he hardly had time to step back and regain his perspective.

So, as he turned back the page in the sooty notebook to June, he marveled at the figures he was adding up: $30,042 on June 21; $25,285 on June 27; June 29, exactly two weeks after the fire, he wrote down $34,616. He usually noted a month's worth of sales on each last day of the month, but this time he was curious about something else. He wanted to know how much money had come in since the June 15 fire. When he added it up, the two-week tally about floored him. Not because of the amount. It was the familiarity of the number. The one that had been bouncing around in his head every time he entertained thoughts about the future; or about walking away from it all. The number was $151,874. It was just enough to pay off the loan. It was symbolic, if nothing else. Plus, when he did total the month, he was amazed to learn at $244,307, it was the best sales month the company had ever experienced. And it gave Bob the incentive to keep his options open.

Of course, since Bruce Cullison hadn't demanded that the loan be paid off in full, Bob realized he had two things going in his favor – time and money. He had the grace of time to pay off his debt, and he had the promise of revenue if he could just figure out how to keep making the product his wholesale customers wanted. And he had another gift he cherished. He had the unwavering love of his wife to sustain him, the backing of his friends, and the encouragement of those around him. Some were employees and regular visitors to the mill store. Others he barely knew, and was touched by their compassion.

One of the groups that surrounded Bob and Charlee with kindness was the Milwaukie chapter of Kiwanis International. The Moores had been active club members for many years, and had developed several lasting friendships. Charlee was the outgoing president of the Kiwanians, as the women were called, and a gentleman named Dennis Gilliam was president of the men's club. Bob and Charlee got to know Dennis and his wife, Marie, quite well, as they worked together on club projects, such as support for a nearby battered women's shelter. It was Dennis and Marie who showed up at the Moores' home the day after the fire to pray and console them. Their bond was so great that two years later, Dennis left a twenty-nine-year career in the printing business to work side-by-side with Bob, first as General Manager and ultimately as a partner in the business, with the title of Executive Vice President of Sales & Marketing.

There were many loyal customers, too, who tracked Bob down to express their feelings and ask about his future plans. One of those regular visitors to the mill was a woman named Lori Sobelson. When she heard about the fire on the news, she said she and her husband were "just heart-broken." The next day they dialed the phone number of the mill and were surprised Bob answered (the company phone rang at the warehouse, as well as the mill).

"I remember so distinctly my husband saying that it sounded like Bob was near tears. We could tell he was very upset, and we really didn't know what to say. We told him we called to let him know we were concerned as customers; that we hoped he would find another way to have a store and see the business come alive again. We said we would be watching, and promised to follow him wherever he went."

Like hundreds of others who had been coming to Moores' Flour Mill for the past nine years, Lori had vivid memories of her experiences there. "It was so unique. The smells. The wooden floor and the old worn-down wooden steps. I would stand and watch Bob mill the flour. One day I asked him if I could have the flour that just came off the millstone, and he said, 'Yeah.' I watched him fill the bag and thought, 'this is so cool.'"

Lori was like many of the other women who shopped at the mill store. She loved to bake. And she would bring her out-of-town guests to meet the friendly miller and take a tour of his pride and joy.

"Over the years, I got to see the business grow like crazy. I became very familiar with the products, and got to know Bob and Charlee pretty well. I bought all my flours and grains there; and fruits, nuts, coconut, and stuff like that, just because most of it was so unique. I would bring my friends from out of town who were big King Arthur flour fans, and they thought Bob's products were great. So when the fire came, oh my gosh, I cried."

Customers like the Sobelsons and the Gilliams, who for years had enjoyed the convenience of buying their old-fashioned oatmeals, pancake mixes, and breakfast cereals from the neighborhood mill store on Roethe Road, now had no other option than to scour the store shelves and bulk bins at Fred Meyer Nutrition Centers looking for the tell-tale stone ground products they knew came from Moores' Flour Mill.

But there was a problem. As those bulk bins emptied, there was no more product to fill them back up. Well, not exactly. There were no more *Bob's Red Mill* branded products to replenish the stock. But there were some other locally milled flours, grains, mixes, and cereals available. Two competitors in particular had been following the plight of Bob Moore with keen interest. And they were more than willing to step in and not only fill those empty bulk bins with their stuff, they were very interested in talking to the Fred Meyer buyers about replacing Bob's Red Mill shelf presence with their own branded products.

It was the late '80s, and America's eating habits were changing. The fast food craze was finally facing some real competition. The idea of eating fresh, local, and additive-free food was gaining in popularity. It was an exhilarating time to be in the oats and flour business. But with no mill to grind the oats and wheat, and no equipment to package it, was Bob Moore even in the oats and flour business anymore? With no building, did Moores' Flour Mill even exist? And with no money, how were Bob and Charlee going to survive?

A couple days after the fire, thousands of Oregonians who watched Channel 2 news with Paul Linnman heard the answer. As fifty-nine-year-old Bob Moore stared blankly into the camera, he replied to the TV newsman's question about what the future of Moores' Flour Mill might be:

"I really don't know what I'm going to do, Paul. I just don't know."

THE CRX LADY

CRAIG RATZAT KNEW HE DIDN'T WANT TO GO THROUGH THIS AGAIN. He had considered what it would take to rebuild, and then told Bob he wanted out. Bob remembers trying to reason with his partner of nearly nine years. "When he got back in town after the fire, he was really shook up, more so than I think I was. He said something like, 'Bob, I'm out of here.' He had a new wife now, but I talked to him like he was a little kid. I said, 'Craig, you are not out of here. Now that's all there is to it. You're a hard worker. You're an honest man. Give me at least a year.'"

Craig got talked into it. But he had a stipulation. He wanted out of the partnership, to be bought out. And as a salaried employee, he wanted a guaranteed paycheck. He would give Bob one year, not a day more (a year and a day later, Craig went to work for one of their competitors). The two partners settled on a price for Craig's interest. He had paid $1,400 for thirty percent of the fledgling business (and over the years had increased his share of ownership). They agreed on a buyout of $89,000, with monthly payments over a certain term of years. Because of the divorce, half the money would go to his ex-wife. Knowing the straits of Bob's financial situation, Craig agreed to his former partner's request to restructure the repayment schedule and allow him to make interest-only payments until his bank accounts were on a more solid footing. The answer to Bob's same request to Craig's ex-wife Gail arrived in a letter. She would allow him no grace. Ignoring his current financial plight, she demanded he stay current with his principal and interest payments. Bob still burns today over that affront.

There were a lot of reasons to consider just walking away from the business. He was nearly sixty years old, an age at which many men start thinking seriously about retirement. There were business loans, a mortgage, home remodeling bills, and living expenses to consider. Some facing similar financial obligations declare bankruptcy. There would be a tremendous uphill battle to fight to rebuild the business, maintain customers, and recapture market share. Many sixty-year-old businessmen might lack the stamina and fortitude to continue.

As he contemplated these things in the days after the fire, one name kept popping up. He couldn't get Dave Geiter off his mind. He remembered the meal at Sweet Tibbie Dunbar's where he and Charlee had treated the employees to a nice dinner in celebration of a particularly successful week. Dave had brought a new girlfriend, and was excited to introduce her to Bob and Charlee. The Moores were among the many guests who celebrated Dave and Eileen's wedding several months later. That stream of consciousness led to the names of the other employees of Moores' Flour Mill who were caught in limbo. His employees were the most important part of his business. Was he going to turn his back on them, or was he going to keep the team together? Some kind of chemistry was happening in his brain. The cloudy, uncertain future was starting to clear up for him. Dave didn't realize it, but his employ had a profound effect on Bob Moore.

"The night of the fire, David and Eileen were standing there with me and Charlee, and we were talking about our combined future. Over the next several days, I was experiencing such a profound range of emotions concerning David. His presence impacted me and my plans. Because of him, I knew I was going to have to do something to make this business permanent and serious. David was the turning point, one of the main causes of continuing after the fire."

Of course, Bob had other reasons, too. Whether it was the company's financial obligations, the threat from the competition that was nipping at his heels, or his competitive nature, he felt driven to figure out some way to keep the business afloat. Once the decision was made, he had some very pressing issues to deal with.

Safeway had already dropped Moores' Flour Mill as a supplier of whole wheat flour for its bakeries. But Bob still had Franz and Williams, as well as a couple of other small area bakeries. And, of course, there was Fred Meyer. Bob didn't have their bakery business, but, "I really busted my butt to keep their retail." But to keep the Bob's Red Mill brand on the shelves of Fred Meyer Nutrition Centers and the other stores that carried his line of products, he needed to solve his production crisis. Fortunately, due to the company's growth in the first two quarters of 1988, Bob had already commissioned his real estate guy, Don Ossey, to find bigger space in which to operate. That search was accelerated once Bob determined to move forward. The criteria included a minimum 20,000 square feet of industrial space in the Milwaukie area. While Ossey went about his business, Bob got creative on the production side. The three sets of millstones he salvaged were inoperable and would take weeks (if not months) to restore, so he needed a temporary solution. He knew right where some millstones were operating. In fact, he had installed them himself. Bob called his son, Robert, and asked if he could share the use of his mills in Redding. Bob's idea was not to interfere with Moores' Flour Mill's daytime operations, but what about sending someone down to run them at night if they were available? Robert thought that was doable, and was happy to help out.

Bob immediately dispatched Dean, his warehouseman/firefighter. With orders in hand, Dean moved into a spare bedroom at Robert's house, and began the every-night task of milling and mixing products (which Bob bought from his son), packaging them in fifty-pound bags, palletizing them, and shipping them north. Every day, Dean would talk with Bob by phone or receive a fax detailing the night's fulfillment.

"I just told my customers we could fill their orders. It was a day-by-day thing – so much 10-grain cereal, so much Scottish oatmeal, so much this, so much that; and you've got these orders, and it gives you a direction. It gives you a focus; it gives you something to look at. 'Okay, got that done; good. What do we do next? Let's see, well, the next time we get an order for that, we better do such and such.' So, you try your best to focus on what you can do."

That short-term focus, and the team's "can-do" attitude, more than got the company through its most difficult time ever. There was no letdown in orders, and even with no production capacity of its own, Bob's Red Mill (as the company was henceforth known because there was no more Moores' Flour Mill in Milwaukie, Oregon) did something remarkable. The business not only averaged more than $270,000 a month in sales over the last half of 1988, December finished at an all-time high of $322,307, and the year was the company's best-ever at $2,763,384 in total sales.

In the meantime, Ossey had found two contiguous 5,000-square-foot spaces to lease in an industrial complex on International Way in Milwaukie. Across the way, another 20,000 square feet with a loading dock would soon come available, providing the relocated company up to 30,000 square feet.

While Dean spent night after night producing product to ship to the company's warehouse on Roethe Road, Bob and the rest of the crew spent day after day building out a new mill room, packaging area, storage space, office, and storefront. In less than five months, the new facility was up and running. On November 16, just in time for Thanksgiving, Charlee had the Bob's Red Mill store open for business, selling $232 worth of product after a 153-day layoff.

Bob and Charlee had lots to be thankful for that Thanksgiving. Even though they had lost their precious mill in the fire, almost all of their customers stuck with them. There had been enough inventory on hand in the warehouse to fill in the gap between the end of production on June 14 and a few days later when Dean started shipping product from Redding. And Mom and Dad were thankful their son had graciously taken Dean into his family's home and allowed him to run the mills down there at night.

But probably nobody was as thankful (or should have been) as the mentally unstable woman who was suspected of burning down Moores' Flour Mill (an estimated $500,000 worth of damage). She had ultimately been arrested and pled guilty to three felonies and three misdemeanors. In one of the felonies, she admitted to the judge she had deliberately set the July 31 fire that caused an estimated one million dollars in damages to the Vineyard Plaza, a shopping mall less than a mile from Moores' Flour Mill. Her punishment? Probation. And she had to enroll in a year-long behavior-modification center. On the Hawaiian island of Oahu.

Here's what Bob and Charlee learned about the person they suspect is their arsonist:

Kathleen Susan Anders was a twenty-seven-year-old Californian who had spent time there in a mental institution. She lived in a Southeast Portland apartment, and according to a Clackamas County Sheriff's report titled "The Correlation Between Anders and the Alarms from January to May of 1988," she set off at least fifty burglar and fire alarms along McLoughlin Boulevard and 82nd Avenue in Clackamas County.

According to Deputy David Byrne, who worked the graveyard shift for the Clackamas County Sheriff's office, "She was prolific; I don't think she took a day off." She became so familiar to sheriff's deputies they dubbed her the "CRX Lady," because she drove a 1987 silver CRX Honda. In her car she usually carried a crowbar and gloves, sometimes a knife or a pellet gun. But the tool of choice for her trade was usually a large rock she would pick up near her intended target and then throw through a window. She rarely, if ever, entered the premises, and was typically gone by the time the responding officer arrived.

The Field Contact Reports filed by police told the story of her prowling activities: "In area of burglary with crowbar, flashlight and gloves in trunk." "Suspicious vehicle in area of alarm." "Parked at car wash just sitting in car." "Parked behind mower and saw shop." "Stopped at intersection for several minutes." "Out of car behind Sherman Williams Paint store." "Prowling Tiara Spas."

She was, according to Ken Stewart, her attorney at the time, trying to put herself in danger with the police. "I don't think she was trying to harm others, but she was self-destructive. Sometimes when she was carrying a fake gun I believe she was trying to commit suicide by cop." Stewart told the judge at Kathleen's sentencing she had an attention deficit disorder and hyperactivity in an adult state; that she used cocaine; that she started breaking windows because she was bored. Stewart, now a judge with Clackamas County Circuit Court, remembers Kathleen as a delightful, highly educated young woman. He said in his twenty-seven years of private practice, her case was the most bizarre of all. "She drove the cops nuts," he said. He also described her as a very fortunate woman, because her death wish didn't come true.

In the weeks leading up to the fire at Moores' Flour Mill, Kathleen ratcheted up her repertoire. For five months she had been breaking windows, setting off burglar alarms, and getting under the skin of Clackamas County's finest. Her plate glass playground was getting boring.

Like a drug addict who needs that higher high, Kathleen decided to elevate her crime spree to the next level in order to satisfy whatever demon inside her head was telling her to do bad things. So she started setting fires. At first, it was trash cans and dumpsters that she would torch. Several were reported in May and June. But these small contained fires in back lots of businesses along McLoughlin and 82nd didn't bring out the armada Kathleen was expecting. There was more fizzle than flair to these backyard bonfires. Sure, she would light some paper and boxes on fire and watch them burn. But, dammit, where were the firemen and their big red trucks with the loud horns and blaring sirens? She would just have to show them she meant business. So the next time she fired up one of those dumpsters, she pushed it up against the wall of the building.

Oh, she kept up her old habit, too. She just added the new twist to keep it exciting. On the ninth of June she threw a rock through the front window of J.P. Services, Inc., and for good measure came back two nights later and blasted another one. She hit Tech Audio a second time, too. Her hit list also included Far West Federal Savings, Champion Auto Parts, Oak Grove Disposal, Discount Tire Center, Associated Body & Paint, Smith Brothers Photo Supply, Scotsco, Neighbors Pharmacy, and Tiara Spas (twice). And these are just some of the businesses she ultimately admitted to burglarizing. She even tried to break into Wiley Security, the company who serviced the alarm systems in most of the buildings she damaged. No word on what she hoped to accomplish by sneaking into the alarm company she kept so busy, but she told the arresting officer she "was walking in the area and may have bumped against the door."

Bob Moore doesn't know how many times his and Kathleen Susan Anders' paths must have crossed. But they surely did. With all the early morning commuting she did from Multnomah County to Clackamas County, she, too, must have been a regular customer at the Bomber. Undoubtedly, while she was there gassing up the Honda after a night of her favorite activity – target practice along McLoughlin's window pane alley – Bob and the boys were inside the restaurant having breakfast. As an early riser, Bob must have driven past the CRX Lady countless times as he headed south on River Road or McLoughlin Boulevard on his way to the mill, just as Kathleen was wrapping up her nightly ritual and driving north on one of those two roads that led back to her Southeast Portland apartment. Both knew for sure she had been on Roethe Road, and specifically, right across from Moores' Flour Mill. On June 12, sitting in Deputy Byrne's patrol car right down the street from Roethe Road, Kathleen admitted to throwing a rock through the front glass door of Sassi Chassi. The back part of that building was used as warehouse space for Moores' Flour Mill.

Technically, Kathleen was never accused or convicted of the June 15 arson fire that destroyed Moores' Flour Mill. She did admit to parking across the street from the mill about 2:30 a.m. on May 21, and setting off the burglar alarm in the building adjacent to the mill warehouse. After midnight on June 12, she got pulled over on River Road at Vineyard (almost rock-throwing distance away from Moores' Flour Mill) and confessed to more than twenty acts of criminal mischief in the area. Shortly after midnight June 14, *someone* pushed a dumpster up against the side of Moores' Flour Mill and torched the place. On July 31, a suspect (later determined to be Kathleen) returned to the scene of the 3 a.m. fire set at the Vineyard Plaza, according to James Hart, assistant chief and fire marshal for the Oak Lodge Fire Department. He told a reporter "we are actively looking for links" between that person and the mall fire, as well as several other recent fires that were set in commercial trash bins and dumpsters. *Oregonian* reporter Steven Amick wrote, "Hart stopped short of saying the same person set a June 15 fire" at Moores' Flour Mill. All everyone knew was when Kathleen left Oregon to attend Habilitat on the resort island of Oahu, reports of window breaking and fire setting of businesses in Clackamas County stopped.[6]

All Bob would say about the slap on the wrist the woman he suspects burned down his mill got was, "If she hadn't burned down my mill, I probably would still be operating my little company out of that old building."

The other thing Bob was very thankful for that Thanksgiving was Ossey had found a buyer for his mill property. He had bought it for $95,000, but that was with a building on it. With just a barren lot, he thought he might be able to get $70,000 or $75,000 for it. Ossey got him $165,000.

"Later when we talked about it, I told Don I didn't think the property would be worth as much without that building on it. He said it was worth

---

6 According to Stewart, Kathleen was very open to him in admitting her criminal involvement, but she vehemently denied burning Moores' Flour Mill. Because of her staunch denial, Stewart said he felt comfortable taking the chance to allow federal authorities to give her a lie detector test regarding the mill arson. She apparently passed, because police dropped her as a suspect in that fire. He says he knows that flies in the face of all the circumstantial evidence, adding, "I suppose we'll never really know." What he does know is after Kathleen got out of Habilitat, she was arrested for setting a dumpster on fire near a business in Honolulu. Because this was a violation of her probation, the district attorney's office was going to ship her back to Oregon. Stewart was able to intervene and got her off, as long as she paid restitution. The last he heard, Kathleen had married a Honolulu police officer.

way *more* with that old wooden building gone. 'Bob,' he told me, 'You are the only person in the world who could see any value in that old building.'"

But there was a problem that November. A big one. As soon as Moores' Flour Mill was up and running in suites 5444 and 5446 in that industrial park, Bob knew it. It wouldn't work. It wasn't practical. It wasn't big enough.

"I mean, while we were setting it up, and wiring it, and getting this machine working, and that piece of equipment operational, I was asking, 'Where are you going to put this? Where are you going to put that?' Just as we were moving in, I realized even with the 20,000 square feet across the way, we were in trouble."

Then, seemingly out of the blue, another *John Goffe's Mill* library book moment. Bob was driving up International Way about a quarter mile from his undersized – and definitely interim – location, when he saw a pickup truck parked alongside the road. There was a guy with a posthole digger walking up this grassy knoll by a large building.

"Instinctively, I pulled over to see what he was going to do. And as I was walking past the truck, I looked in the bed, and there was this big sign: FOR SALE – INDUSTRIAL – 50,000 SQUARE FEET."

The wheels started turning immediately. He knew the option of his 30,000-square-foot mishmash of industrial space down the road wasn't going to be viable. But what would he do with a 50,000-square-foot building? That was more than double the size of the combined Roethe Road mill and warehouse. And he should probably lease; he certainly couldn't afford the $900,000 price tag he learned the owners wanted. But, hey, he thought to himself, it won't hurt to look at it.

Walking around that 50,000-square-foot building on International Way in Milwaukie that November of 1988 gave Bob the same kind of butterflies in his stomach he experienced ten years earlier when he and Charlee had stumbled upon the old feed mill on Roethe Road. He hadn't yet called his real estate guy to give him the phone number on the "For Sale" sign, but he knew he would. First, he wanted to get a closer look for himself. What he could see through the windows left him breathless.

"Oh my gosh, look at all that space," he remembers repeating over and over. At every window on the four sides of the tall structure, he would peek in, and exclaim again to himself, "Will you look at all that space!" By the time he got around to the side that had a row of offices with expansive window views, he crossed the line from observer to planner. "Oh my gosh, what do you suppose...?" he asked no one in particular.

As Bob expected, Ossey told him he probably couldn't qualify for a loan on a nearly one-million-dollar real estate transaction. So, he said he would keep looking for him. He also told Bob he wouldn't want the property anyway because of a deal-killing stipulation tied to the purchase agreement. Turns out the land had major environmental issues due to chemical spills that had contaminated the soil. Whoever bought the property would have to pay for expensive environmental studies, most assuredly a costly clean-up, and then spend who knew how many years dealing with the Department of Environmental Quality to get a clean bill of health.

Just months after wrestling with its own disaster, Bob's Red Mill was in no position to tackle another one. But, for some reason, Bob wasn't convinced he should just drop it. He felt compelled to delve deeper into what he couldn't shake was an opportunity looking for a solution. What he discovered would have sent most entrepreneurs running in the opposite direction.

As Bob understood it, Blount Inc., a neighboring manufacturer known in Oregon for making chain saw parts and equipment, expanded next door and built a factory for Red Head Fasteners, a leader in concrete anchoring technology. ITW (Illinois Tool Works) apparently acquired the patent for Red Head Fasteners, renamed the brand ITW-Red Head, and continued making the mechanical and screw anchors on the site. At some point, Toshiba became interested in the property and tried to buy it. But first, they had to conduct an environmental study because of the extensive use of chemicals in the fastener-making process.

"My understanding was that study cost them about fifty thousand dollars, and they found it was just a mess. A total mess. So, they broke the contract with ITW and walked away."

Obviously, if a huge international company like Toshiba couldn't make the deal pencil out, Bob knew a small local business like his didn't stand a chance. Why bother? He obviously couldn't afford the $900,000 asking price; there was no way he could come up with the fifty grand to do his own environmental study, even if he did want to pursue the opportunity. He was way out of his league. But, sometimes the little guy can out-maneuver the big boys. All he had to do was get creative. In his mind, he was committed to getting that building. For his employees. For his customers. For his future.

Of course, he couldn't *buy* the property. If a company as large as Toshiba wasn't interested, probably no one would be. As an astute businessman, Bob knew ITW would ultimately be forced to resolve the contaminated soil issue before they could sell. But, as far as he knew, there was nothing wrong with the building itself. Bob's Red Mill didn't need the couple acres of parking out behind the building; it needed thirty- or forty- or fifty-thousand square feet of manufacturing space.

Every day on his way to work, and then back home again, he would drive by the dormant building. If a man could lust after brick and mortar, Bob would have had to plead guilty. He couldn't stop thinking about the possibilities. One day, as he was driving by, he noticed the Toshiba foreman's truck parked there. Probably just wrapping things up on the deal that went south, he thought. As he walked past the pickup, he looked inside, and there it was. The environmental study. Just lying there on the seat. The foreman was nowhere to be seen. Impulse overtook him, and he peeked inside. Within a few minutes, he had gleaned the information that ITW didn't want any prospective buyer to know. It was worse than anyone imagined; a very serious environmental hazard. It would take many years and many millions of dollars to clean up that poisoned acreage.

"I was there when they finally uncovered one of those great big underground tanks. A four-inch pipe was supposed to be dumping chemicals and solvents from the plant into the tank. But the ground must have shifted or something, because the pipe had come loose from the tank and all this nasty, oily, stinky crap was just oozing right into the ground."

Armed with the information they needed, Bob and Don Ossey contacted Frank Donovan, ITW's land manager, and began negotiating for a lease deal with an option to buy. It was the same kind of arrangement he had had on the old mill property, and it had worked out well when he and Charlee were able to buy it. Frank was actually quite happy someone would consider renting the building. Otherwise, he would be sitting on an empty factory producing no income, while ITW paid millions to clean up the land.[7] Undaunted that the facility was twice the size of the Roethe Road mill, Bob signed a five-year lease, which came with a five-year renewal option. It also included an option to buy the building in the first five years, starting at $1 million and escalating to $1.25 million by 1994 (stipulating, of course, the DEQ had cleared the property).

Sitting in his office within the 325,000-square-foot current home of Bob's Red Mill, Bob says, "I had the same feelings with that 50,000 square feet as I had when I looked at this, walking through this. It was overwhelming for everybody but me. I just knew it was the right size."

For the second time in less than six months, Bob and team moved their entire operation. This time, it was only a couple of blocks, from 5444 to 5209 S.E. International Way. But the one-ton millstones still weighed the same. And the mill room still needed to be built out. There was a lot more room for them, but the packaging lines still had to be installed. The ceilings were about twice as high, but they still had to construct the grain elevators and buckets, as well as the platforms to store the raw products. One of the biggest differences was the large open rooms that would be used for the office and the store. But all the furniture, shelving, equipment, and products still had to be loaded and unloaded.

"I don't know where we found the energy to get that interim space up and running, only to find, like in a month, that it was just too small, that it wasn't going to work. We just couldn't do that much business in

---

7 Bob estimates ITW paid about three million dollars to get a clean bill of health from the Department of Environmental Quality. The clean-up project took more than seven years.

that location. That is all there was to it. Almost at the very moment we got slightly organized at the industrial park, we started moving into the new place. It was ridiculous. You just can't believe how mixed up all this got for a year or two after the fire. I mean, I would wake up in the middle of the night and hear voices in my head, because there was just so much going on. It was crazy. And then we moved into 50,000 square feet. Charlee and I thought, at the time, this property would be all we would ever need for the rest of our lives. But, then, of course, the business starts growing, and growing, and growing."

CHAPTER 24

OFF AND RUNNING

B OB MOORE LOST A LOT IN THE FIRE, BUT NOT HIS LOYALTY TO HIS employees or their commitment to him. He didn't want to lose any of them. All who wanted a job, had a job. A few chose to go in other directions, but in January, 1989, when Moores' Flour Mill started operations in their new building, the core team was intact. Dave Geiter got the new mill room up and running again. The millstones had survived the fire, and were now well into their second century of operation. Dean Hauck had gone from managing a meager 10,000 square feet of warehouse space to triple that in the 50,000-square-foot factory. The packaging crew was stable. And, of course, Charlee capably managed the store and office duties.

The big question mark was Craig Ratzat. He was integral to the business, but had basically given Bob his one-year notice shortly after the fire. He was no longer a partner – more like the plant manager – and was in the process of having his partnership bought out. Bob was hoping Craig would change his mind and stay, but he couldn't gamble on such a key position. He needed to do the prudent thing, and plan for his departure, even while he would do everything in his power to keep him. As the end of a very tumultuous year wound down, Bob welcomed 1989 with great relief. Six months ago, it looked like he was done. The vultures were circling. Other manufacturers wanted what he had – a stronghold in the niche business of supplying whole grain foods to regional grocers. Financially, he had taken a major blow, essentially breaking even with the loss of his building and the insurance payout. Like a boxer, he had to decide whether he was going to get back up after being knocked down and finish the fight.

"When I look back at my life, especially after the fire, I can see moments in time where I just kept pulling the track up and shifting it a little bit this way; and then kind of backing up and putting the track down in a different direction. But as heavy as it was, and as difficult as it was, I was bound and determined to keep showing up, to keep moving forward. I just don't know how in the heck I did it."

Business since June 15 had been a tenuous month-to-month guess as to whether he would keep all his customers and have enough products to keep up with their orders, even if they did stay with him. Entering 1989, he certainly had enough space now to double, or even triple the output. And, because he was in a lucky bargaining position with the beleaguered Frank Donovan of ITW, he and Don Ossey had negotiated three months' free rent on his lease with an option to buy. So, there was some grace in the first quarter of the year that seemed to propel the company forward. Plus, with their windfall profit from the sale of the mill property, Bob and Charlee were in a decent financial position. And, the "oat bran craze" was still peaking, so, fortunately, there didn't seem to be any slowdown in the demand for healthy, natural products. This breathing room provided Bob just what he needed in the second quarter of the year – time to focus on finding a new general manager, someone who hopefully would become his partner.

"I don't mind sharing my life with partners, especially partners who take on a major responsibility in the company. In fact, I've never really been interested in doing this business without competent partners."

A notorious list builder, Bob had written down several names of potential candidates. One, in particular, kept rising to the top. And when he found out Dennis Gilliam was looking for new career opportunities, he pounced. Bob had known Dennis for nine years, ever since he joined the Milwaukie Kiwanis Club in 1980. Dennis, a twenty-nine-year veteran of the typography and printing business, was contemplating a career change in early 1988, and because he admired Bob's entrepreneurial skills so much, he asked him to lunch one day to get his opinion on a touring company he was considering starting. Bob doesn't remember whether he had a strong opinion about the new business idea, but he did tuck away the confidential knowledge Dennis was planning to make a job change.

Their friendship and mutual admiration for each other grew through their experiences in Kiwanis. Bob, a committee chair, had witnessed Dennis's progress as program chair, to overseeing the weekly bulletin, to becoming president, winning a Kiwanis International multiple service award along the way. And it was Dennis and his wife, Marie, who cared enough for Bob and Charlee that they showed up at the Moores' home the day after the fire to share their love and support.

When it became clear to Bob that Craig was not going to hang around a day longer than his one-year commitment that expired in June, he met with Dennis and offered him the GM position. The salary offer was less than what Dennis had been making at Paul Giesey Adcrafters, so they negotiated a bit, and after Bob spelled out the opportunities to earn more, Dennis accepted.

"He was just the guy I needed; a very solid person; and he has been a great blessing to me," Bob praises. "I knew he wasn't going to be a plant manager like Craig, but I had the mechanical skills to handle that side of the business. The company needed his twenty-nine years of sales, marketing, and management experience; and from that standpoint he has done a great job, a super job. It was a marriage made in heaven."

Dennis took the proverbial ball and ran with it. He familiarized himself with all the facets of the business, and honed in on the sales and marketing aspect. He took over the Fred Meyer account. He produced the first mail order catalog. He developed all-new sales and marketing materials. And he helped the company turn the corner by recommending Bob's Red Mill attend a national industry trade show called Natural Products Expo. The twice-a-year show (West is held mid-March in Anaheim, and East usually in September or October) brings together coveted buyers and distributors with manufacturers of natural and organic products. Expo West, which debuted in 1981 with 3,000 attendees, provides mom and pop shops, as well as regional and national players, a platform to promote what's new, and, hopefully, initiate sales.

"We never would have been able to make this company go if it hadn't been for Craig, but I doubt if he and I ever would have thought about going to Expo West," Bob observes. "When Denny and I went down there in 1990, that's really when this company got kick-started."

But first, they needed a trade show booth. Bo Thomas, who had come on board as Maintenance Manager about the same time as Dennis Gilliam, was tasked with building a 10 x 10 booth. He had a background in construction, and sort of a relationship with Bob. Bo had worked for Sassi Chassi, the van conversion company located next door to Moores' Flour Mill warehouse on Roethe Road. He remembers Bob stopping by once on his way to the warehouse and listening to him play the piano (turns out they both played a mean boogie-woogie).

But the impression Bo made on Bob was more vivid. One afternoon, when Bo's wife, Nancy, stopped by Sassi Chassi with their three kids to pick up her husband's paycheck, she took the youngest one into the office with her and left the other two boys in the car…with the key in the ignition. Jared, the oldest, started the car, put it in neutral, and the car rolled backwards down the hill and into a shallow creek. When Nancy came back outside, the car was gone. Bob, who doesn't miss a thing, saw the would-be tragedy unfold from across the street, and noted Bo's calm demeanor when he discovered his boys safely seated in the semi-submerged vehicle.

A couple years later, Bob was on an outing with Charlee to the Oregon coast and stopped at a clock shop in the community of Bellevue near McMinnville on their drive home. In the conversation he struck up with Scottie Glenn, the proprietor, Bob mentioned he had recently lost his maintenance man, and was looking to hire a replacement. It just so happened Scotty was Bo's father-in-law, and he recommended his son-in-law, who was quite the whiz at building things. Bob remembered the calm piano-playing dad, and suggested Scotty have Bo call him. They connected, and over dinner at Tebo's Restaurant in Gladstone, Bo accepted Bob's job offer.

Bo had custom-designed the interiors of hundreds of vans, even an ambulance, over the six years he worked at Sassi Chassi. But he had never built a trade show booth before. The wooden contraption he fabricated "must have weighed a ton," Bob guesses. He had to buy a trailer just to haul the huge panels, and pulled the heavy load in his 1982 Oldsmobile Brougham all the way to Anaheim.

"How does a business grow? You take a chance like Denny and I did. We drove twenty-two hours straight. We never quit. As soon as we got there, we set up that crazy booth in this terrible location they give first-timers – clear in the back of the Convention Center, next to one of those big sliding doors. We had no broker, no distribution system whatsoever. We didn't even have a price sheet; just a printout of our product list. We went down there just to see what the heck it was all about; to get the lay of the land. But what an exciting event it turned out to be! People wanted our stuff!!"

While Charlee and Marie, who had flown down to Anaheim, played tourists, Bob and Denny worked the booth. On the first day of the show, they made a connection that would forever change the complexion of the company.

"Everything was so casual because we didn't have any planned meetings, or even expectations, but I had come back to the booth after walking around a bit, and Denny was all excited, and says, 'Guess what, I found just the right guy for us! His name is Ben Roditti.'"

Later on, when Ben returned to the booth, he shared how his company, Quality Brokerage, had built the nationwide business for Stone-Buhr, a Seattle manufacturer of artisan baking products, and that his firm was let go when Stone-Buhr got swallowed up by a larger outfit. He then proceeded to tell Bob and Dennis how he had gotten all the Stone-Buhr products into nearly every store in America. "I know everything there is to know about those buggers who fired me," he told them. "And I need to be your national broker."

"Of the five billion people on the face of the earth in 1990, Ben Roditti was the *only* person who could pull this off – the only person in the world – and he walked right into our booth," Bob exclaims.

They framed their new broker relationship with Quality Brokerage at the show, and the national push of Bob's Red Mill products across America was under way. The Moores and the Gilliams went to Disneyland to celebrate. Before they left Expo West, they met Suk Lee, who owned Vitamin City, a health food store in San Dimas, California. Mr. Lee "wanted everything we had, so I had to tell him how he could get it," according to Bob. "I told him we could ship product directly to him, but he said it would be better to work through a distributor. When I told him we didn't have one, he said to wait a few minutes; that he would be right back. He came back, dragging one of the buyers from Nature's Best, and told him he wanted our line of products."

Nature's Best, which has become the largest privately owned wholesaler-distributor of health and natural food products in the country, immediately added Bob's Red Mill as a customer, initiating a strong relationship that exists today. Mr. Lee was so excited to learn about Bob's Red Mill, he bought all the products Bob and Dennis had brought as samples to the trade show. That certainly lightened the load for the twenty-two-hour return drive, a ride punctuated with lively discussion about the very bright future of the company.

Dennis sums up that initial Expo West experiment and resulting windfall of new business with, "Nothing ever happens unless you put yourself out there. You've got to put yourself out there."

Buoyed by the success of that first trade show experience, Dennis developed a marketing strategy to mine the resources of other trade-show

opportunities. One that really clicked was the National Food Distributors Association trade show.[8]

"In my first year or two with the company, I thought we would be a
strong regional player, and continue to have good sales. Then I went to
the NFDA show, and that is when, in my mind, I made the transition,
thinking, 'Hey, we can absolutely go national.' All we have to do is put
our head down and plow, and we can take this thing national."

At the show, Dennis was able to set up meetings with distributors
who had relationships with buyers from grocery stores and chains in different parts of the country. He had dozens of fruitful one-on-ones, and
when he got back to the office, Bob asked him to make a presentation to
all the employees, about twenty-five at the time. He taped together about
two dozen sheets of paper, pasted the four-foot-by-four-foot square on
the wall, with notes about each meeting in every eight-by-ten-inch box.
Then he asked people to randomly pick a box, and he would give a run-
down on the specifics of that particular distributor meeting. After about
two hours of hearing all the new business opportunities, the staff went
back to work, awed by the potential.

"That report, I believe, really iced it for the whole company," Dennis
explains, noting Bob's is still working with every one of those distributors
he met with at NFDA. "Everyone believed we could become a national
company with distribution in every part of the country. We were off and
running."

Off and running, but with pennies jangling in their pockets, not
silver dollars. The moving, the rebuilding, the hiring, the new marketing
effort – everything was taking a toll on the company's depleting financial resources. Bob, always the one to write down every single day's sales
numbers on his monthly calendar, had made his last entry on February 8,
1989: $207 in retail sales; $11,195 in wholesale, for a total of $11,402.

---

8 The National Food Distributors Association later changed its name to the Specialty
  Food Distributors and Manufacturers Association, and eventually became part of the
  National Association for the Specialty Food Trade.

Nothing special. Maybe that's why he stopped writing it down. The total for January, 1989, was only $241,210, less than what they sold the month of the fire. It wouldn't be until 1993 that the company would even equal what they did in 1988. It would be five years of tough going.

According to Dennis, "Everything I did, I always had this picture of being careful of our bottom line, because we bumped along for the first six or eight years: 'Are we going to make it, are we not going to make it?' 'Oh, had we seen this financial report six months ago, we might not have made it. But we didn't see it, so we're still here.' That kind of stuff. We would joke about it."

"Those first several years," Dennis adds, "I was – both of us were – very conscious of being careful with dollars. We were very, very frugal. Bob has been a master at buying used, for pennies on the dollar, and then cleaning up and re-using stuff. I have always appreciated that. I like doing that with furniture, too. So, we were a good fit there. Bob, he would buy a whole pallet of air locks for ten dollars each, and he *knew* they would be worth a thousand dollars – I'm not exaggerating. He knew they'd be a thousand bucks. And over and over and over, Bob has done this, and that's how he built the business on a shoestring."

An example of how Dennis incorporated frugality into his business dealings turned out kind of fun. It, in part, created his identity as a colorful representative of the company. As he was making arrangements to attend a trade show in Milwaukee, Wisconsin, he chose the cheapest airfare, but it caused him to stay over an extra day (the cost with the additional hotel night was still less than the next best round-trip airline ticket, so…). A fan of bowties ever since his daughter, Karen, had given him his first one, which she found at a New York vintage clothing store called Alice Underground, Dennis came up with the idea to put a "Looking for bowties" ad in the classified section of the *Milwaukee Journal Sentinel*. After he got back to Oregon, a lady called to say she had seen his ad and was interested in selling the hundred bowties her deceased husband had worn. They agreed on two bucks each, and sight unseen, Dennis became the proud owner of thirty or so used bowties he culled out of the shipment.

"A couple months later, she called me back, and asked me if I wanted her husband's underwear. How can you not love a sweet lady like that?"

A dead ringer for Orville Redenbacher, with his signature bowtie, white hair, glasses, and ready smile, Dennis forever earned his Bob's Red Mill persona as the bowtie-wearing, popcorn tycoon look-alike. And, he admits, a tradition might not have been born had it not been for his frugal adventure on a company business trip.

Even though money was tight, both Bob and Dennis recognized they needed someone really good to manage the company's finances.

"Bob has always been good about building the right kind of team," Dennis says. "He was always aggressive about going after really good people. He worked hard at it. We both worked hard to find the best financial person. We couldn't afford it, but we couldn't afford not to do it."

John Wagner heard about the opportunity through Phil Bayha, Bob's Red Mill's local broker. He was the Controller for Pacific Seasonings, the fifth family-owned business he had worked for. He didn't know if he could handle a sixth, especially when the salary offer Bob made would have set him back to what he was making six years prior.

"I explained to Bob I had been through these family businesses where when somebody gets tired, they sell out and I'm out of a job; or one of the family members dies, they sell, and I'm out of a job," John relates. "You help build the company, and they end up with all the money. I told him I wanted an equity interest."

Bob knew if he wanted to attract and keep top-level professionals, he would have to consider multiple partners. He had been in a three-way equal partnership with his sons, and he had invited Craig Ratzat to be a minority partner. He was very comfortable with the concept of Dennis Gilliam as a future partner, and he was open to offering John the same opportunity. However, he was adamant about relinquishing power of the final say-so.

"I'm a big believer in not having anybody working for you that you can't fire," Bob says. "No matter who they are, no matter how big they are in the business. Because you could get into a knockdown, drag-out disagreement, and bust the company all to pieces. I wasn't going to let that happen. And it hasn't. Part of the reason it hasn't happened is I was thinking about it in advance."

They shook hands on the promise of an equity interest, "a gentlemen's agreement that most of my business friends said I was crazy to accept," according to John, "They said, 'Get it in writing.' Well, I took a risk, but I felt confident because Bob and Denny share the same values I have, and I knew I could trust them."

The starting salary was another issue, however. Bob offered the same compensation he was getting, adding, "Well, when we can afford a raise, you can give it to yourself, as long as I get the same." John agreed, figuring the company had enough upside to it, and over the long run he would make out okay. November 1, 1993, was his first day as Vice President of Finance.

According to his future partner, Dennis, "We both took less than what we had been making, but Bob's story was a very compelling one. I think it was a little bit easier for John, though, because we had already begun to turn the corner. When I came on board, I didn't even see a corner that we could turn."

One of the first things John did was put together an estate plan for Bob and Charlee. Bob didn't have any life insurance, so, as a prerequisite for a partnership structure, John set up buy-sell agreements. Once they were in place, and a valuation of the business had been done, Dennis and John each bought an equal number of shares in the company, becoming minority partners, with Bob the majority stockholder. Now, John could focus on the numbers. His assessment of the company's financial situation in 1993–94 was with such a large facility, sales were about two to three years behind the cost structure of operating the business. In other words, they weren't at the break-even point. They needed more volume, but that would take time. So, John worked on improving the margins. A penny here, a nickel there; a slow process, but in the long term it would pay off. For the immediate future, the business strategy all three agreed was necessary was an aggressive sales effort. Yes, they had outside help with their broker and distributor network, but what they lacked was an in-house sales professional to oversee all sales efforts.

One had knocked on Bob's door a year earlier, but Bob sent him to see Phil Bayha. Robert Agnew wasn't interested, however, in working for a brokerage firm. He went back to food service distributor Rykoff-Sexton, where he had worked the previous three years, and bided his time. A year later, he tried again. He had seen Bob and Dennis exhibiting at a Northwest Foodservice trade show in Portland, and stopped by their booth to pick up one of their product lists. When he got home and read down the list, he told himself, "I could sell this stuff all day long and not feel bad about what I did."

Back at the office on Monday, "after a particularly frustrating client call," Robert walked down the street to a payphone and called Bob. "As a salesman, I was in a business where you close. There is no black and white. When Bob got on the line, I said, 'I need to see you. I need to see you tomorrow at 8 a.m.,' and that was it. Bob was like, 'Well I can't do that,' but then he said to hold on and he got off the phone, and when he came back, he said, 'Okay, be here tomorrow at eight o'clock.'"

Robert's timing was perfect. The partners were on the lookout for a seasoned sales professional, preferably one with food experience. Robert had four years with Rykoff-Sexton. Plus, he sold radio advertising before that, and they figured if he can sell air... Bob offered Robert the job of "Sales" (that's what it would say on his business card). Robert accepted, and asked if he could squeeze in a week's vacation before he started. Bob, tossing a dose of his hard-ball sales pitch back at him, said, "I want you in now."

Robert, who eventually would become a fourth partner, remembers saying to himself on the drive home, "I have arrived." It was March of 1994. In a way, Bob's Red Mill, too, had arrived as a company. They were back on track with their revenue generation, finally hitting the $3 million mark at the end of their 1993 fiscal year (September 30), after posting in the mid–$2 million range for the previous five years. The three key positions – GM/marketing, accounting, and sales – Bob had worked so hard to fill were more than adequately staffed. The company was beginning to grow into its 50,000-square-foot building, and was already looking for additional warehouse space in nearby industrial complexes. They had just fulfilled their initial five-year lease agreement, and heading into their renewal term, Bob and his partners were seriously considering executing on the purchase option. The twenty-five employees who less than a year earlier had been introduced to the notion of Bob's Red Mill as a national company now firmly embraced the fact. They were, indeed, as Dennis Gilliam predicted, off and running.

CHAPTER 25

THE MAGIC DOCUMENT

LIKE A FOOTBALL TEAM DOWN BY THREE TOUCHDOWNS AT THE HALF, Bob's Red Mill came charging out of the locker room and ruled the second half. Devastated by unforeseen events in the first half, they relied on good coaching and solid players to re-tool the playbook. After tweaking their strategies and putting some new personnel on the field, the team roared back in the third quarter with a momentum that allowed them to catch and overcome the competition. Arrowhead Mills out of Texas was a dominant force to reckon with, but only crossed over with about ten percent of Bob's Red Mill products. They were moving strongly into puffed cold cereals – away from Bob's Red Mill's line of products – and with their focus on organic, their products were spendy. Stone-Buhr had a strong presence nationally with its five- and ten-pound flours, but was vulnerable since losing its sales force.

The bottom line, in the game of dominance in the niche of stone ground whole grain products, was Bob's Red Mill, with its complete product line, had the advantage. The up-and-coming national contestant was offering ninety-eight SKUs (stock-keeping units), incorporating all twelve common grains that were stone ground into flours, meals, farina, and cracks. These grains were also mixed into thirty different cereals, five bread mixes, five muffin mixes, and four pancake and waffle mixes. There were a variety of specialty flours made from stone ground rice, beans, and lentils. In addition, there was a full line of soup mixes, nuts, seeds, dried fruits, sweeteners, milk powders, pastas, rice, beans, and other related natural food products. Bulk products were available in five-, ten-, and twenty-five-pound bags, and smaller sizes were offered in triple-laminated cellophane burst-resistant packages made from biodegradable wood cellulose.

And Bob took pride in setting his company apart from the competition by dedicating the manufacturing of natural foods the natural way – by using huge slow-turning, hundred-year-old millstones grinding the bran, endosperm, and germ in a cool fashion that preserved the nutritious oils. And, as he likes to say, "One hundred pounds of goodness goes in, and one hundred pounds of goodness comes out." The company even built a miniature grist mill to demonstrate this process, and brought it to trade shows, grinding various grains right in their booth. The creative tactic worked, helping Bob's Red Mill stand out among the hundreds of other exhibitors. Dennis's strategy to "put our head down and plow" was working. The company was swiftly building a brand name. He led the effort to develop more alliances with key brokers and distributors. Following a three-year-long courtship, they landed the giant Chicago-based KeHE Food Distributors, Inc.

"KeHE showcased our entire product line," he says. "They basically functioned as our marketing department, opening doors to accounts in several new regions. Suddenly, we started getting calls from people we had never heard of before."

At their first Expo East trade show in the Fall of 1994, they picked up the other big distributor, Tree of Life, which had major inroads into the East Coast. Later that year, Gourmet Award Foods in Minnesota became a distributor, choosing twenty-nine products to market in specialty grocery stores. "The distributors loved us," Bob points out. "Our line was attractive to them because we were a one-stop shop that could bring to their warehouse every conceivable grain product. There just was no other single complete whole grain supplier in the country."

The natural and grocery trades weren't the only market segments the rejuvenated brand Bob's Red Mill was going after in the early 1990s. They had four other customer profiles they were targeting. The specialty market was small, but had a lot of potential. As early as August, 1994, the company's first foreign customer, a specialty foods buyer from Saipan, placed an order. There was also huge potential in industrial, but Bob's Red Mill didn't have the capability to supply flour in bulk for tanker truck distribution. But they were doing a brisk business selling whole wheat flour to small, medium, and large bakeries in the West. Mail order was in its infancy stage, but annual catalogs were being distributed to an ever-growing mailing list. The Mill Outlet Store, as they were now calling their retail space, had expanded its offerings to include bread and pasta machines, as well as fresh-baked muffins and coffee. It had a growing regional customer base.

From time to time, Bob would also try sampling, handing out baked or cooked products to local grocery store shoppers. Except for one early faux pas, that type of outreach was a tiring, but successful venture. In a personal, handwritten letter to their Fred Meyer buyer (their largest account at the time), Bob wrote:

> Dear Julie,
>
> I had the privilege of spending last Wednesday, Thursday, Friday, and Saturday doing a hands-on milling demonstration at the new Fred Meyer store on Walker Road in Beaverton.
>
> I came away from this 10- to 12-hour-a-day experience a little fatigued, but absolutely ecstatic over the customer response to the actual milling display, and to my "pitch" for the in-store bakery and the nutrition center.
>
> And then – I got a call from Phil Bayha yesterday. He informed me of your over-hearing my response to a customer's question of where

they might get large bulk quantities of my products, and I told them, "At the mill."

The nutrition centers have a very efficient and well-used system of special orders from Bob's Red Mill. They may order any of our products in any size their customer may wish, simply by calling the mill. The product will be on the store's next delivery.

I knew this. It was stupid of me to indicate anything else! This was the first time since our disastrous arson fire that I have been out doing PR work. I just lost perspective. And I am profoundly sorry. You have my solemn promise that nothing of this sort will ever happen again.

Frankly, Julie, the milling demo was the most fruitful selling tool I have ever had the opportunity to be a part of. It attracts almost every shopper's attention. When I finally thought of it (after two days), I put a small display of Bob's Red Mill pre-pack products beside the operating mill, along with some five-pound bags of flour (which customers kept asking for). They all sold like the proverbial hotcakes.

There is no question in my mind that this is a very positive way to impress shoppers with the uniqueness of Bob's Red Mill products. I can be counted on to repeat this demo wherever and whenever it is timely and practical for both of us. My very best.

Regards,
Bob Moore

He didn't get fired. But he didn't get invited back anytime soon to do another in-store demo at Fred Meyer. On everything else, the company was hitting on all cylinders. As Bob wrote in an internal company document at the time, "Our growth is limited only by our imagination and energy, and both are in abundant supply." There were five mills running on two shifts, and the mills were operating at about a seventy-five percent capacity, which meant there was more production possible with their current set-up. Bob had purchased two additional stone mills, and they were standing by, ready to be put into operation as soon as the demand called for it. The company had borrowed $200,000 to fuel its growth, which in Bob's visionary mind, included construction of a separate mill store/bakery/restaurant.

"This is my life's desire," he wrote, "to build a replica water-powered mill of historical significance that will be a tourist destination for families and out-of-town guests." Bob envisioned a facility that would pay homage to the nearly 200 water-powered flour mills that existed in Oregon in the late 1800s. He also felt a place celebrating the history of the state would fit nicely with other local tourist attractions, such as the End of the Oregon Trail Interpretive Center in nearby Oregon City. Inwardly, he knew it would satisfy his longing to see his beloved red mill rebuilt. But, he also recognized that his personal desire to resurrect one of his dreams was not reason enough for the company to pursue it. It would have to make financial sense. Ultimately, he would need to sell the concept to his partners, and convince them of its viability. Bottom line, it would need to be a profitable venture.

Being the long-term planner he was, Bob started down the path that would lead to the realization of his dream, and prepared to knock off the first obstacle in his way. He would need to secure the land on which to build up to a 30,000-square-foot facility. He had his eyes set on the two-acre parcel of land across the street from the building they were leasing. It was a paved parking lot, stretching all the way from International Way south to Highway 224, and it was included in the lease deal with ITW. It had become a bone of contention between Bob and Frank, because the lot was being used as a dumping ground for the contaminated soil in the environmental clean-up. There was a thick layer of the heavy clay soil covering most of the two acres (Bob's Red Mill employees could only use the front row of the lot for parking their vehicles). Every couple of weeks or so, a tractor would pull up and turn the dirt over, apparently allowing the gaseous solvent residue embedded in the soil to dissipate. "It was a real mess; they were always in our way," Bob groused about the two-year ordeal.

Finally, the day came when the Department of Environmental Quality declared the site clean. This meant ITW, after a one-year waiting period, could sell the property with a certified note attesting to the completion of the environmental clean-up. Bob received a copy of what he deemed "the magic document," and immediately called Frank. He wanted to know what it would take to purchase the property. Frank suggested they both get an appraisal, which they did. They each came in close to $1.4 million.

"I thought that was a good deal," Bob says. "I talked to John and Denny, and they agreed. So, then we learn we have to wait a whole year, which is fine. I mean, we are doing okay. We are all busy. We're going to trade shows, and selling stuff, and growing like crazy."

Sales attested to the crazy growth: $4.4 million in 1994; $5.4 million in 1995; $6.8 million in 1996; $7.4 million in 1997.

In 1998, right before the one-year waiting period was over, Bob approached the company's bankers at U.S. Bank to gauge their interest in loaning the partnership (Bob and Charlee, along with their two senior partners Dennis and John, had formed a separate limited liability company, Triad Grain Group, to buy property personally) the money to buy the ITW property. Once again, each got an appraisal. They both came in about the same again. But that wasn't as surprising to Bob as was the amount – $2.4 million! The property value had increased a million dollars in less than a year.

"I can remember sitting in my office, and calling Frank. I told him I thought we might finally be in a position to buy the property, and I asked him for his price on it. He said, 'Well, I thought we had a price.' I remember very distinctly saying, 'Oh yeah, Frank, I have it right in front of me – $1.4 million.' 'Right, right, right,' he said, '1.4.' I told him we were going to start trying to get the money, and would he send me a letter holding to that price for six months. 'Yeah, of course I will, Bob,' he said. Now, he should have gotten another appraisal, because it had been over a year, but he didn't. I think because this piece of property had had tons of problems, and was such a pain in his neck, he just wanted to get rid of it."

Knowing he would be in a very favorable position with the bank, Bob came up with a creative strategy and presented it to U.S. Bank. He wanted to borrow $1.4 million on a property for which the bankers knew they could get $2.4 million. Would they accept the difference in valuation – $1 million – in lieu of twenty percent down?

"I remember there were two of them, and they both got a big kick out of it. They kind of looked at each other, and the guy said, 'Well, we can loan you up to eighty percent of the value of the building, and that's $1.92 million, so I can't see a reason in the world why we can't loan you $1.4 million.' And that's what they did. We didn't have to pay anything down to get a loan on the purchase of the property."

Now that he had locked up a facility in which to grow, Bob was determined to fill it to capacity from a production standpoint. He added the two mills that were on stand-by, giving him a total of seven. There was still plenty of room to reach 100% utilization, and Bob wanted to get there as fast as possible. The infrastructure was in place. Internally, operations and production were running like well-oiled machines. It was time to harvest their overhead. Bob was confident he wouldn't have to add too many more employees or equipment to increase output by fifty percent, maybe more. Bob's Red Mill ended its 1998 fiscal year at $8,107,816. He went to Denny, and threw down the challenge: What would it take to double sales in five years?

CHAPTER 76

MY LIFE'S DESIRE

B OB MOORE DID NOT GET A "YES" MAN WHEN HE HIRED DENNIS GIL-
liam.

"Bob used to come into my office and say, 'Boy, we sure are different, aren't we?'" Dennis recalls. "But that's what he wanted – different
thinking. And, believe me, that's what he got."

On growing sales – possibly doubling revenue in five years – there
was mutual buy-in. The "how" was up to Dennis. One of the marketing strategies he had already put in place was the hiring of a local
PR/Advertising agency in October, 1997, to help "tell the story of Bob's
Red Mill." Koopman Ostbo Marketing Communications specialized in
the maturing natural and organic products marketplace, having worked
with other Northwest food manufacturers such as Kettle Foods (makers
of Kettle Chips) and Pacific Foods of Oregon, known for its soymilk,
soups, and broths. The Portland firm had been successful with its media
relations campaign, placing local news stories about the company, as well
as new product introductions and articles about Bob and Charlee in the
national trade press. With Bob's challenge in mind, Dennis favored taking
the proactive marketing program to the next level. He asked Koopman

Ostbo Marketing Communications to come back with their recommendations for advertising the brand. The stated goal was to make Bob's Red Mill the number one hot cereal in the Northwest, and then go national.

The agency recommended a transit ad campaign on Portland's TriMet bus and light-rail system, supported by radio spots. The breakfast-themed slogans included, "No Grain, No Gain," "Life Insurance You Eat," and a pancake version with "Stack the Odds in Your Favor." The campaign ran during the first quarter of 1999, and included a cause-marketing component, soliciting donations of coats and jackets that were given to a homeless shelter. Bob's Red Mill employees, including Bob and Charlee, manned sampling stations along the public transit routes, providing a hot breakfast for Portland's morning commuters.

Sales continued to rise, breaking the $10 million threshold in 1999 for the first time (up twenty-nine percent from the previous fiscal year). Dennis and John didn't know if the scare-tactic known as Y2K was an aberration or if people would continue to stock up on their dry goods into the next millennium, but they stuck with their strategy to increase the annual marketing budget as revenues grew. They were preparing for a big push – national advertising for the first time in the company's history. But, first, they wanted to hear their agency's thoughts on the packaging – was it ready for prime time, in their opinion?

"It needed an overhaul," says Koopman Ostbo Marketing Communications principal Craig Ostbo. "At the time, the packaging featured a line-drawn caricature of Bob wearing an apron. It kind of had that old Smith Brothers' Cough Drops look. We felt strongly it needed a more contemporary photo of Bob – looking like he does every day – with his glasses, white beard, bolo tie, and trademark driving cap. We did some research, and outside of Portland, people would say, 'You mean there really is a Bob?' We advocated for Bob's picture on every bag, because Bob is the brand."

Koopman Ostbo also expressed concern that the current positioning of the Bob's Red Mill brand – to some as a hot cereal, to others as stone ground flour – was limiting the brand's reach. The agency proposed repositioning the brand as "Whole grain foods for every meal of the day."

"Positioning the brand broadly across many categories – for breakfast, lunch, and dinner – turned out to be extremely beneficial," Ostbo adds. "It was perfect timing, too, as the Bob's Red Mill brand would end up playing a major role in a momentous food trend in America – the whole grain movement."

With the new packaging and position statement being implemented across the entire product line, Dennis felt confident it was time to advertise nationally. He opted first for the niche market of gluten-free living, targeting print publications whose readers had special dietary needs. Seeing a boost in gluten-free sales, he carved out a larger ad budget for magazines serving the community that came to be known as LOHAS (Lifestyles of Health and Sustainability). This bigger audience segment – not yet the mainstream – was made up of people who focused on health, fitness, sustainable living, the environment, and personal development. Turns out this group of people was larger than anyone at Koopman Ostbo Marketing Communications or Bob's Red Mill expected. Sales went through the roof: $12 million in 2001, and nearly $15 million in 2002.

Bob and his team became big believers in marketing, and as they continued to grow, they relied on their agency for all their outsourced marketing activities, including public relations, advertising, graphic design, printing, copywriting, and media buying. Later, Bob would tell a reporter at a prestigious businessmen's breakfast event he spoke at, "Koopman Ostbo took my brand to the moon."

With sales and marketing in good hands, Bob could turn his attention to his "life's desire" – construction of a mill store/bakery/restaurant. He would call it the Whole Grain Store & Visitors Center. It would have an operating waterwheel. And it would be painted bright red, just like his mill that had burned down. He had the green light from DEQ that the two acres of land across the street from the manufacturing plant where he wanted to build it was clean. The only obstacle was dealing with local government agencies on permitting issues and a morass of red tape. Wes Tarr, Bob's good buddy and "Construction Doctor," counted fifty-two appointments he had with city, county, and municipal government bodies over a long list of "don'ts" and "can'ts" in the project's long pre-planning stage. Frustrated with the lack of movement, Wes finally went to the "office" of the mayor of Milwaukie. Jim Bernard, whose father, Joe, had been mayor before him, took meetings at the same place his dad did – in the back shop of Bernard's Garage.

Wes, who had worked with the elder Mayor Bernard on several Milwaukie construction projects in his seventy-seven years, said, "Jimmy, you want us to put a good building on that piece of property, a nice building in there, or do you want it to be blackberries? You've got a choice. Every time I go to the city, they say I can't do this and I can't do that; it can't be this color, or it has to be this far set back. I'm tellin' you, Jimmy, Bob is not going to do this project; he is going to move it someplace else if he can't put what he wants where he wants it."

Wes' stern, but grandfatherly approach worked. Mayor Jim volunteered to walk over to city hall with him, and with his pro-business approach, became an advocate for not losing the tax base and job-generating project to another city.

"The city manager and I worked with our planning department to figure out how we could make the project a reality," Jim says. They tackled zoning changes to allow for larger retail space in the Omark Industrial Park area, worked on altering parking lot standards, and coordinated with TriMet to determine if they could adjust setback requirements. Things started moving forward again, but there was another hurdle – the property in the past had been considered a wetlands area. Any changes to the site would have to involve the Department of State Lands Wetlands Program, whose job it was to protect and manage Oregon's wetland resources. That would have opened a whole other can of worms, if Wes hadn't learned that one of the indications of a wetlands area was the existence of cattails. His crew got busy one morning before the inspector was to arrive, and what do you know, there were no cattails to be seen when he got there. The inspector mandated some additional drainage, but that was it. The project could move forward, as far as the State was concerned.

During the lengthy process of getting approvals, Bob and Wes spent months visiting stores, bakeries, and restaurants throughout the Portland area to gather ideas about the building's design. Theirs was a three-in-one combo plate plan, and none they had seen quite fit the bill. But the massive feel, large beams, high ceilings, and overall sturdy look of a McGrath's Fish House was the direction in which Bob was leaning.

"I kind of had a picture in my mind what he wanted, and then one night it all came together," Wes explains. "I woke up at one in the morning, went down to my dining room table, got out my drawing stuff, and drew up a building for him. I took it over to him that morning, and laid it on his desk. He said, 'That's exactly what I've been looking for. This is what I want. Where do we go from here?' I told him, 'We start spending money!'"

The site prep alone had cost almost half a million dollars, and the estimated cost of construction was north of two million dollars. Originally, Bob envisioned the Whole Grain Store & Visitors Center would be a prototype for at least three other similar outlets in the Portland metropolitan area, and possibly more throughout the region. But cost overruns and the headache of dealing with the bureaucracy of local government dampened his enthusiasm. He would build one store, and it would be spectacular. One of the marquee features of his dream facility would be an eighteen-foot-tall operational waterwheel. That's what powered the flour mills of old, and it was Bob's tribute to the craft he loved. He would build it front and center on the 15,000-square-foot building. Actually, Wes built it, and he didn't charge Bob a dime. It was his gift to his old friend. Plus, he had fun doing it. Bob wanted the waterwheel made out of redwood, so Wes found a guy that had a huge pile of redwood logs. He went out there with a list of specifications (a lot of the boards would have to be cut eighteen inches wide and two-and-a-half-inches thick to accommodate the curvature of the wheel), and had truckloads of the sawed pieces delivered to his house. He had never built anything like it before, so he decided to construct it in his backyard to make sure it would work, and then he would disassemble the entire structure and rebuild it at the store.

For months, neighbors would stop by and gawk at the Noah's

Ark–like project going up in the Tarrs' backyard. One day, when it was nearly done, Bob came over, and, maybe giddy in his excitement, jumped inside the eighteen-foot-high wooden wheel, and started walking on it. Like a hamster inside his exercise toy, Bob got the wheel turning faster and faster. Pretty soon he was jogging to keep up with the momentum, but the faster he ran, the faster the wheel turned. It almost carried him upside down before he got it to slow down.

"That thing was so big and heavy, you just couldn't grab onto it and stop it," Wes says with a smile. "I yelled at Bob to turn around and run the other direction; that was the only way it was going to slow down. I remember the neighbor kids sure got a good laugh out of that one." Wes ended up using a chain and padlock to secure the waterwheel so no one else would attempt Bob's Cirque du Soleil "Wheel of Death" maneuver.

Without further mishap, Bob's Red Mill's Whole Grain Store & Visitors Center opened on October 30, 2003. Bob and Charlee made their grand entrance in "Clara," their 1931 Ford Model A, as a Dixieland jazz band played in the background. The fanfare also included the release of twenty-five white doves in recognition of the company's twenty-fifth anniversary, a ribbon-cutting ceremony orchestrated by the North Clackamas Chamber of Commerce, and a speech by Mayor Jim Bernard. Once inside, the crowds filled the aisles to witness the unveiling of a billboard-sized wall mural depicting the history of Bob's Red Mill.

The Whole Grain Store & Visitors Center has been a popular destination since day one. Tour groups arrive by bus to see displays of historic milling equipment and a working stone mill using century-old French buhr millstones. Shoppers can purchase all of Bob's Red Mill's more than 300 products – many in bulk – and browse a large selection of baking aids, kitchen tools, and cookbooks. Diners enjoy breakfast and lunch ordered at the deli counter, as well as freshly baked breads, muffins, and cookies prepared in the made-from-scratch bakery. There's also a classroom with full kitchen where cooking classes and demonstrations are held.

CHAPTER 17

PEOPLE BEFORE PROFIT

B OB MOORE LOVES SPECIAL OCCASIONS. HE TIED THE OPENING OF the Whole Grain Store & Visitors Center to the twenty-fifth anniversary of the company's founding. And four years later, on his seventy-eighth birthday, he did something remarkable. Sales had been on a tear, with an annual average increase of 24.8% in year-over-year numbers since 2003. In 2007, sales topped forty-five million. But before the year ended, Bob had made a decision. Even with a separate leased warehouse that gave him more than 100,000 square feet in which to operate, he was convinced Bob's Red Mill would need more space. A lot more. Once again, he put his real estate guy, Don Ossey, on notice. What Ossey came back with floored the management team, everyone except Bob. He had found more space all right – 325,000 square feet to be exact. It was the old Meier & Frank warehouse, a building so large it had seven acres under one roof. It sat on seventeen acres, and it was located less than a mile east of the company's current location. People cautioned Bob that it was just too much space and too expensive to lease. They would never grow into it, and most of the warehouse would sit vacant, some said. But Bob had a vision. And maybe no one but he could see it. He believed very strongly the company would continue to grow, and that tripling the size of their operation was the right thing to do. So, on February 15, 2007, Bob signed a lease for the property. And, not just any lease – it was for thirty-five years! To see it through to the end of that term, Bob would have to live to 113. But, he didn't do it for himself, and that's why he proclaimed that day the best in all of his seventy-eight years (except for marrying Charlee, of course).

"Signing that lease secured the future for my employees," Bob says. "I did it for them, so they would have a job for as long as they wanted to work."

The move itself was monumental (at a total cost of $2.5 million), but preparing the cavernous concrete building to host a food manufacturing company was a massive task. Just the cleaning and painting took untold hours, with more than 11,000 gallons of white paint applied. But Bob and his team approached the task at a feverish pace. And the transformation was unbelievable. What had been dingy, dirty, and dark now sparkled. Every inch of wall and ceiling was bright white. Where nothing had been illuminated for decades, brilliant lights shone on acres and acres of storage racks, manufacturing equipment, packaging lines, and nearly 20,000 square feet of newly remodeled office space. And, important to the company's huge gluten-intolerant audience, a 23,000-square-foot dedicated gluten-free manufacturing facility was built out. As a testament to Bob's vision of growth for the company, 160,000 square feet of distribution space was set aside to feed trucks that could pull into the forty loading bays.

Moving into their new "world headquarters," as Bob dubbed it, was one of the proudest moments of his life. He had built mills in a Quonset hut, a newspaper office, a wooden chicken feed building, and a fastener factory that was chemically tainted. But this – a beautiful blocks-long structure more than twenty-five times bigger than his mill that burned down – was the crowning glory. As Bob would say at the grand opening ceremony, "This should take care of our needs for the next ten to fifteen years." He was usually right, but not this time. It would be much sooner than that when he would call Don Ossey with a familiar request.

The public was invited to the May 1, 2008, grand opening of the new Bob's Red Mill world headquarters, and event planners figured they would serve free pancakes to maybe a few hundred community members. Nearly 3,000 came. They didn't necessarily show up for the free food, but it was the open invitation for guided tours of the facility that drew such a large crowd. The opportunity to see the inner workings of a real flour mill was too unique to pass up. The public's fascination with the historical displays of milling equipment and the operation of the slow-turning millstones was an eye-opening experience to the company's marketing experts. In the days and weeks following the grand-opening ceremony, they noticed many of the people who had taken the tour were showing up at the Whole Grain Store & Visitors Center, and buying stuff. Light bulbs started going off: Offer more tours, *sell more product.* For people outside the Portland metro area and Oregon who wouldn't necessarily travel to see the place, invite local, regional, and national media for a tour, and have them share with their respective audiences, which will *sell more product.* It was brilliant. And it worked. Plus, giving personally guided tours to dignitaries and media was one of Bob's favorite things to do. Soon, the company was offering weekday 10 a.m. tours of the plant. And Bob, sometimes in a golf cart to speed up the process, was giving several tours a day.

He loved showing off his operation, letting visitors hold small mounds of the freshly ground flour or corn in their hands after it had cascaded from the millstones. He would give them a sample of corn grits or steel cut oats or whatever was coming off one of the sixteen packaging lines. He would wow them with a seemingly unending exploration of the vast warehouse. And a walk through the squeaky-clean quality control lab with all of its top-of-the-line testing equipment was always impressive. But his favorite part – what he enjoyed doing the most – was introducing his people, and letting every dignitary or media person know what a great job they were doing.

The Grand Tour

Bob likes to start the expanded version of his plant tour at 10 a.m., and it usually wraps up about 2 p.m. or later. Lunch at the Whole Grain Store & Visitors Center, as well as a goodly amount of time spent perusing the aisles of products, is always included. But, first, there's a protocol. Guests climb a set of stairs to the lobby, reading welcoming comments attached to poster-sized photos of Bob and Charlee along the way. Long-time receptionist Bonnie Rothenfluch provides the greeting, which is often interrupted by incoming phone calls and her very patient, *"Bob's Red Mill, this is Bonnie,"* iconic response.

The journey traditionally begins in Bob's second-floor corner office. It's there where this lover of people, millstones, history, photography, and books can point to items and artifacts that help tell his story. There's a picture of his great-grandfather, Jacob Yost, riding in a parade on a horse-drawn wagon with "Yost's Yeast" emblazoned on the side. Is it mere coincidence Bob's bloodlines on his mother's side dealt in the business of baking? A collage of family photos covers a cork bulletin board, a display Bob points to often as he tells tales about his upbringing, military career, jobs he had, places he lived, travels with Charlee, and activities with his boys. A glass-covered picture frame features certificates of achievement, military commendations, and business cards – chronicling his service and career life from U.S. Electrical Motors to Bob Moore Mobil Service to JC Penney Auto Center and Moores' Flour Mill in Redding. None of it seems boastful. It's simply his way of sharing his life with his guests. And everything has meaning, including the Bible verse above his door: *Then I hated all my labor in which I had toiled under the sun, because I must leave it to the man who will come after me. And who knows whether he will be wise or a fool? Yet he will rule over all my labor in which I toiled and in which I have shown myself wise under the sun. This also is vanity.* (Ecclesiastes 2:18–19) And probably the most meaningful of all is the book *John Goffe's Mill*, usually lying face-up on his conference table, just like he found it that fateful day in the Redding Public Library. Bob often sums up his preamble to the tour by picking up the book by George Woodbury, and saying, "This is how it all got started."

Then, with an energetic, "Let's go on a tour!" he bounds out of his chair, calls for Nancy, his executive assistant, to join them, and they're off. Nancy Garner, a petite woman usually wearing a monogrammed Bob's Red Mill logo sweater, brings camera and a special skill on the brisk walk. Sometimes it's their first stop or maybe their last; oftentimes both. They head downstairs to the two pianos located outside the plant's break room. Out comes the sheet music, and the two musicians perform – in perfect synchronicity – vintage jazz songs like "Ain't Misbehavin'," "After You're Gone," and "Who's Sorry Now?" Many times, the smiling guest is invited to sing along or sit in if he or she knows how to play the piano. Either way, it's five or ten minutes of lightness and impressiveness. How many business people signed up for a factory tour are serenaded by an eighty-one-year-old CEO and his beautiful assistant?

The first tour stop is a trip down Memory Lane, as Bob leads guests past displays of his old milling equipment. Stopping to share a story or two, he points out photos of faces and places woven into the company's history, and draws their attention to news articles and pictures of the June 15, 1988, arson fire that burned down his mill. The original millstones from the fire are there, providing a testimony to their resilience. The point isn't lost on visitors that as go the stones, so goes the company. They live on, maybe roughed up a bit, but they both survived. The displays and wall of memorabilia from the past set the stage for the present. Strategically placed picture windows along the wall that defines the manufacturing plant provide glimpses into what employees are doing right now – cleaning, grinding, mixing, packaging, and moving the multitude of Bob's Red Mill products. The views from the fifteen large plate glass windows not only give tour members a peek at a bunch of equipment and bags of grain, they show off something that is much more important to Bob – his people. Whether the production line workers, maintenance crews, or warehouse guys feel "special" because people are watching them perform like they were on stage or not, their boss wants them to be seen.

Because they're real. They are important to him. And they prove something many of his competitors with their walled-off production areas can't demonstrate – this is a genuine stone ground milling operation that doesn't hide behind the veil of being just a marketing company. Bob's Red Mill Natural Foods® is an authentic brand, with more than 200 *real* people, grinding millions of pounds of *real* whole grains, mixing them with *real* ingredients, and packaging them in clear, transparent bags. Many have tried to steer him away from the see-through cellophane packaging, but Bob is firm in his belief that that kind of transparency is beyond a function of packaging. It's about an open relationship he has with his customers. They can trust him, and they can trust the authenticity of the Bob's Red Mill brand.

Before entering the production area, Bob takes a detour to point out two of his favorite departments. The first is the Label Department. It's just a small office and rows of storage racks with thousands of printed and stick-on labels, but to Bob it represents the breadth and scope of his company. Every time he checks in with Label Coordinator Raisa Gorban, he can get an update on the number of SKUs. This gives him an indication of how many products with their multi-sized packages the company is producing. When he started the business, there was a handful. In the early '90s, there were about a hundred. It wasn't that long ago the total was in the mid-three digits. With the international market for Bob's Red Mill products growing at a remarkable rate (more than seventy countries as of 2011 carried his products), at last count there were 1,269 SKUs. Bob was never in business for the numbers, but the wide variety, to him, meant security. If demand were to drop off in, say, flaxseed meal (not likely, as it is the company's number one seller), the sheer scope of having 360 other products to sell was a safety blanket.

The other reason Bob liked to visit the Label Department was Raisa. If he were ever to admit to a having a favorite employee, this buoyant Ukrainian would be it. She was always smiling, eternally upbeat, and just fun to be around. Of course, he loves all his people. They're what keep him going, the reason he shows up to work early and sometimes stays late. He wants to get to know them personally, to hear their stories. If his arms were long enough, he'd stop by on each of the three shifts working twenty-four hours, six days a week, and give everyone a group hug. Raisa's story – and her special relationship with Bob – is undoubtedly similar in nature to that of scores of other employees:

At thirty-eight, she moved with her family from the Republic of Moldova (located between Romania and Ukraine) to the United States. She arrived in Portland on December 25, 1995, a Christmas present not only to herself, as she was delivered from a life of poverty and repression, but a gift to all who came in contact with her bubbly and appreciative personality. With her limited command of the English language, she was able to land a job at McDonald's, making (to her) an unbelievably high wage of five dollars an hour. She had been there less than two weeks when her manager one night at closing time told her to clean out the refrigerator and throw everything in the garbage. She cried all the way home because of the waste of food. Another American tradition that brought her to tears was a sightseeing visit to a popular Portland-area Christmas lights exhibition. Thousands enjoyed the brightly lit homes

PHOTO CREDIT: NANCY GARNER / BOB'S RED MILL NATURAL FOODS, INC.

Raisa Gorban, with a picture on her desk of her best friend

along Peacock Lane, but to the woman whose government allowed only three hours of electricity per day, it was overwhelming.

After working several months at a restaurant she felt was too wasteful, Raisa applied for a job at Bob's Red Mill. She and her Ukrainian friend Lubov filled out applications and sat in the lobby waiting for their interviews. As she sat there, she saw on the wall dozens of framed articles, each with an image of a bespectacled and bearded man wearing a cap.

"I was sitting on the bench, and I saw his picture everywhere," she said. "I knew he was the boss, but I didn't expect to see him alive. Because for me, boss, owner, is somewhere that you cannot see," she added in her unique style of English.

When Bob walked by, she did a double-take, looking up at the pictures on the wall and back at the man towering over her. Then she jumped up, and declared, "YOU'RE BOB! Oh, I want to work for you!" When Bob asked what job she wanted to fill, she replied, "I don't know; I just want to work for you."

Just then, Brian Miller, the human resources manager, returned with the two women's applications in hand. "Hire her!" Bob said, and then turned to leave. As he was walking away, Raisa ran after him, and grabbed his sleeve. "Bob, Bob," she tugged. "My friend needs a job, too." Raisa remembers Bob standing there, laughing so loud she says it sounded like thunder. "He looked at me, and he looked at Lubov, and he said, 'Hire both,' and then he left. Today we are close, close friends. He's like my best friend."

That was October, 1996, and Bob has been a special person in Raisa's life, and in her family's life, ever since. When her oldest daughter Liliya got married, Bob and Charlee were at the wedding. When her second daughter, Inna, wed, the Moores were there. "He's in my family, you know," she said with a laugh. "Both he and Charlee are amazing people; I love them both," she lavishes.

She also loves her job. "Maybe because I am an immigrant, but when I arrived at Bob's Red Mill, I just opened the doors, and the walls held me. I feel like I am at home – like Swiss-fit home! When I take a vacation, it's so funny, because I'm always talking about Bob's Red Mill. My husband laughs at me, but he knows how I love this company. I thought that, maybe, I love it here because there are such good people around. I've never met bad people here. I've never had any problems. Nobody ever tried to make me feel bad, or put me in an uncomfortable situation, no. I feel like at home. You know, at home everybody loves you; nobody wants to hurt you; nobody makes you feel uncomfortable. Here, the same."

When Raisa moved into a new office as Label Coordinator, she took to wearing several sweaters. One day when Bob stepped in, he asked her why it was so cold. "I said, 'Bob, the heater doesn't work.' He asked me, 'Did you tell this guy?' I said yes. 'Did you tell that guy?' Yes. Then Bob said to me, 'Why didn't you tell me?' I thought, 'Bob is the big boss, why should I bother him with heaters?' Anyway, the next day, the guys from some company outside came and fixed it. Later, Bob came and said, 'Okay, Raisa, how are you?' I said, 'Bob, I can make eighty degrees in here! Thank you very much.' He said, 'Raisa, any problems, anything you need, just come to me and tell me.' I think he is a special man; but not only because he is so good to me. He's good to everybody."

Bo Thomas, the head of maintenance – Bob's other favorite department – can attest to the "good to everybody" sentiment. So can his wife, Nancy, and their four kids. All four of the Thomas children graduated from college, basically on a maintenance man's salary. When he hired Bo, Bob asked him to name a goal he could help him achieve. His maintenance man said he wanted to earn enough to pay for all his kids' college expenses, and he wanted his wife to be home with the children through junior high school.

"It was May, 1990, and my kids were little," Bo remembers, "when Bob sat me down, and he gets out a piece of paper and a pencil, and he starts writing down numbers – what it would cost to put four kids through college over the course of the next twenty years. He laid out a salary with raises, and a certain amount of guaranteed overtime each year. He basically made a promise to me that it would happen."

At the company's annual "State of the Mill" meeting on August 16, 2010, Bob gave one of his shortest speeches ever, primarily due to the emotional nature of his comments. He shared with the group that Melinda Thomas, Bo's youngest daughter, had just graduated from the University of Oregon, the fourth of the Thomas kids to earn a four-year college degree.

"Bo, we did it," Bob announced to his assembled team. "We got all four of those kids through college. And every person here – everyone at Bob's Red Mill – had a piece in making that happen. And if I don't say another thing, I think that is a milestone for this company; it is such an important thing."

The maintenance department – with its welders, electricians, and mechanics – is where Bob feels the most comfortable. He and Bo fabricated hundreds of pieces of equipment there over the years. Today, the team of fourteen builds and repairs everything for the company, mostly one-of-a-kind machinery that started as an idea in Bob's head, and ended up on the production floor. It's where Bob earned his reputation as the epitome of a tinkerer, someone who likes to get his hands dirty fixing or building a piece of equipment. He loves to hang out there with "his guys." Especially Wes Tarr, the man Bob calls his sweetest and oldest true friend.

PHOTO CREDIT: NANCY GARNER / BOB'S RED MILL NATURAL FOODS, INC.

Wes Tarr, Bob's long-time friend and "Construction Doctor"

Fiercely independent, the "Construction Doctor" maintained his own business and contractor's license well into his seventies. Bob's Red Mill was his main client, and had been since Wes helped renovate the original mill back in 1979. Add in the home improvement projects the Moores hired him to do, and Bob/Bob's Red Mill pretty much captivated his entire working career. It was a career that almost ended in 1996 when Wes was diagnosed with lymphoma, a type of cancer involving the immune system. Doctors said he would likely live only six to eight more months, unless he underwent a radical experimental treatment program. "They asked me if I was against being a guinea pig, and I told them I was not against anything that might keep me alive," Wes explains.

Even though the cancer had spread to his lungs, the treatment seemed to work. But his wife, Opal, says that's not what kept him alive. A few years later, when Bob had asked Wes to build the Whole Grain Store & Visitors Center, he declined, telling Bob he should hire someone else because he probably wouldn't live to see the project completed. But Bob, sensing a tone of resignation in his friend's voice, wouldn't take "no" for an answer. He kept pestering and pushing Wes to get back in the game. The persistence paid off, and Wes put his tool belt back on. Ten years later, he's still working. That, says Opal, is what saved her husband's life. Wes admits he's tried to quit the construction business two or three times since, but each time Bob has talked him out of it. When he finally gave up his contractor's license, Bob came to the rescue again. On March 15, 2007, he put Wes Tarr on the Bob's Red Mill payroll. Wes was eighty-three.

"When Bob wanted me to come on steady, I told him I'm too old to punch a clock or go to a bunch of meetings," Wes relates. "He said that was fine, that I could work whenever there was something for me to do. The last couple years have been awful near steady, because there has been a lot to do. But, I just charge him for whatever hours I work."

Sometimes, Bob admits, he just likes to have Wes around so they can have a cup of coffee or talk about their favorite shared hobby – restoring old cars. Wes found Bob his first Model A at a swap meet. He has two now – Wes has three – and the two friends never run out of stuff to talk about when it comes to restoring or driving their cars. One of the best trips Bob said he ever went on was with Wes and Opal to the 100th anniversary of the REO (Ransom E. Olds) Motor Company in Lansing, Michigan. Wes took the 1933 REO Flying Cloud Sport Coupe he had restored from the frame up (one of only three in existence and valued at more than a quarter million dollars), and Bob and Charlee followed in their motorhome. The two couples spent six weeks driving on the back roads of the country's mid-section – a first for Bob. He had seen a lot of grain in his life, but never like the fields of corn and grain he saw up close in Iowa and Illinois. Wes said it was a thing of joy to see the look of absolute amazement on his friend's face.

There's one more part of the plant tour that doesn't require hairnets, and that's a quick trip outside to see where grain is temporarily stored in seventeen 100,000-pound metal silos, and where trucks loaded with raw products disgorge their loads into an intricate pneumatically pressured piping system. Great care is taken at several stages in the processing system to ensure purity, beginning as soon as the trucks arrive. Loads can be rejected before ever reaching the inside of the building if exacting criteria are not met. Back inside the grain-cleaning room, visitors for the first time see the grain as it cascades through a network of screens and filters designed to remove rocks, twigs, and any foreign material. Quality control is a high priority, with samples regularly tested by cereal chemists in the high-tech testing lab. Once the grain is clean, the rest of the process – from raw product in the front door, to packaged product out the back door – is remarkably simple. The most important thing that happens in a kernel's journey through the Bob's Red Mill manufacturing plant takes place in the mill room. It's here where wheat meets stone, where corn and quartz collide. It's where the magic occurs. But, it's not magic at all. The process is too simple for words. The whole grain goes into the hopper. Millstones slowly turn and grind the grain. Stone ground grain comes out. Sometimes, it's mixed with other ingredients. Other times – as in the case of popular items such as whole wheat flour and flaxseed meal – one-hundred percent of the goodness that went into the mill goes into the package.

What distinguishes the product – what sets Bob's Red Mill apart from the big-time corporate flour producers – is the difference between a *whole* grain and a *processed* grain. Simply stated, a processed grain is a whole grain missing its most nutritious parts. The edible section of every whole grain – known as the kernel or wheat berry – is comprised of three distinct parts: the bran (provides fiber, B vitamins, and trace minerals); the germ (antioxidants, vitamin E, B vitamins, and healthy fats); and the endosperm (carbohydrates and protein), which amounts to about eighty-three percent of the kernel weight. The big manufacturers of enriched white flour process out the bran and the germ – the good stuff – and then, as Bob so eloquently puts it, "they add back in a whole paragraph of chemicals and garbage." They do it, he says, to give flour a finer texture and improve shelf life, but what happens is, they remove dietary fiber, iron, and B vitamins, leaving "no nutrition to speak of."

In a Statement of Purpose Bob is willing to share with anyone, he writes:

> For a century and a half, the simple basic task of feeding our western world's population an available and fundamentally life-sustaining diet of whole grains has been made merchandise of by the millers of our lands, who remove the bran and the germ from virtually every kernel milled. By promoting and touting the "white" portion of wheat, rice, corn, barley, rye, and buckwheat as an "elite food," and the only "digestible" portion of grains, they have done our bodies a great disservice.
>
> The millers have always been able to establish very profitable animal feed businesses along side their white flour mills. They sell the vast tonnage of bran and germ they remove to the cattle industry to fatten up animals for the meat-packing industry. Is there a problem here? I think so! Even though grains have developed into a very lucrative business throughout our lands, by removing the fiber and the life-giving wheat germ

from the entire food chain, their selfishly profitable action started our nation slowly but surely on the path to the ill health and life-long obesity we are experiencing in America today.

Concern over these issues as we were raising our three boys brought my wife and me into the whole grain business. It is keeping wholesome, uncomplicated, "simple" grains continuously available to the people of our land that has caused us to ensure the continuity of Bob's Red Mill.

This Statement of Purpose makes us what we are: Basic, Whole, and Simple.

The document is signed by Bob Moore.

Enjoying a bowl of hot, steaming Scottish Oats (his all-time favorite, by the way) one morning in his office, Bob pauses to proclaim, "Say what you want about breakfast cereal, but oats are God's gift to man for his breakfast. They really are. This is the most uncomplicated cereal the world could ever come up with. You take oats out of the field. You grind them between two stones. You cook 'em in water. Then you eat them. I don't know of anything that is simpler than that."

In a twelve-month period ending their 2010 fiscal year, Bob's Red Mill produced ninety-one million pounds of simplicity. Their modern Skjold mills from Saeby, Denmark, run twenty-fours a day in three mill rooms. These newer mills use the same quartz millstones as Bob's first generation of mills, but operate quieter, smoother, and cooler. They are also configured differently, with a stationary stone on top, and a rotating stone on the bottom, "the only improvement in millstones in thousands of years," according to Bob. At optimal speed, they can produce 600 to 700 pounds an hour. They fill 2,000-pound "super bags" that are transported to one of sixteen packaging stations. Most of Bob's Red Mill's 200 employees work on the packaging line, operating form-and-fill machines that at full capacity could kick out an average of 345,000 pre-printed cellophane bags of product every twenty-four hours. The bags are sealed in four-pack cardboard boxes, stacked 343 units to a pallet, and fork-lifted to the warehouse. Some of the packaging lines are assigned to fill larger bags, such as five-pound flour bags, as well as twenty-five- and fifty-pound sacks for bulk sales.

The fastest-growing segment of the company's sales – and more than thirty percent of its revenue – is its gluten-free line. The milling room and packaging areas for its fifty gluten-free products are housed in a dedicated facility, which means the space is actually a separate, but attached, building with its own air system to protect against any cross contamination. Gluten is the common name for the proteins in specific grains that are harmful to persons with celiac disease, which is a lifelong inherited autoimmune condition affecting children and adults. These proteins are found in wheat, rye, barley, and their derivatives. When people with celiac disease eat foods that contain gluten, it creates a toxic reaction that can cause damage to the small intestine, and often a loss of their ability to absorb crucial nutrients. It's been reported about one in 133 Americans is afflicted with celiac disease.

Bob's Red Mill is a nationally recognized leader in gluten-free foods. The company was the only whole grain manufacturer invited to speak before the U.S. Food and Drug Administration panel working to define national standards for gluten-free product testing and package labeling. According to Roger Farnen, Quality Assurance Manager, Bob's Red Mill adheres to the highest gluten-free standards, taking samples from 2,000-pound batch units, and conducting R5 ELISA (enzyme-linked immunosorbent assay) lab tests on every one of them (between 60 and 160 tests every twenty-four hours). In addition, all shifts perform continuous random testing on the production lines. The stringent tests follow the most rigorous protocols (including the Codex Alimentarius for international standards) to ensure the purity of all gluten-free products. The gluten-free facility is also dairy and casein free in an effort to better serve allergen-sensitive consumers, he added. Yvonne Fyan, Customer Service Manager, reports the highest volume of consumer calls her team receives involve questions about gluten-free products. "They typically rave about the variety of gluten-free products we offer, and how we have helped change their lives, because now they can enjoy pizza, cakes, cookies, brownies, and other baked goods they couldn't eat before," she says. Consumers are directed to the Bob's Red Mill website to access gluten-free recipes from noted author Carol Fenster, Ph.D., as well as extensive information from registered dietitians, health professionals, and lifestyle experts.

As Bob's guided tour winds through the mill rooms and the packaging areas, one of the most common questions or observations deals with cleanliness. The place is spotless! Logic would say grinding and mixing hundreds of tiny particles of grains would create a dusty, dirty environment. Anyone who's been in their own kitchen when flour is used to bake cakes, breads, or cookies can attest to the dusting of white powder covering apron, countertop, appliances, floor, and faces. But, here, in a huge factory that hosts the processing of nearly one hundred million pounds of powdery substances a year, it's remarkably clean. And the company's safety record is just as spotless. They are a voluntary participant in the Hazard Analysis & Critical Control Points (HACCP) program, a management system in which food safety is addressed through the analysis and control of biological, chemical, and physical hazards, from raw material production, procurement, and handling, to manufacturing, distribution and consumption of the finished product. The national program basically ensures its participants perform their processes and procedures in the proper manner, and maintain a clean facility.

Following a recent HACCP audit in which the company improved four percentage points over the previous excellent year, the man charged with making everything run smoothly, Director of Operations Dennis Vaughn, celebrated by ordering 150 pizzas for workers on the three shifts to enjoy. Nearly everyone in the company (except marketing and finance) reports to him.

"I am extremely proud of our employees for the caring attitude demonstrated by each and every one of them," Dennis says. "So, I like to honor them with employee appreciation events. Sometimes, it's strawberry shortcake for everybody; another time, Cold Stone ice cream. Management has served them Italian dinners. We do a lot of things for them."

Add a generous monthly profit-sharing program to the top of that list. When a month is profitable (and nobody at the company can remember one that wasn't), the company's finance department adds up the sales, and determines what the expenses were. What is left over at the end of the month is profit, and a percentage of that profit is shared with all employees. The program is based on a three-month rolling average, so what is paid out in August was based on May, June, and July's performance. "It breeds loyalty," Dennis understates. "It also helps the employee to want to do a good job. They want to do a good job because the more profitable we are, the more pay they get. This is what Bob's intent has been from the beginning – if the company is profitable, you are going to share in it. If it is not, well, then you are not going to get as much money."

The way the company is committed to treating people extends beyond its happy workforce. Suppliers, sales people, and grocery store customers are treated like royalty.

"We run this business like it was a 1950s service station," Dennis shares. "We come out with our white uniforms on, wearing our white hat. We will check the air in your tires, we will check your oil, and we will wash your windshield. We provide excellent service for a quality product, and we still believe that the customer is always right."

That service-oriented connection reaches out to the 168 or so farmers and suppliers that do business with Bob's Red Mill. Bob and his managers believe if you are doing business with somebody, you are going to have a much better relationship if you are shaking that person's hand. "That personal relationship is very important to us," says Purchasing Manager Neil Koberstein. "If you just deal with them over the phone, you never really have that same connection as you would when you have gone and met that person, and shaken their hand. At that point, you have more ownership in the relationship. So, that is what we do. We try to go out every year, and meet some of our farmers and suppliers."

Koberstein says those trips have been as short as thirty miles away to nearby Forest Grove to visit a soft white wheat farmer, to as far away as Canadian farms in Saskatchewan and Manitoba to see oat processors, hemp growers, and flax fields.

"I believe a lot of companies enjoy working with us because we are a very truthful, honest company," Koberstein explains. "And that goes both ways – we like working with honest, down-to-earth people, too." He cites an example of the camaraderie Bob's Red Mill enjoys with its customers when he welcomed a Canadian contingent to the plant by playing their national anthem on the piano as they walked in. "You know what," he points out. "That was pretty cool."

Dennis Vaughn describes that just as important as having a personal relationship with suppliers is getting to know "the people that put our product in stores. Of course, our sales team meets the buyers, but we want them to come here; we want them to get the full Bob's Red Mill experience. We want them to meet Bob, take a tour of the facility, and meet the people who work here. So, when they go back home, they leave here with the feeling we are a family-type organization, where everybody cares about everything we do, and that this is a bunch of good people with whom they will want to do business."

The end consumer, too, is obviously very important to everyone at Bob's Red Mill. Back in 1990, when Dennis Gilliam joined the company and set his sights on becoming a national player, he and Bob thought it would be wonderful if just ten percent of the American population would eat their whole grain foods. Decade by decade they have upped that goal, as they now believe more than a quarter of U.S. households have at least one Bob's Red Mill product in their pantry. Of course, that leaves them with an ambitious seventy-five percent of the country yet to reach. Advertising and an aggressive public relations program have contributed to the healthy twenty-five to thirty percent annual growth in sales over the past decade (boosting sales to more than $70 million in 2009), but, the marketing team, and its agency Koopman Ostbo Marketing Communications, challenged themselves to think bigger, to think outside the box in order to reach more consumers. It was their account rep, Ted Morgan, who presented his big idea back in 2007. It made the group laugh, but they pooh-poohed the recommendation. Morgan persisted, and the next year he brought it up again in a marketing planning meeting.

"Bob's Red Mill should enter the World Porridge Making Championship," he repeated. "That way, if you win, we can claim you have the world's best oats." It must have been a slow day in the "Who's got a better idea?" department, but Dennis Gilliam and his marketing manager Matt Cox bit. When the team looked into it, they discovered no American had ever entered the unusual sixteen-year-old cooking competition held in tiny Carrbridge, Scotland. Mostly, local Scots and a handful of entrants from the United Kingdom had battled for the coveted Golden Spurtle trophy, named after the Scottish kitchen utensil used to stir oatmeal. The rod-like wooden tool is supposed to keep the Scottish national dish from becoming lumpy while cooking. The Scots take their oats seriously, billing the "fierce competition" as one of the country's "most renowned culinary cook-offs" on their website. So, while they had fun with it, the Bob's Red Mill team took their entry into the 2009 competition seriously as well. Scottish oatmeal, after all, was Bob's personal favorite. They enlisted the support of Mark Greco, a local chef from Gravy, a restaurant known for its outstanding breakfasts, to help create an entry in the Specialty category. The American team, represented by Matt Cox, felt they had their best chance to win with their Oregon Orchard Oat Brûlée, a caramelized encrusted concoction featuring Bartlett pears, dried cherries, hazelnuts, and Pear Eau de Vie from nearby Clear Creek Distillery. The traditional porridge category – the one whose winner earned the Golden Spurtle and title of World's Best Porridge – was limited to only three ingredients – oats, salt, and water. It was a foregone conclusion a Scotsman wins in the traditional category.

Following months of practice and preparation – and armed with their own Oregon-made Spurtle fashioned out of myrtlewood (*a Myrtle Spurtle!*) – the Bob's Red Mill team, with the culinary hopes of the USA on their shoulders, flew to Scotland. Matt represented the company in the blind taste test, and wonder of wonders, the judges announced he was the winner! Not in the Specialty category, where they thought they

PHOTO CREDIT: ANDREW STOCKTON

**Matt Cox wins the Golden Spurtle trophy for
cooking the World's Best Porridge**

had their best chance, but in the traditional category with Bob's Red Mill
Steel Cut Oats. Matt and the team returned home triumphant, with the
title of World's Best Porridge, and carrying the Golden Spurtle trophy.
Before they arrived, Morgan and the Koopman Ostbo design team were
already working on new packaging design for every bag of Bob's Red Mill
Steel Cut Oats, the World's Best Oatmeal.

Back at work, Matt was a bit of a celebrity. He had had his picture
taken with Miss Scotland. A photograph of him holding the Golden
Spurtle appeared on the big outdoor screen overlooking Times Square in
New York City. The PR team at Koopman Ostbo had hooked him up with
several media interviews. And he got a big hug from Bob. Well, at least
it wasn't a kiss, like Bob had given him shortly after he started working
for the company. He had moved up to Portland from Humboldt County
in Northern California, hoping his experience working at a natural foods

co-op could land him a job at Bob's Red Mill. He got hired as Dennis Gilliam's marketing assistant, and, used to his laid-back California hippie lifestyle, was admittedly somewhat unkempt with his very casual dress and scraggly beard. He tells the story of how Bob pulled him aside one day in the break room, and told him the history behind his own beard.

"He told me in the late '70s his boys all had these long, shaggy beards, and he just didn't like the way they looked. So, after he moved to Oregon, he decided to grow out his beard – a very trimmed and sculpted one – and then he went back down to Redding, and blew their minds with this big, perfectly shaped beard. He's telling me this long, drawn-out story, and he never said, 'I want you to shave off your beard,' but, somehow, even though he keeps a beard, and that is part of his persona, it occurred to me he did not want me to have a beard, or if I did, at least keep it really neat."

Knowing there was no way he was going to keep a beard as neat as Bob's, Matt elected to shave it off. The next day, they crossed paths in the hall, "And he sees me, stops in his tracks, and just lights up. 'Oh Matt,' he said. 'Your face! It is so neat!' And then he grabbed me and kissed me on the cheek. Everyone was crowded into the break room at that time, and with me still being new and finding my place, it was a little embarrassing." Today, Bob still sports his neat and trimmed beard, and Matt, much more confident in his skin, still chooses not to grow out his.

The Final Stop

Every product that leaves Bob's Red Mill passes through Dean Hauck's department. As the Manager of Shipping and Receiving, his job – and that of his twenty-two employees – encompasses all aspects of stocking, picking orders, and loading trucks. Visitors who tour his warehouse and distribution facility marvel at the size and scope of the operation. Dean, the former volunteer firefighter, who, when he started working for Bob in June of 1987, managed a 10,000-square-foot storage area across the street from the Roethe Road mill, now oversees a place sixteen times larger than that. It's a beehive of activity, with forklifts honking as they sail down wide aisles, trucks beeping as they back into forty docks, and amped voices from several loudspeakers orchestrating the dance. And, with a new $500,000 automated racking system, it is a miraculously smooth operation.

Dean has seen a lot, and heard a lot, over the past twenty-five years. He helped fight the fire that burned down Bob's Milwaukie mill. He was the chosen one to go to Redding and run Moores' Flour Mill at night so Bob could fill orders in Oregon. He persevered through the transition from partner Craig Ratzat to the triumvirate of Dennis Gilliam, John Wagner, and Robert Agnew. He helped move and set up warehouse operations in temporary space after the fire; to the factory on International Way; and to the world headquarters building, where he runs the biggest department space-wise.

Dean got his first job in high school pumping gas at the Flying J on McLoughlin Boulevard, where Bob had an account for his work and personal vehicles. Over the years, while he ran the mill down the street, Bob gained an appreciation for Dean's work ethic. He kept telling him (he was the manager by then), "One day I'm going to have a job for you." When that day came, Bob offered him a dollar more an hour than he was making at the gas station, and Dean accepted. He drove the company truck and worked in the warehouse to start, but Bob had more in mind for the responsible young man in his mid-twenties. As he did with so many others he recruited, he saw the potential for greatness, and he wanted to be a part of pulling the best out of him. He mentored him for two years, and, when he thought he was ready for advancement to a managerial position, he scheduled a time for them to meet. Being the thoughtful planner he is, Bob wrote down his thoughts in preparation for sitting down with Dean:

> Your job is to work into being a first-class Plant Manager of a health food company, and to be a good example of a clean-cut young man who is interested in and dedicated to his employees, our customers, and the success of the company.

Your specific task is to first and foremost lead others with understanding and good management practices. Along with this is to be always watchful for wasted time and practices, so the company will be profitable.

You are a working manager, expected to help out in all places. This is important to your awareness of the various jobs around the business, so that you can understand the various jobs, and make suggestions for improvement. Don't ask someone to do something you are unwilling to do yourself – or don't know how to do yourself. Challenge yourself to do as many jobs as possible within the company, as I have done.

Communicate with me. You are working for me. I am the main person in your working life at the present time. Dialog with me. Discuss things. Be open and talk with me. Keep in mind what your job is – to represent me and the best interests and profitability of this company. This is what you are drawing your paycheck for. And if we are successful – which we will be – you will share in the profit and success.

Bob conveyed those thoughts to his truck-driving warehouseman in 1989, one year after the fire. His advice never rang so true; the same words could have been said – and undoubtedly are being communicated – to every employee today. Especially the part about sharing in the profit and success.

CHAPTER 28

AN EMPLOYEE-
OWNED COMPANY

B OB MOORE RUNS A BUSINESS, BUT TREATS EVERYBODY LIKE FAMILY.
People like Wes Tarr and his three partners are his brothers. His
kids are Dave Geiter and Dean Hauck – and a handful of others like Bo
Thomas, Micky Torgerson, Dianna Kelley, and Lori Sobelson, who have
been with him almost since the beginning. And then he has a wealth of
grandkids – the 200 employees he values so much. Even his relationships
outside the walls of the world headquarters are familial, closer than some
cousins. There's Don Ossey, his real estate expert; John McCormick, his
attorney; and Ken, Craig, and Ted, his PR and advertising guys.

And, he knew in his heart – probably around the time of the fire –
his people were so important to him he would never jeopardize their
future by "selling out," or alter his relationship with them by letting
someone other than himself have the majority interest in Bob's Red Mill.
That heart-felt feeling, that emotional commitment, manifested itself in
the rejection of hundreds of offers over the years to buy his company.
He could have retired a very rich man if he had entertained any of those
propositions. But all that the wooing, cajoling, and flattering accomplished over the years was a steeling of his resolve. Whereas before, maybe

up until the time he reached "retirement age," he had a strong *feeling* about what he ultimately wanted to do with the company, at some point he crossed a line of no return in his mind, and *decided*, with clarity and purpose, that his employees would have the company. At first, when he and Charlee jointly made the decision, he didn't know how it would happen. He just knew it *would* happen. As he was later quoted as saying, "Truly, this was the only business decision I could personally make."

Planning for that eventuality began in his late 70s, shortly after he had secured his employees' job futures with the long-term lease on the new manufacturing facility. Next, he wanted to secure their financial futures. The first step was to approach his partners – Dennis Gilliam, John Wagner, and Robert Agnew – and discuss with them his goal to have the employees own the company. The succession plan sounded good to Gilliam, 65; Wagner, 67; and Agnew, 46, at the time. So, with the help of their attorney, John McCormick, of the Portland law firm, Sussman Shank LLP, the group began exploring their options. They learned employee ownership could be accomplished in a number of ways: Employees can receive stock options or buy stock directly; they can be given stock as a bonus; they can obtain stock through a profit-sharing plan; they can even become owners through worker cooperatives, where everyone has an equal vote. But, after months of research, they found the most attractive option for the company, its owners, and employees, was an Employee Stock Ownership Plan (ESOP).

An ESOP is a tax-qualified benefit plan created by a corporation for the benefit of its employees. It is similar in some ways to a profit-sharing plan (the difference is you get cash on an annual basis from profit sharing, and shares of stock in an ESOP until you retire or leave the company, at which time the stock value is traded for cash). In an ESOP, the company sets up a trust fund, into which it contributes new shares of its own cash or stock to buy existing owner shares. Companies can borrow money from a bank to fund the ESOP, or the business can bankroll it itself (as the Bob's Red Mill partners planned to do). Shares in the trust are generally allocated to individual employee accounts based on their

W-2 earnings. As employees accumulate seniority with the company, they acquire an increasing right to the shares in their account, a process called vesting. When they leave the company, they receive their stock, which the company must buy back from them at its fair market value. That value is determined annually by an independent appraiser.

Once they had determined to move forward with an ESOP as a way to transfer ownership to the employees of Bob's Red Mill, the group hired third-party administrator Pension Plan Specialists, PC, of Vancouver, Washington, to set it up. Through the lengthy and costly process, President Joe Burt spent a lot of time with Bob, which meant showing up at Bob's office at his favorite meeting time – 6 a.m.

"When we first sat down, what he wanted to make very, very clear to me was this plan would be put in place for his employees, so some big corporation, like Kellogg's or General Mills or whomever, wouldn't come in and take over the company," Joe says. "He wanted me to thoroughly understand the ESOP was being done to create tremendous stability and job security for his employees, not to build wealth for any of the partners."

Joe describes as "very generous" the stipulations Bob wanted as part of the plan. That included a three-year vesting term, instead of the more typical six years. But, even more, Bob wanted all of his employees who had already been with him three years to automatically be fully vested as soon as the ESOP was executed. The "prior years of service" credit *immediately* vested more than 100 employees. Joe adds, "It was also exactly in line with his character" to ensure if someone was permanently disabled, died, or retired anytime in a plan year, they would receive their full benefit for that calendar year (most plans require the person to be employed on the last day of the plan year to earn a contribution for that year).

"As you could imagine, Bob was very paternal about what he wanted for his people through an ESOP," Joe explains. "He really wanted this to be a retirement plan, an opportunity to create long-term prosperity for each one of them."

To be eligible to participate in the plan that was ultimately developed, an employee had to be at least twenty-one, employed for a year, and have accumulated at least 1,000 hours of service. Anyone who had previously met those requirements was immediately eligible to participate. When all had signed off on the plan, the Bob's Red Mill group got together with their Koopman Ostbo PR team to strategize how best to roll it out to their employees, customers, and end consumers, as well as the media. Yes, it was a positive move, but some companies that implement an ESOP do so in an environment of immediate changes in management. Bob was adamant there would be no changes in the day-to day operations of the company, and he certainly had no intention of retiring. The strategy team developed specific messaging points for each of the company's target audiences, and then hit on somewhat of a theatrical idea. The company was ready to announce the ESOP in early February, 2010. Bob's birthday was on the fifteenth. Why not combine the two events, and announce on Bob's eighty-first birthday he was giving the gift of his company to the employees?

It was a brilliant strategy. On that Monday, the 200 employees of Bob's Red Mill gathered during the lunch breaks of their respective shifts to ostensibly honor Bob with a cake and a serenade. Instead, they got pizza, and the surprise of their lives. What they heard would alter their lives forever. Effective that day – Bob's February 15th birthday – their status as employees changed to owners. The company, which most of them knew could sell at three to four times its earnings, was theirs. And, as it began to sink in, they would not have to pay anything for it. It was solely funded by the employer. It was being given to them. Truly, a gift.

A gift that didn't necessarily come with a guarantee, the pension plan expert points out. "I did explain to the employees it is not necessarily a guarantee they will have success in retirement. As you can imagine, as the company value goes up, so does their stock price. If the value goes down, so does their stock price. One of the things I really wanted them to understand is they control their own destiny. When you make the mind shift from employee to owner, you start to think of things a little differently. If you are looking for a piece of scratch paper, maybe you grab it out of the recycle bin, as opposed to a brand new piece out of the fax machine.

You start to think, 'What is this going to cost me?' One of the things we wanted them to understand is, they can, by working hard and working smart, influence the value of their retirement accounts. Bob really wanted me to hammer that home with the employees. Up until then, he controlled everything, he took all the risks, and he earned the rewards. He wanted the employees to understand that is what they had now. From then on, they would have the responsibility and accountability – and the incentive to share in the success, and reap some of the rewards."

According to Roger Farnen, Quality Assurance Manager, the opportunity is not lost on staff. "I think the employees, no matter what their position, recognize there are tangible incentives. We all realize Bob is basically passing the entrepreneurial torch to us, and, at the same time, instilling in us that hard work provides rewards."

Bob's Red Mill employees had always been proud of where they worked, and for whom they worked. But their pride spilled over in the days following the ESOP announcement. The letters that went out to the company's "Valued Trading Partners" in advance of the public statement extolled their virtues, with comments like, "We believe we have the finest people you will find in the natural foods manufacturing business. By providing our current and future employees an ownership stake in the company, we are confident we will continue to retain and attract the very best."

And the media attention that resulted from the Koopman Ostbo press release was astounding – nearly 100 news stories that reached one in three Americans in the days and weeks following the announcement. The coverage started the morning of Tuesday, February 16, with an article in Oregon's largest daily newspaper, *The Oregonian*. The headline, "Founder of Bob's Red Mill Natural Foods Transfers Business to Employees," was fairly straightforward, but the ripple effects of the front-page story were like a firestorm. At 8 a.m. on the seventeenth, the producer of *ABC World News with Diane Sawyer* was on the phone with the agency's PR director. They wanted to know if CBS or NBC had run the story, and when they heard "not yet" from the savvy account executive, the producer asked for an exclusive, promising to feature Bob and the ESOP story in prime time on their "American Heart" segment. They dispatched a reporter and cameraman who spent most of the next two days interviewing Bob and touring his facility. In a rare bit of TV news protocol, there was no voiceover from the reporter. Because the story was so powerful, they allowed Bob to tell it himself, a rarity in news reporting.

The nearly three-minute piece ran on Thursday night's broadcast, with a moving introduction from Diane Sawyer, who said, "And now, from the American Heart, a story we really love; hope you do, too." The segment featured dozens of Bob's employees, about whom Bob made this comment, "I don't think there's anybody worthy to run this company but the people who built it." The camera panned the mill room, packaging lines, warehouse, offices, and Whole Grain Store & Visitors Center, and then focused on the man, himself, to tell why he gave the company he built from scratch to his employees. "It's the only business decision I could make," he said, looking into millions of American homes that night. "I could not sell the company; I could not sell the company." Then, he shared a philosophy about business he has embraced his entire life, his core value that places people before profit: "There's a lot of negative stuff going into business today; it's a good ol' basic Bible lesson, and that is that the love of money is the root of all evil. And, unfortunately, our entire philosophy today is just to get all the money you can in whatever way you can, and it's caused people to do a lot of things just for money that they feel in their hearts is not the right thing to do. I've just truly, truly, truly tried to set some of that aside, and do what I thought was the best thing for the group of people who made this all possible."

The TV, radio, and print stories that blanketed the nation that week not only generated tons of congratulatory messages from existing buyers of Bob's Red Mill products, but people who had never even heard of Bob Moore were now fans. The company's customer service department was swamped with emails from around the country:

"I just saw you featured on ABC News. Just want to say I rejoice in your virtue. It is my endeavor in life to be as faithful, hard-working, honest, grateful, intelligent, and generous as you." *Nancy from Alabama*

"Your story warmed my heart and restored my hope for humanity. We are of a different age, when decency and doing the right thing meant something; when a man could accomplish anything with hard work and a good heart." *Ward from California*

"I read the article about you giving your employees your business. I'm not sure if you will ever read this message, but I wanted to say thank you, too. I am shocked to know there are still some KIND people in this world. Everyone is so busy trying to make money to better themselves that they don't take the time to thank those responsible for their success! I commend your generosity! Your act of kindness should be filling the TV stations. Maybe just one other person could learn from the example you set. The only time I've read or saw something this great was when I watched *Willy Wonka and the Chocolate Factory*. Thank you for letting your employees touch your heart and not your wallet. God has a special place in heaven for you!" *Karen from Illinois*

"I want you to know how proud I am of you! Giving your company to the workers was the most generous thing! You are a wonderful Christian and a great American! I applaud you sir and tip my hat in respect to you. I am proud to know you." *Eddie from North Carolina*

"Thank you for being an inspiration to this country that we love. I wish more people were like you and had the best interest of their family of employees at heart. You exemplify the true meaning of leadership. My prayers are with you and your staff for continued greatness." *Fred from California*

"I read about the transfer of the company to the employees and just wanted to tell Mr. Moore that the world would be a much better place if others adopted your philosophy about life." *Tim from California*

"Kudos to you! I have worked in the footwear manufacturing business for over thirty years, and after all this time when push came to shove it was the 'top dogs' who received the prize, and we were pushed to the pavement. I applaud you for seeing the importance in the company. The employees make the company! I wish there were more with your vision." *Julie from Pennsylvania*

"I just wanted to say what a generous and loving heart you have. To share with those who loved you and supported you along the way – that is what life is really about." *Darlene from Texas*

While the media coverage was all positive, including a two-page spread in *People* magazine with the headline, "People Before Profit," not every writer got the story right. Some assumed an ESOP meant the owner was stepping down from running the business, and they reported Bob was retiring. They were wrong. While an ESOP is part of succession planning, and often involves an exit strategy for owners, Bob had made it very clear he was not retiring. The day after the ESOP was no different for him than the day before. He had always been active in the day-to-day operations, and he would continue to be.

"I've gotten to a point in my life where I want to be," Bob explains. "I mean, if the Good Lord came into my office right now, and said, 'Okay, Bob, what is it you want to do in your next life?' I would say, 'Lord, I would like to do just what I am doing right now. I want my same life and my same wife. I couldn't be happier.' It's like that card game where they ask you how many cards you want, and you trade yours in for some others; I would say, 'Thank you, but I will play the hand I was dealt.' I love coming to work! And I don't want to retire. Most business people I have known over the years have had one goal, and that is to get out of the business they are in. My advice to them is, 'For Heaven's sake, do not let go of your job! Keep it.' That's what I have done. I have worked to keep the business I love."

Asked if he had to pick just one thing that stands above all others in the business he loves, Bob does not hesitate.

"If I had to pick one thing about my life today, it would be my people. I love them all. I just love them. And, to me, the ESOP is the ultimate way to reward them for their contributions to our ongoing success and growth. Now, they don't have to worry. They will own the company. Personally, it is a very good feeling. The continuity of this company has been secured."

EPILOGUE

I N DECEMBER, 2011, BOB'S RED MILL NATURAL FOODS WAS VOTED THE Most Admired Company in Oregon over sixty other companies nominated in the Agriculture and Forest Products category. The annual awards luncheon put on by the *Portland Business Journal* attracted more than 800 of the state's top CEOs and business leaders. Only one winner of the more than eighty who were recognized that afternoon at the Portland Hilton Hotel received a standing ovation – Bob Moore.

Bob is no stranger to Oregon's statewide business leaders, who were the ones who voted for the Most Admired companies. In fact, the same group named Bob "CEO of the Year" in 2008. There were many reasons to recognize the company and its leader, such as its astonishing year-over-year revenue growth through the economic downturn (a 32.7% increase 2009 to 2010; and after hitting the $100 million mark on November 17, 2011, a 23.6% increase over 2010 to an estimated year-end 2011 total of $115 million). Or the giving of the company to its employees in 2010, which most Oregonians had read about or heard about on television. But the buzz in the hotel banquet room that afternoon was about Bob and Charlee's philanthropy. What the Moores had done in the previous twelve months was beyond compare, even with Nike and every major bank, hospital, forest products company, and manufacturer represented in the room.

Bob and Charlee had spent much of that year planning how and where to divest themselves of their wealth. Of course, they have always been very generous, not only with their own children and grandchildren, but with their extended Bob's Red Mill family, as well. Their wills amply provide for their three boys, and the grandchildren are well taken care of. Employees cite story after story where Bob and Charlee have personally written them checks and handed them envelopes stuffed with cash. School tuitions have been paid, homes saved from foreclosure, flooded basements restored, medical bills wiped away, cars repaired – the list goes on and on. Much of their community support for seniors, food banks, hospitals, and children's programs is in the form of anonymous gifts. They feel they have been richly blessed, and, in turn, they want to bless others.

For decades, Bob and Charlee have poured their resources of time, energy, and money into the business. Sure, they've taken some well-deserved vacations to favorite destinations in Europe. They've remodeled their Milwaukie home a couple of times, most recently to add extra bedrooms for kids and grandkids. They bought a motorhome, but don't like to be gone for long periods of time. There's the expensive piano and violin they enjoy so much. And, Bob has his 1931 Ford Model A's. But, they'd give all the toys up for a few more years with Annie, their beloved beagle. And a remedy for Charlee's neuropathy, which restricts her mobility.

Until recently, Bob drove a 2001 Ford Windstar to work every day. But, when the partners were required as part of the Employee Stock Ownership Plan to sell a percentage of their shares to the company to fund the trust, he used some of the money to buy a new Ford Explorer with all the bells and whistles. John McCormick, his CPA/attorney, told Bob and Charlee they had two choices to make regarding the balance of the funds they received – pay most of it in taxes to the government, or give it away to nonprofits. The Moores had been planning for a long time which causes and charitable organizations they wanted to support, so, to them, it was an easy decision. Their criteria were born out of their life's pursuit. They would give to those who promoted good nutrition and healthy eating.

They found their first worthy recipient right in their own backyard. Since 1956, the National College of Natural Medicine (NCNM) had been quietly offering four-year graduate medical degrees in Naturopathic Medicine and Classical Chinese Medicine from their campus in downtown Portland. Dennis Gilliam actually brought the school to Bob's attention, and he and Charlee decided to underwrite some scholarships. As they got to know NCNM President David Schleich and adjunct faculty member Dr. Courtney Jackson better, Bob and Charlee ratcheted up their gift to $1.35 million to build a new kitchen/classroom and support a pilot project called "Ending Childhood Obesity." The local community program offers free family workshops that provide nutritional health education and training in cooking and preparing whole grain foods.

Bob had found the cause he would spend the rest of his life and most of his money supporting. Childhood obesity was an epidemic he believed could be prevented through healthy foods and better diets.

"Too many kids and their parents are overweight, and even with all this talk about health care, there has been little discussion about nutrition. All we hear is advertising stuff that is weak in nutrients to kids by the big food manufacturers who are trying everything in their power to give you as little as they can for as much as they can get, because they have stockholders who only care about their bottom line. I am so sick of their greed I could scream! I mean, there is so much evil in this world, and I'm not talking about wars and violence, and things like that – there is plenty of that, too – I'm talking about the high fructose syrup, junk food, and empty calories we're feeding people. That's why I'm in this business, because I believe it so fervently. I just happen to make a living at it, but I would have been just as happy to be in that little old wooden mill down there, right now, at my age, right today, opening the doors in the morning, and starting the mills, and giving tours to people."

But Bob finds himself in a position today to make a difference. So, he went looking for another organization that could join him in his quest to spread the word about the nutritional benefits of whole grain foods and how they could affect the obesity crisis in America. He found a willing partner on the campus of Oregon State University. Bob had been invited to speak to OSU students and faculty as part of the university's day-long "Entrepreneur in Residence" program. He was impressed by the passion of the students in the College of Health and Human Services, and the commitment to nutrition education by their dean, Tammy Bray. When he got home that night from the exhausting presentation, he told Charlee about some of the needs he saw, and they discussed ways they thought they could help out.

On January 19, 2011, OSU President Ed Ray announced at his annual State of the University address the partnership the Moores and OSU had developed. Bob and Charlee would donate five million dollars to establish the Moore Family Center for Whole Grain Foods, Nutrition, and Preventive Health. It was the second largest gift ever given to OSU's College of Health and Human Services, and Ray noted, it came from a family that never attended the university. He said the academic center would build on the college's research on nutrition and childhood obesity, and help promote the health benefits of whole grain foods. It would also provide endowments for the center's director and an additional professor, as well as create an outreach fund to deliver public health obesity prevention strategies.

Bob and Charlee were determined their money would be used to communicate to women who were considering starting a family the importance of a healthy diet, not only for their own bodies, but also for their unborn children. In doing their research, they learned of a relatively new area of study called "developmental origins of health and disease." The concept is predicated upon the assumption that environmental factors acting early, usually in fetal life, have profound effects on vulnerability to disease later, often in adulthood. Bob and Charlee also discovered the once-controversial theory that a baby's future health is heavily influenced by what happens during the first one thousand days after conception was now being widely embraced. Studies conducted by the world-renowned Oregon Health & Science University (OHSU) were showing how poor maternal and early childhood nutrition can increase a child's likelihood of obesity, heart disease, autism, and other chronic conditions. These nutritionally linked conditions, as well as type-2 diabetes and hypertension, have risen sharply along with the post–World War II advent of processed convenience foods that are high in sugar and fat, but low in nutritional value. Experts call this phenomenon "high-calorie malnutrition," and research is proving its consequences can last for generations. When Bob contacted OHSU to find out more about their work on developmental origins, they offered him a tour and an opportunity to meet with some of the leading researchers. He came away very excited. He hadn't been aware of a lot of the terminology or history of the research, but he discovered OHSU was working on the very subject he and Charlee were committed to supporting.

The negotiations with NCNM and OSU and the subsequent donations in the early part of 2011 were taking up a tremendous amount of Bob's time. He was still running the day-to-day operations of Bob's Red Mill, and at the same time he was learning that giving away his money was bordering on a full-time job. Yes, it was his personal fortune, but every time he and Charlee made a contribution, the media and everyone involved called attention to "the founders of Bob's Red Mill." There wasn't – and hadn't been for a long time – any separation between Bob and the brand. They were one and the same. What was good for Bob was good for the company. What was good for the company was good for Bob. He had an excellent management group in place to run Bob's Red Mill, but what he needed right now – for both their benefits – was someone to protect the company's brand image and make sure these significant donations and the recipients involved were doing what they were supposed to do. The responsibility he and Charlee felt – to finish strong, to see their life's work pay off for the people they determined to reach – was too important for them to just write a check and turn their back on the difference the money was intended to make. They needed someone they could trust. Someone who would hold up the best interests of the company, while managing the programs the Moores were supporting. Lori Sobelson was exactly that person.

Lori and her husband Dave were customers of Moores' Flour Mill in Milwaukie for several years before it burned down, and remained so throughout the company's relocations. When there was a job opening announced for Program Director of the Whole Grains Store & Visitors Center, she applied, and got the job. She took on responsibility for helping to manage the store, deli, kitchen, cooking school, as well as the mail order business. She became the top woman manager at Bob's Red Mill, and Bob liked her spunk. Hadn't seen a fireball like her since that little Mary Bierwagen thirty years prior. And when it came to honoring the mission of the company and demonstrating a passion for healthy eating, she was one of the company's best. She believes wholeheartedly in what Bob and Charlee have created. And that's why, as the company's new Director of Community Outreach, she has been entrusted with not only protecting the company's image in the community, but also with overseeing that the Moores' financial gifts are managed appropriately.

Bob needed Lori to quickly get up to speed on the status of the NCNM and OSU projects, because he wanted her involvement in a third, and much larger, endeavor. He and Charlee were so impressed with the work OHSU was doing in the areas of nutrition and childhood obesity, they had committed to donate $25 million to support its research and community outreach efforts.

"Charlee and I have always been inspired by challenge, and I can't think of a tougher challenge than changing people's behavior when it comes to their diets. My hope in partnering with OHSU is that we can motivate people – especially mothers-to-be – to make the kinds of changes that promote their own and their babies' health."

On September 16, 2011, at the opening reception for the Developmental Origins of Health and Disease's Seventh World Congress, which happened to be hosted by OHSU that year, the university announced the establishment of the Bob and Charlee Moore Institute for Nutrition and

Wellness. The gathering of top medical doctors and international nutrition experts applauded the largesse of the founders of Bob's Red Mill, but in his remarks, Bob simply credited his people and thanked Charlee for her inspiration. He left them with, "I'd like to go out making a lot of noise. No reason why we can't start something."

ACKNOWLEDGMENTS

WHEN BOB MOORE AGREED IN APRIL, 2010, TO LET ME WRITE THIS book, he said he would carve out of his schedule as much time as I needed. When I suggested we start meeting twice a week, first thing in the morning, I expected the eighty-one-year-old guy to tell me to be in his office at 8 or 9 a.m. After all, that's when I started work; and besides, I drive right by Bob's Red Mill world headquarters on my way to my downtown Portland office. I laughed out loud when he said, "Be here at six!" I thought he was kidding. But when I looked at his partners' serious faces around the conference table, I realized this was no joke. Bob says he is at his best early in the morning, and I have to hand it to him – he was sharp, he was always prepared, and he has a great memory. Plus, he was never late, and he usually got there much earlier than six. I know, because after about the fifteenth or sixteenth interview session, I started arriving ten, fifteen – even twenty minutes early – just trying to beat him to his office. But, he was always there – with a cup of coffee in his hand and a book or magazine in front of him. I finally gave up, and cherished my extra fifteen minutes of sleep. The man has boundless energy, and I guess I have to thank him for that (the opposite would have been a drag that early in the morning). Our three-hour interviews were always lively, with much laughter and pontification. Even a few tears. And some banging of the fist on the desk. He certainly doesn't lack passion. He loves life. Believes in the continuity of it. I appreciated all the lessons. And, thanks, Tatyana, the nice Ukrainian lady who served us a different hot Bob's Red Mill breakfast cereal at every session (I gave up trying to explain that I am part Ukrainian on my mom's side, because she kept saying, "Welcome, welcome," to whatever I said).

Thanks, Nancy, for all the follow-up. Bob relies on you for everything; we could never have gotten this done in a timely fashion without you. Denny, I appreciate all your insights, but most of all, your friendship. Everyone at Bob's Red Mill is truly amazing. I wish we could bottle up the compassion and dedication you all demonstrate at work every day. It would sell like hotcakes (sorry about the lame reference to what you make; at least I didn't say everyone keeps their nose to the grindstone. Okay, I tried not to, but it finally slipped out.).

I must admit, the KO team did a yeoman's job, picking up the slack, and never missing a beat. Craig, thanks for your vision and making it possible for me to get published. Great job, BRM Team of Ted, Vanessa, Robert, Tracy, Darin and Ashley – Bob has told me numerous times you guys are the reason he stays so busy.

My gratitude to the Clackamas County Sheriff's Office, especially Jim Strovink and Lori Vicars, for providing me more information than I could use regarding the nefarious events that occurred along McLoughlin Boulevard the first half of 1988 (maybe another book down the road?). And thank you Clackamas County Judge Kenneth B. Stewart; will we ever know whodunit?

Finally, thank you Bob and Charlee for exemplifying to me how a husband and wife should treat each other, how a father and mother are supposed to love their children, and how partners in business must put their people before profit. I can only hope to love my wife, Karen, better; cherish my daughter, Kristy, more; and have a greater appreciation for my business partner, Craig, and the employees with whom we have been blessed.

On the farm in Elk Grove, California (1961)

David, Ken, Bobby, and friends on the Moore family farm (1963)

Bob Moore at Moores' Flour Mill in Redding, California (1975)

The 1872 mill salvaged from the Boyd Flour Mill (1978)

June 16, 1988 – the morning after an arsonist burned down the mill

One of Bob's favorite pastimes in the world – working on a millstone

The Whole Grain Store & Visitors Center is a
busy place from opening to close

Whole grain
foods for every
meal of the
day; Whole
Grain Store &
Visitors Center

**In front of the
eighteen-foot
waterwheel**

PHOTO CREDIT: NANCY GARNER / BOB'S RED MILL NATURAL FOODS, INC.

PHOTO CREDIT: NANCY GARNER / BOB'S RED MILL NATURAL FOODS, INC.

Charlee and Bob in their 1931 Ford Model A

Signature lineup of Bob's Red Mill gluten-free products

The Quality Control team in Bob's Red Mill's state-of-the-art test lab

Six high-speed packaging lines in the dedicated gluten-free facility

Twentieth year attending the Natural Products
Expo West trade show (2010)

One of the biggest days in the history of Bob's Red Mill Natural
Foods – partners signing the Employee Stock Ownership Plan (l-r
Bob Moore, Robert Agnew, Dennis Gilliam, John Wagner)

Bob's Red Mill Natural Foods – an employee-owned company

ABOUT THE AUTHOR

KEN KOOPMAN IS A PRINCIPAL IN THE MARKETING COMMUNICATIONS agency, Koopman Ostbo Marketing Communications. The Portland, Oregon, firm began working with Bob's Red Mill Natural Foods in 1997. Since then, Ken has spent hundreds of hours getting to know Bob Moore intimately, and, as Ken's business partner, Craig Ostbo, likes to say, "No one else, but Ken, could write this book." Ken is a graduate of the University of Oregon's School of Journalism. This is his first book.

INDEX